Down in the Valley

Down in the Valley

An Introduction to African American
Religious History

Julius H. Bailey

Fortress Press
Minneapolis

DOWN IN THE VALLEY

An Introduction to African American Religious History

Cover image: Black Methodists Holding a Prayer Meeting, 1811–ca. 1813. Watercolor and pen and black ink on off-white wove paper, 6 9/16 x 9 15/16 in. (16.6 x 25.3 cm). Rogers Fund, 1942 (42.95.19). Image copyright © The Metropolitan Museum of Art. Image source: Art Resource, NY

Cover design: Ivy Palmer Skrade

Library of Congress Cataloging-in-Publication Data

Print ISBN: 978-1-4514-9703-8

eBook ISBN: 978-1-5064-0804-0

The paper used in this publication meets the minimum requirements of American National Standard for Information Sciences — Permanence of Paper for Printed Library Materials, ANSI Z329.48-1984.

Manufactured in the U.S.A.

This book was produced using Pressbooks.com, and PDF rendering was done by PrinceXML.

To my best teachers, Jayden and Aleah

Contents

Introduction: The Study of African American Religions

As a young schoolteacher, W. E. B. Du Bois traveled south and happened upon an African American worship service. Reflecting later on what he had witnessed he wrote, "Those who have not thus witnessed the frenzy of a Negro revival in the untouched backwoods of the South can but dimly realize the religious feeling of the slave; as described, such scenes appear grotesque and funny, but as seen they are awful. Three things characterized this religion of the slave,—the Preacher, the Music, and the Frenzy." Du Bois went on to lament the ways this profound religious phenomenon became lost in translation among churches outside of the region.

> The mass of "gospel" hymns which has swept through American churches and well-nigh ruined our sense of song consists largely of debased imitations of Negro melodies made by ears that caught the jingle but not the music, the body but not the soul, of the Jubilee songs. It is thus clear that the study of Negro religion is not only a vital part of the history of the Negro in America, but no uninteresting part of American history.[1]

1. Herbert Aptheker, ed., *The Souls of Black Folk* (Milwood, NY: Kraus-Thomson Organization, 1973), 189–206.

As Du Bois advised, to fully understand African American religions, one must wrestle with the American context within which the traditions grew and transformed over time. In fact, Du Bois's analysis alludes to a central theme in American religious history that undergirds his framing of slave tradition: declension. The earliest Puritan accounts of life in seventeenth-century New England decry the decline of the community's commitment and dedication to religious life. Each subsequent generation failed to meet the standards set by their forebears. As Perry Miller has shown, the second generation of Puritans struggled to live up to and define their own "errand in the wilderness" in America. The creation of the Halfway Covenant in 1662, which extended baptism but not communion until the individual offered evidence of a conversion experience, symbolized the ever-lowering bar that had to be lived up to to be granted entry into the Puritan way of life. As Puritans moved further away in time from John Winthrop's sermon on the *Arbella*, the less "Puritan" and more "American" the communities became.[2] Within African American religious history, the theme of declension begins with the Atlantic slave trade and its potential impact on the retention of African culture in the New World. If African spirituality is presumed to have existed in its purest forms in Africa, if it survived to America (there is much debate surrounding the issue), is it merely a fading shadow of what came before? Notions of what constitutes "authentic" African American religion and which elements have moved furthest from those original sources are fluid throughout American religious history. At the close of the nineteenth century, as Du Bois exemplifies, nostalgia about the purity of slave religion rose to new heights in the face of rising black churches with more formalized institutions and worship practices in the North. The Great

---

2. Perry Miller, *Errand into the Wilderness* (Cambridge, MA: The Belknap Press, 1956).

Migration northward in the early twentieth century romanticized the South that was left behind, and today, there are those who lament the apparent declining role of the Black Church in black communities in the post–civil rights era.

Defining "African American Religions"

Du Bois also eloquently summarizes some of the key issues in the study of African American religious history. One might be called the search for the essence of African American religions. What makes them distinctive and how do you know a "real" manifestation of it from a "debased imitation"? Du Bois notes the elements that he finds essential to slave religion: the preacher, the music, and the "frenzy." In contrast, after the Great Migration, northern black churches are often characterized as being colder, stiffer, more formal, and presumably more Anglicized than their southern religious counterparts. In other circles, slave songs were derided as base superstitions while the musical interpretations of groups such as the Fisk Jubilee Singers were heralded as the "classical" take on the spiritual. These examples illustrate that there has never been one "authentic" African American religion, but rather individuals and communities have produced varied cultural and spiritual expressions that have been understood at varying times from their perspective as the center of African American religious life. Often African American religions are understood as constituting the exuberant black Protestant preacher, emotional worship services, call and response, chanted sermons, and spirituals. While these are components of certain traditions, when extrapolated broadly or defined too narrowly, they inadvertently create an "authenticity" checklist that is far from all encompassing and, by extension, dismisses all of the communities that do not embrace these particular beliefs and practices. While declension and notions of authenticity are a part of the conversation, this textbook moves fluidly between the overarching big picture umbrella concept of "African American religions" and the diversity and variety of beliefs, practices, and traditions that African Americans have brought, created, and transformed in America.

African American religions are a diverse group of beliefs and practices that emerged from the diasporic experiences of the seventeenth- and eighteenth-century Atlantic slave trade that forcefully and tragically dispersed people of African descent across the western hemisphere. The traditional religions that had informed the worldviews of Africans were transported through the middle passage to the shores of the Americas where they were transformed, as they had been for centuries, to make sense of their current context and conditions. Yet, what aspects of African Traditional Religions survived to the Americas? How have African American religions influenced and been shaped by American religious history?

The concept of "African American religions" implies that there is something distinctive about the beliefs and practices of the religious traditions of which African Americans are a part. Yet, only in certain contexts do we apply a racial or ethnic descriptor for not only a particular community, but to an entire approach to religion. This tactic is most often deemed appropriate for the study of minority religions rather than those with a predominately white membership. One might read about Native American religions, but one rarely encounters a book addressing "Caucasian religion." "The Black Church" is often invoked as a category within African American religious history, but one would be hard-pressed to find similar attention to "The White Church." Instead, other traits and categories rise to the fore to distinguish between majority religions, such as traditions, beliefs, practices, denominations, regions, etc. The growing field of Whiteness studies has illuminated the often invisible, but very real expectations and courtesies extended to those in the dominant race. This privilege is demonstrated in the traditional historical narratives that highlight the complexity and centrality of the immigrant experiences of European Americans as they arrive on the shores of America and begin shaping the contours of American religious history. Yet, in the portrayals of the religious histories of many people of color, race is often assumed to be the central uniting and motivating factor for a wide range of worldviews and actions. Although the "diversity" of African American religions is regularly invoked, the presumption of a shared outlook on life stretching back across black communities through space and time is resilient. This monolithic portrayal of African American religions is reinforced by the historical oppression and racism expressed toward particular communities of color in the United States. Legal proscriptions such as slavery and segregation that forcibly separated African Americans from the broader European American society can give the impression that African American religions existed in isolation, preserved in their purity through a type of ideological quarantine. Yet, despite the disparate power dynamics, it is important to keep the focus not only on how the context of America shaped African American religions, but the ways an African presence influenced the course of American religious history as well.

The Impact of the Middle Passage

Few historical events have been as tragic as the "middle passage" that brought slaves across the Atlantic from primarily the west coast of Africa to the New World. Captured as prisoners of war by rival societies, kidnapped, or sold into slavery, African traders marched their slaves, chained together in twos by their hands and feet, to coastal forts where purchasers examined them to determine the best commodities. Branded with the insignia of their new owners,

Africans waited in subterranean dungeons for their ships to depart to the New World, although many would succumb before entering the ship's hull. To maximize economic profits, Africans were packed as tightly as possible with no room to move. Over the six- to sixteen-week voyage, these conditions often led to wide outbreaks of disease including fever, smallpox, and dysentery. Estimates vary, but most sources place the mortality rate somewhere between 25 and 40 percent for the journey to the Americas. Suicide attempts and slave rebellions during the middle passage were common. Only a fraction of African slaves came to North America. For most, the destination was the West Indies. Between 1619 and 1808, which marked the congressional abolishment of the slave trade, over 400,000 Africans were brought to North America, while eight million debarked in South America and the Caribbean.[3]

Given the barbarity of the middle passage, the mid-twentieth century witnessed heated academic debates in the burgeoning study of African American religions over whether slaves arrived to the New World "tabula rasa" or with their traditional African religious systems intact. One of the earliest pioneers in the study of African religious retentions in the New World was Melville J. Herskovits, who identified an extensive range of "Africanisms" in African American religious life in the Americas. While acknowledging the prevalence of African culture in Latin America and the Caribbean, other scholars, such as sociologist E. Franklin Frazier, questioned the broad-reaching presumptions about the retention of African culture in North America. From this perspective, the "seasoning" process during enslavement that sought to purge slaves of their African heritage, intertribal warfare that led to the capture of mostly young men, and linguistic and cultural differences within the slave

3. Albert J. Raboteau, *Slave Religion: The "Invisible Institution" in the Antebellum South* (New York: Oxford University Press, 1978).

population all conspired to allow only the most meager connections to the African homeland that was left behind. Small slave-to-white population ratios, tight restrictions on movement and gatherings, in-group pressure to assimilate, and the destruction of the African family unit were also central factors that scholars pointed toward to conclude that there was a loss of African heritage. Each successive generation born in America increased the distance from a firsthand knowledge of African rites and practices.[4] From this paradigm, the origins of African American religious history begins not on the shores of West Africa, but the plantations of the South and the transformation of European American Christianity within the slave cabins and private moments of worship and devotion. Today it would be difficult to find academic voices suggesting that there are absolutely no cultural retentions or "survivals" that inform African American religions. Yet arguments over the persuasiveness and the basis of certain claims and evidence used to establish connections to Africa are no less contentious. While scholars have not been shy about rendering comparisons between ancient African rites and contemporary African American religious beliefs and practices, there remains a methodological challenge to determine the best manner to demonstrate, substantiate, and validate these assertions. Should African American religions be studied individually or comparatively, and what are the implications of both approaches? If through comparisons, to what should African American religions be contrasted?

The Search for African Retentions

The sheer size and the diversity of beliefs and practices found on the continent make tracing the lineage and religious culture of one

4. Melville J. Herskovits, *The Myth of the Negro Past* (Boston: Beacon Press, 1969); E. Franklin Frazier, *The Negro Church in America* (New York: Schocken Books, 1969).

people group in Africa to a specific region in America a daunting task. However, careful investigation of travel logs, ship manifests, slave rosters, and slave literature has established that most slaves bound for the New World came from West Africa and the regions of the Guinea Coast, Sierra Leone, Liberia, the Ivory Coast, the Bight of Benin, the Gold Coast, Dahomey, and the coastal parts of Nigeria. Some historians focus less on the quantity of slaves taken from a particular region and more on the nature of the influence exerted by particular cultural groups. While acknowledging that the majority of new world slaves came from West Africa, some studies argue that the Bantu of Central Africa perhaps had the most homogeneous culture among imported Africans and therefore had the strongest impact on the development of African American culture.

In order to make the strongest case for the retention of African beliefs and practices in the New World, scholars have argued that despite the ethnic and religious diversity found in Africa, one can find a shared "baseline" worldview that is present across African cultures. If one can locate commonalties of belief and cultural parallels prior to the middle passage, the argument goes, the greater the likelihood that those traditions would survive and thrive in America. Yet, to substantiate this position, too often the byproduct of this approach is a generalized, static, and timeless portrayal of African Traditional Religions. Even further, the raison d'être for African religions in the historical narrative is to foreshadow the emergence of African American religions. The challenge, then, is to locate the shared traits of African religions, while simultaneously recognizing the variety of religious expressions that have existed in Africa and have changed over the centuries and continue to be transformed as other world religions have.

One way to do this is to look creatively at previously unconsidered sources. Historians have scoured advertisements for labor in the early

American colonies, finding records of requests for slaves from particular regions known to have the skills necessary to perform specialized tasks on the plantations. Some plantation owners imported Africans from the Mande and Mano River groups because of their ability with agriculture, specifically rice, indigo, and tobacco. The Senegambians, especially Fulani, who were of mixed Arabic and African heritage, were thought to be the most intelligent ethnicity and therefore would make good house servants and artisans. Even further, certain Africans such as the Yorubas, Whydahs, and Pawpaws were believed to be submissive and therefore less likely to take part in or lead rebellions. Slave merchants who brought their slaves to the marketplace were very precise about the specific point of origin and region in Africa where their slaves came from. In addition, runaway notices from the eighteenth century demonstrate a familiarity with African geography and ethnicities, which included descriptions such as "a very black Mundingo," or "a Congo Negro Slave." Yet, given the demand for particular slaves, these slave traders had an economic incentive to stretch the truth about their trade routes and the origins of their cargo, which in the end may tell us more about their business savvy than the location and influence of particular African ethnicities in America.

Even without establishing a direct connection to a specific region of Africa, the presence of cultural practices that became prevalent in America only after the arrival of slaves can serve as persuasive evidence. In Africa, the Ovimbundu placed baskets, gourds, and instruments that the deceased person used in their daily lives on their plots in cemeteries so they could use them in the next world. Kongo graves often have cooking pots and utensils and bottles adorned on them. In areas of the South, such as New Orleans, slaves left objects on graves to keep the dead from returning to them. In colonial America, slaves often placed their dead facing east, a common burial practice in many parts of Africa. The Igbo put on an elaborate ceremony for months or up to a year after the death of a person to guide the person's spirit to the land of their ancestors. Similarly, throughout Florida, slaves would hold a "second burial" and would not "preach the funeral" until months after a death occurred. The absence of these burial practices among European Americans strongly suggests that they are rituals of African origin.

Establishing the retention of specific African religious beliefs to America can be an even harder task. Margaret Creel sought to demonstrate that the Gullah of South Carolina, as in many African traditions, viewed death as a door between spiritual worlds and expressed little apprehension of death in their triumphant shout songs and theology. Although there are distinctive elements of Gullah Christianity, it is unclear whether the unique interpretation originated from their experience in America or from an African ancestry. For example, the process of "seeking Jesus" in the Methodist tradition was introduced by whites, but the Gullah did so in a unique fashion, instituting a "striving" process that required a long period of self-examination and solitary prayer "in the bush" waiting for the Holy Spirit to speak to them. While the omission of a judgment day in many Gullah versions of Christian songs might indicate that they had little apprehension about death, it might also reflect the precariousness of life as a slave, facing impending and arbitrary threats on their life on a daily basis.

Artistic expressions are also fertile ground for the retention of African culture in America. Musicologists have noted the similarities between the mechanics of delivery, time, text, pitch, call-and-response style, sounds, body movements, hand gestures, facial expressions, and clothing found in African American religious services and those of Africa. Some have asserted that drumbeats are transmitted along distinctive neural pathways during worship services, catalyzing distinctive African and African American religious expressions. In northern Kongo, specialized ritual experts cut designs on the bodies of living fish or turtles with encoded messages to descendants and then released them back into nature, a practice that continued among slaves in New Orleans.

Recognizing that cultural transmission is not a one-way process, scholars have located African influences on white American culture. Sites of cultural exchange include language through the development of a southern dialect, cuisine, with the introduction of foods such as okra that are native to West and Central Africa into the American diet, and familial ties through the close interaction between white children and their African nannies during slavery. In addition to the creation of jazz, scholars have traced the prominent role of the banjo in white Appalachian music, specifically the act of frequently strikingly the instrument on its head while being played, back to a Senegambian technique in Africa. Similarly, scholars have noted that slave "field hollers" are also reminiscent of the yodeling tradition in many parts of Africa.[5]

Historians like John K. Thornton have examined the "African dimensions" of slave uprisings such as the Stono Rebellion of 1739 in South Carolina. Drawing on eyewitness accounts as well as secondhand reports, Thornton argues that the slaves who participated in the revolt were primarily from the kingdom of Kongo (modern Angola), bound together by a shared Christian religion, and likely literate in Portuguese and Kongolese. He attributes the ability of the rebels to secure and handle weapons with skill to a previous military training during a series of lengthy civil wars in Africa. Marching under banners like African soldiers and urging each other on through drumbeats also evidenced a Kongo background according to

5. John Edward Philips, "The African Heritage of White America," *Africanisms in American Culture*, ed. Joseph E. Holloway (Bloomington: Indiana University Press, 2005), 372–96.

Thornton. What outside observers believed to be chaos, disorderly activity, and a generally haphazard attack, Thornton sees as an African military tactic in which units would repeatedly attack, withdraw, and maneuver to weaken an enemy with superior numbers.[6]

Other scholars focus less on establishing one-to-one connections between Africa and the Americas and more on the transmission of a general worldview that informs the perspective and behaviors of African Americans. Charles Long makes the case that although the outer expressions change over time, African Americans share a "characteristic mode of orienting and perceiving reality," a "persisting structural mode," and the common experience of slavery which lays the foundation for the "persistence of an African style." These cultural continuities, Long asserts, are a part of "the involuntary and transformative nature of the religious consciousness." Long concludes that new African American religious expressions "retain an archaic structure in their religious consciousness, and this structure is never quite settled for; it is there as a datum to be deciphered in the context of their present experience."[7] Framed in this manner, to establish an African "survival" in African American religions does not require establishing the physical route that brought slaves to America, but rather the underlying African principles that can be found in African American religious belief and practice.

Scholars have found Long's approach attractive at a number of levels. While historians have located some African voices in early seventeenth-century America, the legacy of the slave trade has made the reconstruction of the African experience an imprecise undertaking. Absent the abundance of traditional written sources

6. John K. Thornton, "African Dimensions of the Stono Rebellion," *The American Historical Review* 96, no. 4 (October 1991): 1101–13.

7. Timothy E. Fulop and Albert J. Raboteau, eds., *African-American Religion: Interpretive Essays in History and Culture* (New York: Routledge, 1997), 21–35.

available for other immigrant groups such as diaries, journals, articles, letters, etc., scholars must bring an unprecedented creativity to fully acknowledge the contributions of Africans to early American religious life. Long suggests a less quantitative and more qualitative approach in which aesthetic sensibilities become just as valuable data as ship logs and ethnographic studies. This methodology is particularly applicable where similarities between African and African American cultures seem apparent, but no direct line of cultural transmission can be established.

Yet, this approach also essentializes the African American experience and worldview. If one's racial outlook is based on a biologically established "archaic structure" that can be drawn upon intentionally as well as "unconsciously," the source of African American religion becomes more innate and less shaped by social and cultural factors. This approach allows an unbroken link between the mindsets that informed the varied struggles in African American history, from slavery, Jim Crow segregation, to the civil rights movement and beyond. Yet, it also challenges notions of race as a social construction that has no basis in biology. Today, scientists say that whites and blacks have more genes in common than those that differ. The DNA of an individual traditionally defined within a particular people group such as African American is often more similar to someone of another race or ethnicity.

Notions of Race in Early America

Early colonial laws demonstrate how futile it can be to assign a biological basis for race. Almost from the arrival of Africans to America, there were interracial unions that produced children. In 1656, in Virginia, in the court case of In Re Mulatto, the earliest judicial ruling that referred to a "mulatto," the court found that the individual's European ancestry had no legal significance, but it was the presence of any ancestry of African descent that determined one's racial status, effectively articulating the notion of hypodescent or as it is more commonly known, "the one drop rule." Many American colonies issued strict laws and punishments for interracial relationships between blacks and whites, particularly if those unions produced offspring. A 1691 Virginia law called for the "banishment" of any white woman who had a child with a "negro" and sentenced the child to a life of slavery regardless of the status of their parents. Who was deemed black varied by colony. The 1705 Virginia legislature prohibited intermarriage if a person was one-eighth African. In North Carolina, the percentage was one-sixteenth African. This meant that a person's racial status could change as they traveled from one state to another. It was not until the 1850 Census that records would distinguish blacks from mulattoes.

Congressional records of the time suggest that part of the reason for this new racial categorization and division was to evaluate the theory of Josiah Nott, a southern physician, who asserted that whites and blacks were from different species. His hypothesis was that if they mated, their hybrid offspring would be physically inferior to those of both pure races. By 1890, census takers were instructed to visually inspect an individual's physical appearance to determine the ratio of black and white blood in their veins. "Black" was defined as having three-fourths or more African blood, "mulatto" three-eighths to five-eighths, "quadroon" one-fourth, and "octoroon" one-eighth or any detectable black blood. Far from scientific, the census takers were presumed to have an almost a psychic ability to detail an individual's racial heritage.[8]

---

8. Christine B. Hickman, "The Devil and the One Drop: Racial Categories, African Americans, and the U.S. Census," in Timothy Davis, Kevin R. Johnson, and George A. Martínez, eds., *A Reader on Race, Civil Rights, and American Law: A Multicultural Approach* (Durham, NC: Carolina Academic Press, 2001), 7-21; Ian Haney Lopez, *White by Law: The Legal Construction of Race* (New York: New York University Press, 1996).

Even holding notions of race constant, comparing African and African American cosmologies comes with its own set of challenges. If certain African values or "unconscious grammatical principles" can be established, they still may be expressed in a distinctive manner across the varied regions of the continent. As an illustration, many African traditional cultures revered the power of twins. However, the Yoruba had a series of complex rites and ceremonial practices to mark the death of twins, while the Igbo killed their twins at birth. Despite this variation in practice and intent, if, as Herskovits has argued, much of African influence on African American behavior "lodges on a psychological plane that lies below the level of consciousness," then African retentions can be located in a range of beliefs and practices including "motor habits," "aesthetic patterns," and "value systems."[9]

New Models for Understanding African American Religions

How American are African American religions? How does one determine the "Americanness" of a community that has been enslaved, segregated, and so thoroughly discriminated against throughout their history in the country? This question is no less relevant than that of African retentions and its formulation is equally complicated. Perhaps it is precisely this distance between America's self-image and the historical treatment of African Americans that can go a long way toward illumining an answer to these questions. Most broad consensus narratives of American religious history tend to strike a triumphant note, touting the country's exceptionalism in addressing issues of religious diversity. This portrayal invariably invokes the unprecedented protections under the First Amendment of the United States Constitution as cementing America's place as

9. Melville J. Herskovits, "Some psychological implications of Afroamerican studies," in *Acculturation in the Americas*, ed. Sol Tax (Chicago: University of Chicago Press, 1952), 153–55; Melville J. Herskovits, *The Myth of the Negro Past* (Boston: Beacon Press, 1969).

the beacon of religious freedom. Yet, for most African Americans, colonial America represented anything but liberty as they labored on southern plantations. Perhaps the cultural encounter between Africans and European Americans outlines the limits of America's religious tolerance. In this way, as David Wills has suggested, African American religious history fills a "gap" between these two cultures. The Great Awakenings of the late eighteenth century with its interracial gatherings and the formation of biracial denominations seemed to foreshadow racial and religious reconciliation. Yet, the issue of slavery and the entrance of racial attitudes and segregated practices into the sacred space of the church and the day-to-day rituals and treatment of congregants led many African Americans to form independent African American churches. Emancipation witnessed biracial support for the education and uplift of the newly freed slaves, who, given the option, often joined historically black denominations or formed their own churches. The civil rights movement, a mission that united many blacks and whites in the cause of social justice, soon gave way to the Black Power movement of the 1970s that sought not to integrate but to challenge institutional racism in America.[10] This interracially linked approach acknowledges the centrality of black experiences and provides an important corrective to volumes written about American religious history that make little or no reference to the contributions of African Americans. Yet, this framework also suggests that African American religions can only be understood in relationship with the majority culture. While it may be impossible to grapple with African American religions solely on their own terms, if a comparative approach is employed, it must also acknowledge the influence of an African presence on the landscape and trajectory of American religious history.

10. Timothy E. Fulop and Albert J. Raboteau, eds., *African-American Religion: Interpretive Essays in History and Culture* (New York: Routledge, 1997), 7–20.

Perhaps African and American identities should not be understood as opposing forces that required struggle to be reconciled, but rather as hybrid cultures that could be drawn upon to greater and lesser degrees depending on the appropriateness of the context. As Iain Chambers and other cultural theorists have asserted, hybridity is the process of cultural mixing where diasporic peoples "adopt aspects of the host culture and rework, reform and reconfigure this in the production of a new hybrid culture or 'hybrid identities.'"[11] In this way, African American religious studies is not so much about the search for African retentions, "Americanness," or the evolution from a pure African culture to a fixed African American awareness, but for a hybridization process that blurs the boundaries of each of these identities that could be drawn upon to make sense of varied experiences in America.

This hybridization process would also complicate the historiography of African American religious leaders that has tended to cluster their perspectives under broad categories to encapsulate their ideologies and to understand their relationship to one another, such as "radical" versus "conservative" or "assimilationists" versus "nationalists." In his 1908 essay, "Radicals and Conservatives," Kelly Miller writes, "Radical and conservative Negroes agree as to the end in view, but differ as to the most effective means of attaining it. The difference is not essentially one of principle or purpose, but point of view." Miller contrasted the efforts of Frederick Douglass and W. E. B. Du Bois which he saw as "radical" with those of Booker T. Washington which he viewed as "conservative."[12] Gayraud S. Wilmore also employed the term "black radicalism" to understand a component of "black religion."[13] While this approach has served as

11. Iain Chambers and Linda Curtis, eds., *The Post-colonial Question* (London: Routledge, 1996), 50.
12. Kelly Miller, "The Negro's Part," in *Radicals and Conservatives and Other Essays on the Negro in America* (New York: Schocken Books, 1968).

an instructive heuristic device, illumining the dynamics of specific historical moments, if held to too rigidly, it can at once maintain ambiguity and reify the boundaries of the concepts, resist acknowledging change over time in an individual's outlook, and accentuate the evidence that supports the presupposition upon which the categories are based. Scholars have extended Manning Marable's classic dialectic between "accommodation" and "resistance" to understand the former as being "influenced by the larger society and to take part in aspects of it" and the latter as "affirming one's own cultural heritage."[14] From this framework and relatively abstract criteria, multiple volumes have categorized Henry McNeal Turner, W. E. B. Du Bois, and Malcolm X, all having embraced a "black consciousness" and practiced "resistance," as "Nationalists," while those African Americans who advocated for and anticipated full inclusion and participation in American society, institutions, and values, such as Benjamin T. Tanner, Booker T. Washington, and Martin Luther King Jr., have been labeled "accommodationists" or "assimilationists." Although careful examinations of the more contemporary black religious thinkers have complicated this characterization, the resistance—accommodationist dichotomy in the study of African American religions has been resilient, particularly regarding the "Back-to-Africa" movements of the nineteenth century. Yet, the disagreements within many black religious communities seemed to be less about the embrace or rejection of a "cultural heritage," than a divergence in what constituted that lineage. For some African Americans, the question of identity centered on the reconciliation of an African past, an American

13. Gayraud S. Wilmore, *Black Religion and Black Radicalism: An Interpretation of the Religious History of African Americans* (New York: Orbis Books, 1998).

14. Manning Marable, *How Capitalism Underdeveloped Black America* (Boston: South End, 1983), 26; Manning Marable, *Speaking Truth to Power: Essays on Race, Resistance, and Radicalism* (Boulder, CO: Westview Press, 1998).

present, and a possible return to Africa. For others, America contained the only history and future location for blacks, and there were many other distinctive perspectives in between.

Continuing Challenges

The dynamic is further complicated by the question of "authentic" voice. Who is able to speak for the African experience in slavery? While the answer to this question may seem straightforward, as demonstrated by the controversy surrounding *The Interesting Narrative of Olaudah Equiano, or Gustavus Vassa, the African. Written by Himself* (1789), the assertion of authority based on ancestry can be tenuous. Given the brutality of the slave trade and the restrictions placed upon enslaved Africans, there are few firsthand writings from their perspective from the tragic and horrific historical experience of the middle passage. According to his autobiography, Equiano was captured in what is now Nigeria at the age of eleven, resold several times, and survived the middle passage to the West Indies, before finally being purchased by an English slave-trading captain in Virginia. After sailing from Barbados, Philadelphia, and England, he purchased his freedom in 1766. He became a sea merchant traveling from North America, the Mediterranean, the West Indies, and the Arctic circle. He settled in England and became an outspoken abolitionist. Having converted to Christianity prior to penning his autobiography, Equiano's work documents the cruelty of the Middle Passage and the slave trade as well as comparing and locating parallels between the many stories and rituals of the Bible with his own Igbo religion. From his prolific publications, Equiano was likely the wealthiest and the most famous person of African descent at the time of his death on March 31, 1797.[15]

Today, Equiano's *Interesting Narrative* still stands as one of the most important and insightful portrayals of the horrors of slavery and the cruelty of the middle passage. Equiano, himself, has come to symbolize and embody one of the few African voices and the most prominent bearer of Igbo culture in North America, providing one of the only direct documented testimonies linking African and African American experiences. However, the recent discovery of Equiano's baptismal and naval records places the site of his birth in South Carolina in 1747, rather than Nigeria.[16] If this is the case, rather than a firsthand account of his African childhood and experience in the Middle Passage, *The Interesting Narrative* represents a literary imagining of those experiences and cultures or possibly his autobiography represents an amalgamation of several individual stories that were shared in the slave quarters in South Carolina. While scholars continue to argue over the meaning of Equiano's autobiography, the debate points to the issue of cultural authority and who is allowed to speak for a cultural group. From the complex religious traditions of West Africa to the growth of black megachurches in the twenty-first century, what constitutes "true" African American religion changes with the time period and the perspective of the observer. The goal, then, is not to determine levels of authenticity, but to point out the diversity inherent in African American religions and the ways particular beliefs, practices, and expressions were important to varied communities at different historical moments.

While early scholars used a number of categories to encapsulate the essence of African American religions, "The Negro Church" or "The Black Church" has been the most enduring. In his work, *The Souls of*

15. Olaudah Equiano, *The Interesting Narrative and Other Writings* (New York: Penguin Books, 1995).
16. Vincent Carretta, *Equiano the African: Biography of a Self-Made Man* (Athens: University of Georgia Press, 2005).

Black Folk (1903), W. E. B. Du Bois popularized the concept of "The Negro Church" and asserted that it was "the social centre of Negro life in the United States, and the most characteristic expression of African character." While Du Bois acknowledged that "the churches are differentiated," he wrote, "but back of this still broods silently the deep religious feeling of the real Negro heart, the stirring, unguided might of the powerful human souls who have lost the guiding star of the past and seek in the great night a new religious ideal." Six years later, Booker T. Washington capitalized the "c" in "The Negro Church" in his work, *The Story of the Negro,* and by 1921, and the appearance of Carter G. Woodson's *History of the Negro Church,* the concept became synonymous with and used interchangeably for African American religion. The notion of a "racial consciousness" that began in Africa and was most vividly expressed in black Christian traditions continued to inform works on African American religious history such as E. Franklin Frazier's *The Negro Church in America* (1964) and C. Eric Lincoln and Lawrence Mamiya's *The Black Church* (1990).[17]

For the most part, broad narratives of African American religious history have continued to be fairly Christian-centered, wrestling with issues such as the attraction of African Americans to Christianity or distinguishing between black and white denominational expressions of the faith. Albert Raboteau's *Slave Religion* connects African Traditional Religions (rhythmic drumming, speech patterns, reverence for water, etc.) and varied aspects of Christianity (worship services, chanted sermons, baptism, etc.) to foreshadow the

17. W. E. B. Du Bois, *The Souls of Black Folk* (New York: Penguin Books, 1996); Booker T. Washington, *The Story of the Negro* (Philadelphia: University of Pennsylvania Press, 2011); Carter G. Woodson, *The History of the Negro Church* (Washington, DC: The Associated Publishers, 1921); E. Franklin Frazier, *The Negro Church in America* (New York: Schocken Books, 1969); C. Eric Lincoln and Lawrence Mamiya, *The Black Church in the African American Experience* (Durham, NC: Duke University Press, 1990).

acceptance of the gospel by slaves. Paul Harvey's work, *Redeeming the South* (1997) on black and white Southern Baptists serves as a contemporary example of the comparative approach. Henry H. Mitchell's *Black Church Beginnings: The Long-Hidden Realities of the First Years*, locates African survivals in virtually all aspects of African American religions including the tradition of spirit possession, "shouting," and the words of slave spirituals; and, like Herskovits, he links the attraction to the Baptist faith to African water rituals. Even further, he asserts that African traditions have been updated, with the familial ties of blood kin in African villages being replaced with the greeting of brother and sister in black churches. The reticence to remove senior members from their leadership positions and the presence and centrality of an all-powerful, providential God are among the parallels that Mitchell locates between African Traditional Religions and the "African American Christian belief system."[18]

Although Christianity is an important component, the religious beliefs and practices embraced by African Americans have been as diverse as the perspectives present in the black community. Yet, the historiography of the field and the introductory African American Religions course syllabus have not always reflected this variety. In general, non-Christian voices in North America rarely appear in the historical narrative before the early twentieth century with the rise of new religious movements such as the Noble Drew Ali and the Moorish Science Temple. In contrast, this text takes an integrative approach interweaving the experiences of members of nonwestern traditions and other traditionally marginalized communities within the broader historical narrative. In this way, Christianity shares the

---

18. Albert J. Raboteau, *Slave Religion*. Paul Harvey, *Redeeming the South: Religious Cultures and Racial Identities among Southern Baptists, 1865–1925* (Chapel Hill: University of North Carolina Press, 1997); Henry H. Mitchell, *Black Church Beginnings: The Long-Hidden Realities of the First Years* (Grand Rapids, MI: Eerdmans, 2004).

"center" with other religious options during slavery such as conjure and Islam. As his autobiography from 1831 attests, Omar Ibn Said, a scholar and trader who was enslaved and brought to Charleston, South Carolina, retained much of his Muslim identity, as did many other first-generation slaves whose names have been lost to us. It is the stories and perspectives of individuals like Said, Jarena Lee, Richard Allen, Sojourner Truth, Amanda Smith, Elijah Muhammad, and T. D. Jakes that aptly demonstrate the inherent diversity of African American religions and the complicated narrative of their growth and transformation in America.

1

West African Traditional Religions

Scanning the table of contents of many contemporary world religions textbooks, if African religions are even included, you will likely still find them classified among the "primitive" or "primal" religions that existed in "prehistoric" cultures and societies. On what basis might some traditions be viewed as the "Great World Religions" and others relegated to a precursor to "modern" history? The answer to this question lies within the peculiar legacy of the discipline of Religious Studies.

The Early "Scientists" of Religion

The mid-nineteenth century birthed what was then referred to as the "science of religion." Among the most prominent of these new pioneers, Friedrich Max Muller has been deemed by posterity as the "father of comparative religion." Muller was a German philosopher who, among other academic accomplishments, translated the sacred Hindu text, the Rig Veda, wrote the celebrated work *Comparative Mythology*, and is said to have uttered the phrase that undergirds the central presumption of the comparative approach to religion: "He who knows one, knows none." While many of his contemporaries viewed religion and science as distinct and unrelated spheres, Muller made the case that one could study traditions, even those with which they were not affiliated, in a manner that did justice to both the scientific method and the communities under investigation. To be truly classified as a science, like his primary field of linguistics had become, the discipline of Religious Studies would need scholars who extended the scope of their studies beyond the knowledge of their own religions.

Several early scholars of religion took up this charge and pursued new information about cultures with a vengeance. The burgeoning field of archeology unearthed relics from long-ago civilizations and dated materials to specific historical eras with an unprecedented precision. Philologists translated sacred texts that many in the West were previously unfamiliar with. Colonialism brought Europeans into extensive contact with a wide range of indigenous peoples. Drawing on this bounty of new information, these early scholars compared religious phenomena from wide-ranging historical periods and vast regions of the world, creating intricate and massive categorical schemes that noted not only general similarities and differences in their traits such as beliefs and practices, but summed up what those traditions were at their essence and in their natural form. They carefully sorted through the data, identified cause and effect, and drew conclusions only after careful and thorough consideration of all "facts." These "scientists of religion" rigorously adhered to the newly formulated standards of evidence collection, objective evaluation, and the comparative approach. They sought to do away with bias and false presumptions, and committed to never taking the assertions of any tradition at face value. Elements of cultures that remained consistent over time, were only cursorily changed, or failed to evolve altogether were deemed "survivals" and were analyzed as a "living fossil" and a window onto the prehistoric mind. The ultimate goal was to discover the "genus 'religion' which underlay the species 'the religions.'"[1]

While the early nineteenth-century western scientists of religion sought to recover the cultures of "lost civilizations," the basis for their classifications were often haphazard, the rationale for the points of comparisons drawn were unclear, and both seemed to change at the whim of the investigator's own idiosyncratic criteria. In the second half of the nineteenth century, Darwin's theory of natural selection through evolution emerged as the central organizing principle for the scientific approach to the study of religion. In addition, Herbert Spencer's *First Principles* (1862) and his notion of "survival of the fittest" extended the realm of scientific inquiry to include the phenomenon of religion. For Spencer, evolutionary principles acted upon all aspects of society, including government, commerce, language, literature, science, art, and religion. Evolution provided a structure to chart the growth and historical transformations of religion. Rather than existing outside of time in the form of divine revelation, religion was understood as a "developing organism" that changed and adapted throughout history. Massive tables and schematics of the world's cultures were reworked into linear charts that traced the ascension of some cultures and religions and the demise of others.

The evolutionary model cemented a hierarchical structure in which, as in biology, religions were believed to evolve from simple to complex, polytheism to monotheism, and primitive to advanced. For example, Sir John Lubbock's *The Origin of Civilisation and the Primitive Connection of Man* (1870) found atheism to be the lowest form of religion and charted the successive stages of fetishism,

---

1. Eric J. Sharpe, *Comparative Religion: A History* (La Salle, IL: Open Court, 1986), 32.

totemism (nature worship), shamanism, anthropomorphism, culminating with ethical monotheism. Morality, according to Lubbock, only existed in the final stage of development. Edward Burnett Tylor would take issue with a number of Lubbock's conclusions, perhaps most notably the lack of religion among "savages." Instead, Tylor located what he termed animism or a "belief in spiritual beings" among the "primitive" cultures. From this discovery, Tylor introduced the notion of "survivals," which he understood as elements of culture, society, or religion, such as animism, that had failed to succumb to the forces of evolution. Therefore, any religious belief or practice that could be found among "uncivilized" ancient cultures necessarily reflected an earlier stage in human and religious development. This concentration on survivals heightened the attention to "primitive cultures" because they were presumed to show the earliest moments of religious formation.

The Early Study of African Religions

Rather than noting the diversity of African Traditional Religions, early scholars drew upon E. B. Tylor's notion of "animism" to establish how these religious elements evolved over time. Tylor first used the term "animism" in an article in 1866 and later in his work, *Primitive Culture* (1871). Tylor's basic definition of animism was "belief in spirit beings." He described anima as fleeting images that animated people, animals, and objects and could move between beings long after their deaths. Animism characterized primitive peoples who presumed that all matter had its own soul and believed in countless spirits. With the rise of evolution, scholars postulated that this notion led to the idea of one spirit having power over a particular realm of nature, which evolved into polytheism, which eventually transformed into a notion of one supreme God reigning over the lesser divinities. As this analysis indicates, many scholars presumed that monotheism was the most advanced stage of evolution, with Judaism and Christianity representing the most superior versions of religion.

In his *Principles of Sociology* (1885), Herbert Spencer used the term "ancestor worship" to describe the ways certain objects were related to the spirits of the dead and how practitioners offered sacrifices to maintain harmonious relationships with their deceased ancestors. As with many such terms, the application was much wider than this definition, referring to almost any African religious ceremony. A number of contemporary commentators have noted the imprecision and inaccuracy of the term "worship," which would be seen as blasphemous for many cultures to ascribe such reverence toward anyone other than God. However, for early scholars of religion magic was seen as a central component of African traditions and closely related to ancestor worship. Magic was understood as humans' attempts to relate cause and effect in the natural world. Through trial and error they slowly realized that their efforts to influence the outcome were futile and eventually turned to a belief in an all-powerful God.[2]

Early Darwinian scholars of religion excluded indigenous traditions from inclusion in what they considered to be the "great world religions" such as Hinduism, Buddhism, Judaism, and Christianity for a number for reasons. An oft-cited rationale was the lack of a written text among many African cultures. Scholarly treatments of African societies often ascribe the term "myth" to their narratives, but, in some cases, were reticent to apply the same moniker to the stories of western traditions. Part of the reason for this distinction is that African Traditional Religions pass down their

---

2. Alexander Begg, *A sketch of the successful missionary work of William Duncan amongst the Indian Tribes in Northern British Columbia, from 1858-1901* (Victoria, B.C., 1910), 29.

histories through an oral tradition, rather than recording it in written texts. Early western observers deemed the former as the less "accurate" of the two methods, equating change over time with less reliability. Yet, the Abrahamic faiths each existed in oral form, in some cases for decades, before being canonized in written form. In many African societies, narratives that convey religious and cultural history are nuanced over time to address the needs of the contemporary community. Accuracy is measured by its relevance in guiding and speaking to the present concerns of the community.

Early scholars also tended to frame African Traditional Religions as localized "ethnic" traditions and "tribal practices." In some cases, Darwinian theorists even postulated that because the people of Africa were so "savage" and "uncivilized," their religious beliefs and practices had to have been imported from somewhere else. Early missionaries such as William Duncan described indigenous communities as "barbarous, materialist, childish, and inarticulate," and "almost stupefied with brutish ignorance, with the instincts of man in him, but yet living the life of a beast."[3] This tone continued, though not as glaringly into the twentieth century, when many western scholars included African traditions in their studies, not as important in and of themselves, but as a point of comparison to confirm the superiority of the traditions espoused by the scholars engaging in the investigation.

To qualify as a world religion, some argued, the tradition must be "revealed" rather than what E. E. Evans-Pritchard called "natural" religion. This premise contradicts the ways many Africans understand religion as a "way of life" in and of itself, exemplified by the lack of term for "religion" in many African cultures. Others made the case that African religions should be excluded from consideration

---

3. Laurenti Magesa, *African Religion: The Moral Traditions of Abundant Life* (New York: Orbis Books, 1997), 1–34.

as world religions because they are not "redemptive religions" anticipating the soul's redemption in an afterlife or lacking an emphasis on morality issues. "Primitives," they asserted, lacked both the imagination and emotion to do so. Others maintained that to be a world religion the tradition must proselytize.

Despite their complexity and diversity, African Traditional Religions, for the most part, continue to be excluded from inclusion among the "great world religions" in contemporary textbooks. While early Darwinians scholars provided explicit criteria for their understanding of African Traditional Religions as "primal" and "primitive," present-day authors rarely explain, justify, or feel called to elaborate upon the placement of African religions in the "premodern" section of the text. While some suggest that these terms can be rehabilitated and reemployed despite their historically pejorative use in the early study of religion, only selected cultures continue to be placed into the "primal" categories. This extreme localization and emphasis upon the "ancientness" of African religions prohibits any consideration of the ways these beliefs and practices changed over time, engaged other religions, and influenced other beliefs and practices. In this way, African Traditional Religions are often portrayed as a static body of tenets and rituals rather than living and growing world religions.

On what basis do certain traditions warrant inclusion as a great world religion? The need for binary categories often leads to divisions such as eastern and western religions in textbooks, which complicates the placement of African religions if they are allowed to be lifted from the "primal" categories. If the criterion is the number of adherents, there are over the 25 million adherents in Yoruban-derived traditions around the world, such as Afro-Cuban Santeria, Candomble in Brazil, Shango traditions in Trinidad, and Voodoo in Haiti. One could make a strong case that not only should African religions be considered world religions, but that Yoruba religious culture alone would constitute one of the largest and most vibrant of the world traditions. Yet, because this globalization did not occur through missions or conquest, it provides a seemingly more complicated model to map onto the religious landscape of world religions.[4]

Although the evolutionary categories claimed more objectivity than previous models, their classification schemes were no less wedded to the religious outlook of the particular investigator, which usually placed their own tradition as the final stage in religious development. Christianity and Judaism, the religions of western, industrialized nations, were most often placed in the advanced categories, while the beliefs and practices of indigenous cultures were relegated to the "primitive" category. Today, few scholars would assert a Darwinian paradigm to understand religion, yet its influence upon the periodization of the evolution of religious traditions has left an indelible mark on the study of African religions. This legacy can still be seen in many contemporary textbook treatments of African Traditional Religions as a type of "survival" from the nascent period of the study of religion.

African Traditional Religions

Religious life in Africa is incredibly diverse and even further variegated at the local level. It is estimated that there are over 2,100 African languages and dialects. With a continent the size of Africa, which is equivalent to the geographic mass of the United States, China, Western Europe, India, and Argentina combined, it would be safe to say that variety characterizes the religious landscape of Africa. Cultural and regional comparisons are complicated by the

4. Jacob K. Olupona, *Orisa Devotion as World Religion: The Globalization of Yoruba Religious Culture* (Madison: University of Wisconsin Press, 2008).

fact that most African societies do not have a separate word for "religion," blurring the boundaries of the sacred and secular. From this perspective, it would be a misnomer to attempt to divide a person's daily activities from their spiritual life. As such, many western religious concepts do not easily translate to the African context. With those cautions in mind and acknowledging that there will always be exceptions to any generalization, traversing the vast continent of Africa, there are religious components that the majority of communities hold in common.

Most African Traditional Religions have a central figure (God), intermediaries (divinities, spirits), religious leaders (medicine-people, mediums, diviners, priests), and a profound respect for the departed (ancestors) and the natural world. God is often understood as the creator of the earth and all that is in it. In most societies, God is believed to be omniscient (all-knowing), omnipresent (everywhere at once), and omnipotent (all-powerful). However, the moral attributes of God are less precise. While many traditions regard God as essentially good, kind, and merciful, others have a more ambiguous characterization, connecting and holding this higher power responsible for a wide range of calamities, misfortunes, and illnesses that fall upon individuals, families, and in some cases, entire communities. If God is all-powerful, the reasoning goes, he or she could prevent all incidents of evil, but, for purposes often unknown, allows them to occur. For example, the Katanga people describe the nature of God as, "the Father Creator Who creates and uncreates." Because God is often viewed as governing and reigning over the world, many societies invoke images of a King, Ruler, Lord, Master, or Judge to depict this authoritative role.

Although in many cultures, God is portrayed as male, matriarchal societies like the Ovambo and the southern Nuba understand the supreme deity as Mother. The creator figure in many sacred narratives is referred to in female terms or is referenced as Mother. Nigerian stories trace the origins of humans to the mother-divinity Eka-Abassi. In eastern Africa, narratives describe a virgin woman named Ekao who fell from the sky and whose offspring were the first humans. If not divine, women still play central roles in many oral traditions. The Akposso (of Togo) relay stories of Uwolowu (God) first making a woman on earth and bearing the first human being with her. The Tutsi (of Rwanda) pass down a narrative of the first man and woman in paradise who are incapable of having children. For help they pleaded to God, who used clay and saliva to create a small human figure. God instructed the woman to place the figure in a pot for nine months and to pour milk over it twice a day. Once the person was fully formed, she removed the newly created person from the pot. The rest of humanity was created in a similar fashion. Many narratives across Western Africa describe a male and female couple descending from the sky as the founders of human society. In some cases, women are created out of parts of the man's body or subsequent to the appearance of the first male. In many West African sacred stories, women are inventors or discoverers of new elements. In some cultures, women are credited with discovering fire and foods and their preparation. While in some regions the female God is credited with cherishing or nursing humankind, for the most part, the powers ascribed to God in patriarchal and matriarchal societies are virtually indistinguishable.

Most sacred narratives describe some tension between God and people. In some cases, a message is sent by God but somehow does not reach the intended people, is changed by the messenger in some way, or arrives too late. Others speak of a test that God placed before the original people and they somehow were unable to fulfill it, which accounts for the origins of death, misfortune, suffering, and God's separation from humankind. Some narratives cite familial disputes or animals as the cause of the downfall of humans. Some sacred stories describe women as the cause of the separation between God and people. One Pygmy (Bambuti) narrative is reminiscent of the Adam and Eve account in Genesis. The story relates that God put in place a rule that people could eat from all the trees except one. A pregnant woman desiring the fruit from the forbidden tree urged her husband to retrieve the fruit. He did so, but the moon, which was watching, relayed the deed to God who brought death into the world as punishment for the disobedient people. An Ashanti story (of Ghana) describes a woman who, while pounding *fufu*, the national food, built a tower of mortars to try to reach God. God moved higher and higher into the sky and the woman had her children build the tower higher still. The tower came within one mortar from reaching God, so the woman had her children remove the bottom mortar and place it on the top. As a result the tower fell, killing several people. Stories that explicitly place the blame on women for the fall of humankind, however, are relatively few in West Africa.

African societies differ in the day-to-day interaction with God, divinities, spirits, and ancestors. In some traditions, God intervenes and is an intricate part of human history. In others, the Creator sets the world in motion and allows the spirits to take authority over certain aspects of the world. These intermediaries, a step removed from the highest realm that God occupies, are autonomous beings free to roam the earth at will and to participate in the daily affairs of people. Some groups such as the Yoruba have thousands of spirits and divinities, while others only venerate a few such as the Bambuti who focus on Tore, who is in charge of death, and the Dinka who emphasize three: Macardit, the explainer of suffering and misfortune; Garang, who can fall from heaven and enter humans; and Abuk, who oversees women and their daily work. In some cultures, these entities maintain control over certain natural phenomena such as the rain, rivers, clouds, or the winds. Like God, spirits and divinities have a wide range of personalities and temperaments and can be both a positive and negative influence on an individual's course in life. Ancestors who have passed away within the last five generations can also impact the fortunes of their relatives. Within this liminal period between life and the final afterworld, with an ability to speak both divine and human languages, ancestors can serve as mediators between individuals and the next realm, discerning the requests of God, divinities, and spirits. As the keepers of tradition, ancestors can be relentless in ensuring that their descendants adhere to the letter of the law, causing anything from minor disruptions to catastrophic events if familial and community customs such as burial rites are not appropriately carried out. This ancestral connection inextricably links Africans to the land and adds an additional dimension to the spiritual and physical toll the Atlantic slave trade took on those persons ripped from their homeland and forcibly shipped to the New World.

The complexity of these various supernatural entities is described in African sacred stories that describe the personalities of the gods, divinities, and spirits, their spheres of influence, and their relationships to one another. This religious understanding is passed down orally from generation to generation through stories, proverbs, commentaries, songs, and prayers. The Shilluk convey the creative nature of God by describing his use of clay to form the first humans, referring to him as the potter, molder, and maker. Through an account of the stern punishment bestowed upon the first humans for eating the forbidden yam, one Chagga narrative warns of the spirits' abilities to bring sickness, misfortune, wars, and even death when people transgress God's will.

Scholarly treatments of African societies often ascribe the term "myth" to these narratives, but, in some cases, are reticent to apply the same concept to the stories of western traditions. Part of the reason for this distinction is that African Traditional Religions pass down their histories through an oral tradition, rather than recording it in written texts. Early western observers deemed the former as the less "accurate" of the two methods, equating change over time with less reliability.

The interrelationship between God, divinities, spirits, the ancestors, and the living are undergirded and reinforced by intricate systems of sacrifice and offerings performed to maintain harmony. Sacrifice and offerings range from gifts of food and everyday objects to the presentation of an animal's life. Gods, divinities, and spirits have idiosyncratic favorites that convey special reverence such as offerings of eggs and wine in the Akan and Ashanti cultures. When these rituals are done to honor the ancestors, the action is sometimes characterized as "ancestor worship," but might be more accurately cast as a deep and profound respect for those who have passed away. Societies vary about the recipient of these sacrifices and offerings. Some focus on appeasing the divinities and spirits while others venerate God. For example, the Abaluyia describe God as "the One to Whom sacred rites and sacrifices are made or paid."[5] While sacrifice and offerings are made throughout the year, they almost always accompany formal ceremonies and occasions such as births, naming rites, circumcision, weddings, funerals, and the harvest season.

There are a range of religious specialists whose primary duties and training are to maintain harmony between individuals in society and the supernatural and earthly realms. Sometimes pejoratively characterized as "witch doctors," these medicine-people, mediums, diviners, and priests all perform specialized functions and play central roles in African Traditional Religions. In some societies, these titles are only artificial distinctions since their roles overlap and their work

5. John S. Mbiti, *African Religions and Philosophy* (Portsmouth, NH: Heinemann, 1990), 59.

is so closely connected. Medicine-people or "herbalists" are called to the profession and undergo extensive training from as early as five years of age to learn their craft. The primary concern for medicine-people is the eradication of sickness, disease, and misfortune. Most often, the cause of this negativity can be traced to the spiritual working of one person against another. The medicine-person's task is to uncover the source of the affliction or the catalyst for the misfortune. Cures take a range of forms from the use of powders or roots, chanting, sacrifices, or a prescription to avoid certain foods or people. The medicine-person is part doctor and part psychologist as he or she diagnoses not only the physical or spiritual ailment, but why that particular illness befell the individual at this moment in time. The medicine-person also has a duty to protect people and therefore can create charms and applications to ward off harm. The medicine-person's influence on society is seemingly endless, extending to a person's ability to find love, be successful in business or politics, or thrive as a student. Because of their sacred knowledge, medicine-people are entrusted with safeguarding the community from impending and future threats.

While in some African societies medicine-people are distinguished from mediums, diviners, and priests, in many communities the duties are so closely linked that they are virtually inseparable. Mediums provide a vehicle for communication between humans, ancestors, spirits, divinities, and God, serving as mediators between this world and the next. In some cultures, there is a division of labor in which mediums receive the supernatural message describing the source of the wrongdoing or disharmony, and the medicine-person discerns and provides the appropriate cure. Mediums have the ability to be possessed by the divinities, spirits, and ancestors and, in some cultures, can enter into a trance at will. Like medicine-people, mediums often receive intensive instruction, many times sequestered apart from the rest of the community for a substantial period of time in institutions similar to convents or monasteries. As symbolic religious leaders, African royalty are often presumed to embody the prosperity of the community. Diviners can tell the future and, in some regions of Africa, are believed to influence the forces of nature. Priests perform similar functions as the other religious leaders, but tend to be associated with specific temples and are responsible for the care and performance of the religious ceremonies and practices of that sacred space. Each of these religious specialists is a guardian of sacred knowledge essential for the continuance of tradition, the maintenance of orthodox practices, and contributing in a myriad of ways to the future well-being of the community.

Women play a central role in the religious activities in West Africa. In many societies, women are the ones to offer prayers for their families and their communities. In many areas, there are female priests, mediums are predominately women, and, in some societies, women are understood to be more open to experiencing spirit possession during rituals. Female healers most often handle the medical needs of women and children in the community. Prayer is the most universal of the religious actions that is understood to be under the charge of women. Mothers in the Aro of Sierra Leone offer a prayer for an ill child to departed ancestors in the hopes that they will act on their behalf. Banyarwanda women whose husbands are fighting in a war pray for their protection and that of their fellow soldiers and their safe return home. The Maasai women (Kenya and Tanzania) perform sacrifices, offerings, and prayers to God for rain. The prayer is wide-ranging on the behalf of animals, people, and nature at large, since all require water for their survival. After childbirth, Pygmy mothers express gratitude to God. They say prayers to dedicate their baby to God. The mother and father lift the baby to the sky and pray. Women of the Barundi who are unable to have children often pray to God for help. Women are also essential to many rites of passage. Among the Ashanti in Ghana, when girls have their first menstruation they hold a ceremony. Mothers pray that their daughters will grow up healthy and happy and with the ability to bear children.[6] In every aspect of West African Traditional Religions, women have led, participated, shaped, and influenced the development of beliefs and rituals.

African Religions in the Americas

While debates over African retentions in the New World have historically been quite contentious, few would disagree that the persistence of African religious culture is more pronounced in South America and the Caribbean than in most regions of North America. Yet, even in Latin America, African-derived religious beliefs and practices were transformed within this new cultural context. Religions such as Candomble, Voodoo, and Santeria are mixtures or hybridizations of elements of multiple cultures that were synthesized into distinctive traditions. African religions were transported to the Americas in the hearts and minds of captured slaves, despite harsh conditions and often stringent laws designed to strip away cultural and religious connections to their homeland. Yet, as they had for centuries before, Africans reshaped and reevaluated their religious cosmology in the face of new challenges to the community.

A number of factors came together to make Latin America particularly fertile ground for the preservation and growth of African Traditional Religions. When Candomble was founded in Bahia in northeastern Brazil in the early nineteenth century, Catholicism was

6. John S. Mbiti, *African Religions and Philosophy* (Portsmouth, NH: Heinemann, 1990); Laurenti Magesa, *African Religion: The Moral Traditions of Abundant Life* (New York: Orbis Books, 1997); Benjamin C. Ray, *African Religions: Symbol, Ritual, and Community* (Upper Saddle River, NJ: Prentice Hall, 2000).

the officially recognized religion, one that has historically incorporated indigenous practices within the tradition. The Atlantic slave trade routes to Latin America would last a generation longer than they would to North America, providing an influx of Africans who were only recently separated from their homelands and their African Traditional Religions. The cruelly high mortality rate and minute birth rate coupled with an imbalanced gender population created the need for continual importation of new slaves from the West Coast of Africa. Bahia as a main port for the disembarkation of slaves created a region with an unusually high proportion of African-born slaves. The urban setting of Bahia and the high African-to-white population ratio lent itself to less direct supervision over slave communities. The strategy imposed by many municipal governments to encourage the retention of African tribal identities in the hopes that old animosities would divide slave communities actually served to incubate and nurture the rich African religious heritage of slaves.

Although the practice of Candomble had been banned after colonization, elements of Catholicism paralleled those of African-derived traditions. In particular, many Catholic saints held similar attributes as the divinities within Candomble. In Bahia, the distinction between Saint Barbara and Shango, both associated with thunder, became blurred. The mother figure of Iemanja and Mary became closely tied among practitioners of Candomble. The trickster Eshu-Elegba melded with conceptions of Satan and the devil. Gods portrayed as warriors also blended together in the Afro-Cuban cosmology as Oshossi became identified with St. George or St. Michael the archangel. Orunmilla, who employs a rosary-like amulet for divination, was inseparable from St. Francis. Some historical treatments have suggested that Catholicism served as a public mask that enslaved Africans put on to shield and protect their continued practice of indigenous African religions or that they syncretized Catholicism and African Traditional Religions. While plausible assertions, one must be cautious not to unintentionally delegitimate the experiences and worldviews of those who genuinely accepted the Roman Catholic faith. Even further, the presumption that the central traits of the traditions could be easily conflated simplifies the nature of both religious systems. Perhaps as they had for centuries before, a general African openness to other traditions allowed slave religious practice to be informed by both their present Catholicism and their African heritage mutually reinforcing one another rather than displacing one or the other.

Like African religions in general, Candomble reveres a pantheon of divinities known as orisha (orixa). In Africa, orisha were associated with particular cities or nations: Shango in Oyo, Yemanja in the Egba nation, Ogun in the Ekiti and Ondo nations, Oshun among the Ijeshas and Ijiebus, and Oshala-Obatala in Ife, whose temples were maintained by local priests. Traditionally, the individual would venerate the divinity from their hometown. The Atlantic slave trade displaced this home-centered system that merged sacred communal space and place and instead put the onus on the individual to follow the rules and keep the traditions alive. In Africa, there were institutions to regulate and maintain worship practices, to inform each person of their particular role, and priests to officiate over ceremonies and to sacrifice and present offerings to the orisha. In Brazil, the responsibility for maintaining a proper respect and relationship with the gods shifted from the temple to a personal obligation and commitment to adhere to correct practice. In addition, the diasporic experience of African Americans complicates the relationship between devotees and the orisha and raises questions about orthodoxy that would likely not have been a historical concern in Africa. For example, can non-African practitioners of Candomble be possessed by the orisha if they are not directly descended from an ancestor? These issues coupled with a distinctive South American context led to creative adaptations as practitioners navigated unforeseen complexities and formed new orthodoxies. Some communities nuanced the criteria to be possessed by a spirit from a direct bloodline to an ancestor to a more spiritual connection formed by having similar personalities and temperaments.

Few African-derived religions have been more widely and inaccurately portrayed in popular culture than Vodoun or Voodoo. Video shelves are lined with B-movies depicting "Voodoo dolls" and spell-casting witches as the villain or eerily scary or mysterious characters in films. In reality, Voodoo, the Dahomean word meaning "spirit" or "deity," is a complex African religious tradition. While there were practitioners of Voodoo throughout the African diaspora, its presence is most clearly visible within North America in regions that have had sizable Roman Catholic populations such as Louisiana and Maryland. As a religious system, it is highly structured with a hierarchy of deities, skilled priests and priestesses, and devoted apprentices and participants. In Africa, the training to be a Voodoo priest or priestess was extensive, often requiring monastic practice for as long as nine months. Although receiving less formal training, the local herbalists in Voodoo specialized in diagnosing the source of spiritual and physical ailments. Through the careful use of herbs these practitioners could ascertain who had placed the bad medicine or juju on the person and offer the appropriate cure. Voodoo practices were intricately interwoven with the Fon culture in Africa, which has a prevalent belief in witches or azeto who have the power to exert control over inanimate objects as well as the living. Those conditions that seemed to be immune to normative cures were often attributed to the azeto. In New Orleans, this diverse religious system was melded into the Damballa, the snake cult. As in Africa, the process of initiation as a practitioner was detailed and lengthy, being completed over several weeks or in some cases years depending on the devotee's progress and mastery of the skills. Once trained, the initiate must be presented to and accepted by the central deity, the "Great One" or "Great Spirit" symbolized by the serpent, to gain membership in the community.

The early history of Voodoo in America was characterized by strong female leaders such as Marie Laveau and Marie Saloppe. The first recorded New Orleans voodoo priestess was Sanite Dede, who led the most prominent community from 1822 to 1830. However, as the practice of Voodoo became more widespread, there was no central locus of power as initiates formed their own communities and founded independent sects. As with other African traditions, Voodoo transformed over time in both structure and practice. By the late nineteenth century, lyrics to songs originally devoted to specific African gods and Voodoo priests and priestesses became tributes to the tradition as a whole. The term "Voudou," which had been synonymous with Marie Laveau's snake cult, entered the vernacular to refer to any male Voodoo leader. While priestesses had proliferated in its formative period, Voodoo witnessed a demographic shift in which men filled the majority of its leadership ranks. Animal sacrifices that were essential to accessing the power of the blood of offerings were replaced by various foods and liquids in ritual ceremonies. By 1940, many Voodoo practitioners facing unwanted scrutiny withdrew from the public eye. This void would be filled with popular culture portrayals that reduced Voodoo beliefs and practices to commercialized memorabilia and tourist souvenirs. Yet, there remains a vibrant Voodoo community in the Americas and throughout the African diaspora.

The African–Cuban religion of Santeria was brought to the Americas primarily by the Yoruba of southwestern Nigeria. Like other African Traditional Religions, Santeria has a pantheon of divinities. Santerians have a supreme God, Olodumare, who is also known as Olorun. He is the main source of ashe (ache), the spiritual energy that pervades the universe and everything in the world. Olorun works through the orisha, the other divinities, delegating certain responsibilities and assigning certain spheres of influence. Olorun and the orishas communicate their requests and desires for humankind through prayer, sacrifice, offerings, and spirit possession. Orisha have idiosyncratic personalities and aesthetic sensibilities such as favorite numbers, colors, foods, and days of the week. There are countless orisha. Elegba is the owner of the roads and doors and functions as an intermediary between the human and the divine. During prayer and ritual ceremonies, Elegba is often invoked first to open communication to the supernatural world. Ogun, the God of war, iron, and labor, embodying violence, creativity, and integrity, is envisioned as wielding a machete to clear the roads. He is also understood metaphorically to strengthen the lines of communication after Elegba initiates contact, and has final control over life and death. Ochosi, the hunter, scout, and protector of warriors, provides guidance and direction to human destiny and serves as a personal advisor. Obatala, the father of the Orisha, humanity, and creator of the world, is the source of all that is pure, wise, peaceful, ethical, moral, and compassionate and, therefore, is the enforcer of justice. Shango is a warrior and ruler of thunder and lightning. Oya, an ex-wife of Shango, reigns over the winds and presides over the dead and the gates of the cemetery. Oshun controls the waters and is affiliated with culture and fine arts. Yemaya (Iemanja) is an unknowable and merciful mother of all, and guides the seas and the lakes. Babalu Aye is associated with disease; the sick pray to him for healing. Orishaoco arbitrates between the orisha and nurtures the crops, agriculture, and gardening. Osain, the doctor of orishas, controls medicines and herbs. The Ibeyi, the children of Oshun and Chango, oversee the acquisition of material possessions. Orunmila, known for imparting the wisdom and powers of divination, is essential to the work of the priests.

Although animal sacrifice often overshadows other components of Santeria, ebo ("sacrifice") really has much broader connotations and applications in the tradition. Animal sacrifice is generally reserved for rites of passage such as birth, death, and marriage, to overcome serious illnesses or misfortunes, or the initiation ceremony of a priest. Offerings can range from elaborate culinary dishes, fruits and vegetables, or small votives. The devotee receives instruction from the orisha about the appropriate gift, behavior, or action that needs to be taken. Animal sacrifices must be performed by a santero (priest). Celebrations usually accompany the ritual action such as bembe (drumming parties). Members honor the orisha by playing specific rhythms and acting out their distinctive dance, which can bring on the spiritual possession of the priest or participants and open the channels to ashe. As with other African traditions, the ultimate goal of each component of ritual is the restoration or preservation of communal harmony.

While this chapter has sketched some of the overarching traits that are shared by many West African communities, it is important to note that religious life in Africa has never been static. With the establishment of colonial governments and the onset of modernity, West African religions have continued to transform, adapt, and meld aspects of varied traditions over time as they have for centuries. Lifecycle rituals such as birth, adulthood, marriage, and death are still marked by indigenous religious beliefs and practices. While formal weddings and civil unions are growing in popularity, many still validate their marriages according to traditional West African ways. While members of mosques and churches are given Muslim or

Christian funerals, bodies are often still prepared according to traditional burial practices. In Ghana, items that the departed may need on their journey to the next world are often placed in the coffin. As modernity and western missionaries have made their way across the continent, many West Africans have resisted the notion that conversion to another religious tradition entails leaving all of their indigenous practices behind.

This trend is perhaps best exemplified by the rise of African Independent Churches and African Initiatives in Christianity (AIC). Formed as a response to Eurocentric "mainline" historic churches in Africa and driven by charismatic leaders such as Garrick Braide of Nigeria, William Wade Harris of Liberia, and Simon Kimbangu of Congo, many contemporary West Africans have sought to make Christianity more relevant to the African context. Translating the Bible into ethnic languages, exercising charismatic gifts, and emphasizing prayer and healing, the spontaneous worship of AICs is deeply rooted in indigenous African culture.[7] Far from timeless, West African Traditional Religions are as diverse and fluid as any of the world's religions.

7. Mbiti, *African Religions and Philosophy*; Magesa, *African Religion*; Ray, *African Religions*.

2

The Religious Life of Enslaved Americans

From Puritan New England with an African population of three percent to South Carolina with estimates at over 60 percent in 1750, the demographics of colonial America had an immeasurable impact on the day-to-day reality of enslaved Africans as they arrived in America. As in South America, regions with a substantial Roman Catholic population seemed to mesh much more closely with the African religious ethos than predominately Protestant areas. These factors, coupled with the inconsistencies and tensions inherent in nineteenth-century justifications for slavery and the Atlantic slave trade, complicate our understanding of the religious experiences of slaves in early America.

The Compatibility of Slavery and Christianity

The questions raised by proslavery advocates and abolitionists ranged from the theological and philosophical to the pragmatic. Is Christianity consistent with the institution of slavery? Why would a just God have allowed slavery to exist? Why would slaves adopt the religion of their oppressors? From Frederick Douglass's perspective there was "slaveholding Christianity" and the "Christianity of Christ." The former could be used to justify beating and mistreating slaves and attending church on Sunday as the model of piety. In contrast, "true" Christians, according to Douglass, had a deep and abiding faith in the equality of all humanity and opposed the oppressive institution of slavery.[1] One of the justifications for the slave trade as it came under increasing criticism by abolitionists in the nineteenth century was that absent this exposure to Christianity on the plantations of America, African "heathens" would have died without having ever heard the gospel. Yet, even putting aside the fact that African Christianity had existed for centuries before European colonization, if evangelization was the central concern, missionaries, as had been common practice for years, could have ventured to Africa to spread their message. Instead, Africans were packed tightly as cargo in slave ships and transported to America where plantation owners were reticent to offer the Christian message to their slaves.

There were a number of biblical passages that could be invoked to argue for or against slavery. In fact, in terms of quantity, there are more verses that assume the existence of slavery than those that directly advocate for its eradication. Abolitionists drew upon biblical passages that they believed opposed slavery.[2] Others followed the

1. Frederick Douglass, *Narrative of the Life of Frederick Douglass, An American Slave* (Boston: Anti-Slavery Office, 1845), 77–82, 118–25.
2. Some of the regularly cited biblical passages include: 1 Cor. 12:13, "For we were all baptized by one Spirit into one body—whether Jews or Greeks, slave or free—and we were all given the one Spirit to drink"; Gal. 3:28, "There is neither Jew nor Greek, slave nor free, male nor female, for you are all one in Christ Jesus"; Col. 3:11: "Here there is no Greek or Jew, circumcised or uncircumcised, barbarian, Scythian, slave or free, but Christ is all, and is in all." Other ancient biblical passages were invoked to substantiate African slavery. Noah cursed Ham and his lineage for seeing him naked in Gen. 9:25–27: "Cursed be Canaan! The lowest of slaves will he be to his brothers. Blessed be the Lord, the God of Shem! May Canaan be the slave of Shem. May God extend the territory of Japheth; may Japheth live in the tents of Shem, and may Canaan be his slave." Some interpreted the "mark" placed on Cain by God after his expulsion from the Garden of Eden for killing his brother as a racial designation. Genesis 4:10–15 reads, "The Lord said, 'What have you done? Listen! Your brother's blood cries out to me from the ground. Now you are under a curse and driven from the ground, which opened its mouth to receive your

logic of proslavery biblical interpretations to unexpected places. Daniel Goodwin, a minister from Philadelphia, argued that if Jesus did condone slavery it would have been white slavery since that was what Roman slavery consisted of during his time. If that were the case, proslavery advocates would have to abandon the racial justification underlying the institution. However, many asserted that Jesus would have agreed with American beliefs that whites should not be enslaved. Other biblical passages seemed to assume a compatibility between Christian doctrine and slaveowning.[3]

Objections to slavery, at times, required further extrapolation from the biblical passages. In Paul's Letter to Philemon, he returns a runaway slave, Onesimus, to his master, but rather than mandating his emancipation, Paul subtly suggests that it was divine fate that had brought him into his care and that he might be more helpful to the Christian cause if he were no longer a slave.

> I appeal to you for my son Onesimus, who became my son while I was in chains. Formerly he was useless to you, but now he has become useful both to you and to me. I am sending him—who is my very heart—back to you. I would have liked to keep him with me so that he could take

brother's blood from your hand. When you work the ground, it will no longer yield its crops for you. You will be a restless wanderer on the earth.' Cain said to the Lord, 'My punishment is more than I can bear. Today you are driving me from the land, and I will be hidden from your presence; I will be a restless wanderer on the earth and whoever finds me will kill me.' But the Lord said to him, 'Not so; if anyone kills Cain, he will suffer vengeance seven times over.' Then the Lord put a mark on Cain so that no one who found him would kill him."

3. Ephesians 6:5–9 states, "Slaves, obey your earthly masters with respect and fear, and with sincerity of heart, just as you would obey Christ. Obey them not only to win their favor when their eye is on you, but like slaves of Christ, doing the will of God from your heart. Serve wholeheartedly, as if you were serving the Lord, not men, because you know that the Lord will reward everyone for whatever good he does, whether he is slave or free. And masters, treat your slaves in the same way." In a similar vein, 1 Tim. 6:1–2 advises, "All who are under the yoke of slavery should consider their masters worthy of full respect, so that God's name and our teaching may not be slandered. Those who have believing masters are not to show less respect for them because they are brothers. Instead, they are to serve them even better, because those who benefit from their service are believers, and dear to them. These are the things you are to teach and urge on them." Other biblical passages seemed to send mixed messages. First Corinthians 7:21 states, "Were you a slave when you were called? Don't let it trouble you—although if you can gain your freedom, do so."

your place in helping me while I am in chains for the gospel. But I did not want to do anything without your consent, so that any favor you do will be spontaneous and not forced. Perhaps the reason he was separated from you for a little while was that you might have him back for good—no longer as a slave, but better than a slave, as a dear brother. He is very dear to me but even dearer to you, both as a man and as a brother in the Lord. So if you consider me a partner, welcome him as you would welcome me. If he has done you any wrong or owes you anything, charge it to me. (Philem. 10–18)

For proslavery advocates this passage sanctioned slavery and justified the passage of the Fugitive Slave Law of 1850, which required state officials to return runaway slaves to their owners. Abolitionists interpreted the Greek word *doulos* as "servant" and not "slave," arguing that Onesimus was more of a free apprentice, employee, or maybe even a brother of Philemon.

With the rise of higher biblical criticism, theological debates grew more specialized. Advocates on both sides of the slavery issue questioned why Jesus said so little on the matter. At a synagogue in Nazareth, in Luke 4:18–19, Jesus states, "The Spirit of the Lord is on me, because he has anointed me to preach good news to the poor. He has sent me to declare freedom for the prisoners and recovery of sight for the blind, to release the oppressed, to proclaim the year of the Lord's favor." This passage could be seen as a literal freeing of slaves or a nod toward the spiritual salvation of those imprisoned to sin. Some noted that Jesus did not specifically address a range of issues that run contrary to Christianity and therefore his silence could not be assumed to be consent for particular behaviors. Others attributed Jesus' silence to the fact that his land, ancient Palestine, did not have slaves. Abolitionists asserted that Jesus' love ethic nullified the slave laws of the Hebrew Bible and pointed to Jesus' "Golden Rule" in Matt. 7:12 and Luke 6:31: "Do to others as you would have them do to you" as a rejoinder to proslavery advocates.[4]

An American legal system informed by Judeo-Christian principles was equally muddled by the ambiguity in the biblical scriptures and the relationship between baptism and the social status of slaves. The Code Noir of 1685 legislated that all slaves brought to French possessions in America had to receive instruction and baptism within eight days of arrival. However, the statute failed to detail whether the acceptance of Christianity elevated the civil status of African slaves. By 1706, six colonial legislatures passed laws that denied that baptism altered the condition of the slave "as to his bondage or freedom." Because many colonies based civic responsibility on religious adherence, these statutes bifurcated the social and spiritual identities of Africans and effectively excluded them from ever attaining full citizenship rights. In essence, according to the courts, accepting Christianity would have no direct impact on their day-to-day lives and their status as slaves.

Yet, even with this legislative assurance, a number of obstacles lay in the way of slave conversion. Geographically, plantations and farms were spread out across the plains and the meager supply of clergy had their hands full ministering to the many small white rural parishes with few resources to spare to missionize slaves. Despite their strong rhetoric to the contrary, slave masters themselves proved to be a barrier to the evangelization of slaves. Although slaves labored six days a week for their masters, plantation owners were still unwilling to relinquish any work time for religious instruction. In addition, concerns that exposure to Christianity would make the slaves rebellious and "saucy" also served as a deterrent to many slaveowners. This reticence on behalf of the slaveholders to extend religious instruction to slaves belies claims that Christian obligation not

4. J. Albert Harrill, "The Use of the New Testament in the American Slave Controversy: A Case History in the Hermeneutical Tension between Biblical Criticism and Christian Moral Debate," *Religion and American Culture: A Journal of Interpretation* 10, no. 2 (Summer 2000): 149–86.

financial gain propelled the Atlantic slave trade. As early as the eighteenth century, colonial legislatures passed laws that extended additional tax breaks for those who owned Christian slaves. Despite these measures, only a small percentage of slaves received religious instruction in the seventeenth and early eighteenth centuries.

The first organized efforts to proselytize African slaves beyond the sporadic and haphazard attempts by itinerant ministers were those of the Society for the Propagation of the Gospel founded in 1701. The SPG employed the tried-and-true methods that had been successfully executed for years for the Anglican Church: intricate sermons, carefully written and composed tracts or small pamphlets highlighting central points of doctrine, and systematic catechism lessons that, through repetition, instilled the key tenets of the faith. Given what we know about the nature of African Traditional Religions, as one might expect, this approach had limited success. For a people whose sacred and secular lives were inseparable, whose ceremonies were filled with movement, joy, spirit possession, drumbeats, and music, one could barely imagine a more diametrically opposite approach to the central questions and practices of religion. Not only would potential converts need to be fluent and literate in English, but they would need the time to study and grasp abstract theological concepts and master them in such a way as to respond precisely to questions formulated by, in most cases, a non-African teacher. The Anglican emphasis on deliberate Christian nurture that often required a lengthy period of spiritual maturation did not mesh well with the daily duties of a slave. Africans who were only allotted one day to farm for their own subsistence had little extra time to devote to spiritual instruction. Some slaves likely rejected Christianity as the religion that undergirded the system that oppressed them. This sentiment was driven home by the hypocrisy of many slaveowners who self-identified as Christian, yet beat and treated their slaves cruelly. The SPG had little success with African-born slaves, and those who did understand religious instruction did not always accept Christianity.

This is not to say that slaves wholly rejected Christianity. Scholars have coined the term the "Invisible Institution" to refer to the private and secret religious practices of slaves that occurred outside of the watchful eye of their masters. Gathered in slave quarters, brush arbors, woods, and other isolated locations to prevent detection, slaves transformed Christianity to meet their spiritual needs. Some risked beatings or even death to attend these meetings. To deter sound, pots where placed outside of these meetings and may have also been a symbolic connection to African practices learned in their homeland. Rather than the repeated message of "Slaves be obedient to your masters," enslaved Africans found a message that provided hope and empowerment to make it through their daily struggles.[5]

Conjure

Existing side by side and sometimes interwoven with Christianity were other religious options such as *conjure*. Conjure is an umbrella term for a range of African Traditional Religious beliefs and practices that were transformed within the context of America. As in Africa, conjure is a worldview in which misdeeds are punished, good is rewarded, and supernatural forces are at work and can be harnessed for benevolent or malevolent purposes. The world is understood to operate in a coherent manner. From this perspective, there are no random acts, just undiscovered rationales currently unknown to the individual. For example, if you bit your tongue while eating a meal and hurt yourself, a practitioner of conjure would likely not chalk the experience up to an accident, but would question

---

5. Albert J. Raboteau, *Slave Religion: The "Invisible Insitution" in the Antebellum South* (New York: Oxford University Press, 2004), 95–150.

why, on this particular day, would performing such a simple daily act result in harm. A believer would think through their range of relationships and potential enemies and consult a conjurer to ascertain the source of the disharmony. If an individual sought a cure from a priest and the charm or spell did not work, one would not reject the entire system, but might attribute the failure to an incompetent conjurer or question their own ability to perform the rituals correctly, but they would not discard the entire belief system. Conjure, like other derivations of African Traditional Religions, is often labeled as "magic" based or classified as a "primitive" tradition, yet, by analyzing experiential data and causal connections, practitioners take a logical and scientific approach to the problem of evil in the world.

In early America, one of the most pressing uses for conjure was the mediation of the power differential between slaves and their masters. Drawing on their African heritage, slaves enlisted the power of charms and amulets to deter violent beatings and other cruelties at the hands of their owners and overseers. This allowed slaves to have some measure of control over their own lives. Often the effectiveness of a remedy was secondary to the symbolic challenge the practice posed to the established authority. Some cures were protective in nature, while others amounted to outright resistance such as vandalism or theft of the master's property. Conjure spoke to practical day-to-day issues such as health, finances, conflict resolution, retaliation, fertility, and general concerns about the future.

Conjurer practitioners, both men and women, were believed to have special qualities and possess extraordinary powers such as controlling the weather, invisibility, flying, shape-shifting, and communicating with the next world. Conjurers often had physical attributes that set them apart, such as unusual birthmarks or distinctive eye color. Specialists emphasized their individuality by adopting elaborate costumes and accessories. Some conjurers honed their skills over time through careful study or formal apprenticeships, while others felt called to the position and were believed to have been "born with the gift."

Conjurers could discern evil and provide a way to "fix" the harm and offer a cure. Conjurers were believed to have supernatural abilities and had a measure of authority in the slave community based on that power. An aura of mystery usually surrounded the conjurer, as well as other distinctive features such as having a crooked cane, charms, and conjure bag. The spell and ritual used by the conjurer could imbue items such as graveyard dust, bottles, pins, bones, reptiles, horsehair, roots, and herbs with power. A person's regular possessions, such as a hat or a shoe, could be fixed by a conjurer's spell so that the unsuspecting owner would be conjured by contact. Individuals had to carefully dispose of worn clothing, cut hair, and bathing materials because they could be used by an enemy due to their close contact with the body. A wide range of illnesses, injuries, and misfortunes were attributed to conjure. A spell rendered by a conjurer could only be corrected by another conjurer. Conjurers dealt with affairs of the heart and marital issues and told fortunes. Some slaves grew skeptical about a conjurer's ability if a charm did not work, but not about conjure itself. Because their authority rested on their effectiveness, some exploits of conjurers reached legendary proportions. The most daunting challenge facing conjurers was to attempt to conjure whites.

The boundaries between the beliefs and practices of conjure and Christianity were not firm. Slave narratives attest to rituals in which charms were blessed with the phrase, "in the name of the Lord." Catholic symbols were imbued with power by conjurers, and verses from the Bible such as Psalms appeared on conjurer amulets. Herbal cures were often accompanied by Christian images and names from the Bible, including "blood of Jesus" leaves, angel's root, devil's shoestring, and "Adam and Eve" root. It was not unusual for practitioners of conjure to also identify strongly as Christian and see little contradiction between the two commitments. Some Christian slaves did see belief in conjure as incompatible with their faith and discounted the latter as "superstition." Others felt their Christian faith insulated them from the spells and charms of conjurers. At times, conflicts arose over the appropriate uses of spiritual power and what constituted a "good work." Indeed, throughout the nineteenth century, the relationship between conjure and Christianity was often closely intertwined, as examples abound of Christians "hoodooing" rivals. Accounts from white outside observers also acknowledge the power of conjure for those who believe, so much so that laws were passed to restrict the practice.[6]

Slave Resistance

The most prominent slave rebellions in American history attest to the blending of religious elements associated with Christianity and conjure. Denmark Vesey, the leader of a planned slave rebellion in Charleston, South Carolina, in 1822 was known to read and preach from the Bible. Accounts attest to the participation of conjurers in the rebellion. Estimates vary, but records indicate that approximately 9,000 slaves were ready to rebel, before plans of the insurrection were revealed by an informant before the rebellion was even launched. Conjure was intricately interwoven into Vesey's rebellion plot. One of Vesey's longest and closest friends was Jack Pritchard, also known as Gullah Jack. Jack, an East African priest, who was known to practice conjure and possess a "great power and magic," was to play a central role in the proposed uprising. Vesey had a number

---

6. Yvonne Chireau, *Black Magic: Religion and the African American Conjuring Tradition* (Berkeley: University of California Press, 2003); Timothy E. Fulop, ed., *African-American Religion: Interpretive Essays in History and Culture* (New York: Routledge, 1997), 415–31.

of motivations for his planned escape, not the least of which was his abhorrence of the practice of slavery in America and the tight restrictions placed upon the religious life of African Americans. For example, the South Carolina statutes of 1800 and 1803 prohibited African Americans from gathering for religious worship before sunrise or after sunset. By all accounts Vesey's vision for a mass exodus to freedom was intricately designed. It was to commence with the house servants killing their masters while they slept, including the murder of the governor and the mayor to create political chaos. In unison, urban slaves were to take to the streets to their assigned posts. Gullah Jack would head the Angolan contingency while Peter Poyas, a literate ship carpenter, led another group that would obtain weapons from the militia's arsenal as well as horses to secure the streets before the white citizens could assemble to retaliate. As slave families made their way to the coast, Gullah Jack would secure the docks in anticipation of sailing to freedom. Vesey planned the rebellion for years and tightly guarded information, being particularly careful to keep most domestic servants and others who might betray the plot out of the loop. Gullah Jack was essential to the rebellion, giving out "crab claws" to his followers the night of the attack, which was supposed to keep them safe from harm, as well as distributing the poison that was to be emptied into the city's water supply. Despite this meticulous planning, an offhand mention of the plot by William Paul, a minor figure in the proposed rebellion, to Peter Prioleau, a domestic cook, who relayed the details of the rebellion to the authorities, ended the revolt before it got underway.[7]

While it has been debated whether it was a "success," Nat Turner's rebellion clearly qualifies as one of the bloodiest. Launched on August 21, 1831, the uprising culminated with the deaths of fifty-five whites

7. Timothy E. Fulop, ed., *African-American Religion: Interpretive Essays in History and Culture* (New York: Routledge, 1997), 107–30.

and two hundred blacks. Because Turner eluded authorities for two months after the conflict, by the time of his capture, southern white Americans were particularly apprehensive about future slave violence. Although we have few of Turner's own words, slave accounts attest to his abilities as a preacher and prophet. We glimpse Turner's worldview only dimly through the lens of Thomas R. Gray, a white court-appointed attorney who recorded a summary of their conversations in *The Confessions of Nat Turner*. Given the social unrest and hysteria following the rebellion, Gray had a strong motive to paint Turner as a crazy religious zealot and an anomaly among a generally satisfied slave population. Yet, the outlines of Turner's life come through in the narrative.

Early on, Turner not only felt called to be a prophet but his ambitions were confirmed by many in his community including his mother and father. His ability to recall events that occurred prior to his birth and distinctive marks on his head and chest cemented for many that he was "intended for some great purpose." This profound destiny was affirmed by the ease with which Turner learned to read and write. According to accounts, the first time a book was placed in front of him as a baby, he began spelling out the names of the objects displayed before him. Growing up, Turner was exceptionally disciplined in fasting and prayer, and was known for his close reading and deep reflections on the biblical scriptures. After successfully escaping to freedom, Turner returned to Virginia believing that the Holy Spirit wanted him to accomplish great things there for Jesus. Prophetic visions including blood dripping from corn in a field and "hieroglyphic characters" found on leaves in the woods as well as signs such as the eclipse of the sun deepened Turner's conviction that Jesus' return and an exceptional work were at hand. From Turner's reading of these events, God commanded him to slay the evildoers who supported the system of slavery which defied divine will.

The precise events of the uprising may never be fully known, but Gray seems to have embellished on some of the details for dramatic effect and to discredit Turner and his followers. He details that during one night of the rebellion, slave conspirators killed everyone in a house, but forgot that a baby was still alive in a cradle and returned to murder the infant. Gray also describes the violent deaths of women including one instance in which Turner allegedly struck a woman several times with a blunt sword before a compatriot appeared and killed her with an axe. Gray's choice of language also raises questions about whether they originated from Turner. Gray conveys Turner's disappointment that "we found no more victims to gratify our thirst for blood." He also concludes the narrative by depicting Turner as a supernatural oddity, "daring to raise his manacled hands to heaven, with a spirit soaring above the attributes of man; I looked on him and my blood curdled in my veins."[8] While these violent uprisings exemplify direct challenges to the institution of slavery, often their aftermath resulted in increased legal restrictions and violence directed toward African Americans. In some instances, black churches were the target for white retribution and were routinely destroyed and burned to the ground following slave revolts.

Islam

From the seventh century, Islam employed conquest, proselytizing, and trade to establish a global empire. West African Islam emerged from the spread of Islam in the Sudan around the ninth century. From its inception, Islam addressed issues of slavery. The prophet Muhammad after receiving his revelation in 622 CE freed his slaves

8. Milton C. Sernett, ed., *African American Religious History: A Documentary Witness* (Durham, NC: Duke University Press, 1999), 100; Nat Turner, *The Confessions of Nat Turner, the Leader of the late Insurrection in Southampton, Va as fully and voluntarily made to Thomas R. Gray* (Baltimore: Thomas R. Gray, Lucas and Deaver, 1831), 1–21.

and established regulations for slavery. The new religion accepted people of color as equals. Bilal, a newly freed Abyssinian slave, was an early contemporary of Muhammad and was the first muezzin to call Muslims to prayer in Medina.

In one of the early entries in his dictionary in the nineteenth century, Noah Webster wrote, "Of the wooly-haired Africans who constitute the principal part of the inhabitants of Africa, there is no history and there can be none. That race has remained in barbarism from the first ages of the world."[9] Although black Muslim voices in nineteenth-century America are less prominent in the historical records than those of Christians, scholars continue to creatively locate and explore previously unconsidered sources to locate their distinctive experiences within slavery and attest to the power and persistence of Islam in the lives of many Africans. Historians have uncovered the stories of the earliest black Muslims to come to the shores of North America, such as Estevan, a black Moroccan guide and interpreter, who played a central role in the Spanish exploration of Florida in 1527.

The history of African Islam would also feature prominently in the transmission of the religion to the New World. The year 1591 signaled a tremendous change in the practice and prevalence of Islam in West Africa. The fall of the Songhay Empire after the invasion by Morocco to claim valuable salt mines put an abrupt end to West African economic and political power, caused a sharp decline in the black Muslim intellectual center of Timbuktu and the practice of Islam, and witnessed a fundamental change in the function and nature of the slave trade. Arab Muslims enslaved African Muslims in unprecedented numbers. Although slavery had existed in Africa for

9. Richard Brent Turner, *Islam in the African-American Experience* (Bloomington: Indiana University Press, 2003), 11–12; Stephen G. Hall, *A Faithful Account of the Race: African American Historical Writing in Nineteenth-Century America* (Chapel Hill: University of North Carolina Press, 2009).

centuries, it had never been the central component of the African economy. Most often African slaves were sold as a part of political negotiations with other nations and were primarily prisoners of war, criminals, suspected sorcerers, and debtors and took on roles in their new society more akin to indentured servants, such as becoming soldiers. As slavery grew from a cursory element to the center of the West African economic structure, political rivalries grew more fierce and national relations more unstable. With the creation of the Atlantic slave trade, Europeans globalized West African slavery into an industry and means of production in and of itself. The Atlantic slave trade grew so rapidly that it surpassed the entire volume of the Islamic slave trade by 1600. The permanent enslavement and removal of millions of Africans from the continent would leave a devastating and enduring legacy upon the continent of Africa. It is within this context that African Muslims were brought to North America.[10]

There are accounts of African Muslim experiences from autobiographies and biographies in early America. In his autobiography, *A Narrative of the Life and Adventures of Charles Ball, A Black Man*, Charles Ball described an African Muslim on a plantation in North Carolina:

> At the time I first went to Carolina, there were a great many African slaves in the country. . . . I became intimately acquainted with some of these men. . . . I knew several, who must have been, from what I have since learned, Mohammedans; though at that time, I had never heard of the religion of Mohammed. There was one man on this plantation, who prayed five times every day always turning his face to the East, when in the performance of his devotions.[11]

---

10. Edward E. Curtis IV, *Islam in Black America: Identity, Liberation, and Difference in African American Islamic Thought* (Albany: SUNY Press, 2002).
11. Charles Ball, *A Narrative of the Life and Adventures of Charles Ball, A Black Man* (New York: John S. Taylor, 1837); Larry Murphy, ed., *Down by the Riverside: Readings in African American Religion* (New York: New York University Press, 2000), 70.

If Christianity was the religion of the slave master, a justification for the Atlantic slave trade, and a key vehicle for the erasure of an African heritage and culture, remaining Muslim or converting to Islam was a profound act of resistance. Literacy in Arabic, maintaining the five pillars, Muslim dress, and reciting passages from the Quran were both symbolic and practical challenges to the Christian hegemony. On the Georgia Sea Islands, perhaps due in part to its isolated location, the retention of Islam was particularly strong among slaves. One white American, Georgia Conrad wrote, "On Sapelo Island near Darien, I used to know a family of Negroes who worshipped Mohammet. They were tall and well-formed, with good features. They conversed with us in English, but in talking among themselves they used a foreign tongue that no one else understood. The head of the tribe was a very old man named Bi-la-li. He always wore a cap that resembled a Turkish fez."[12] Bilali, a slave on the Thomas Spalding plantation, maintained a deep Islamic identity, giving his nineteen children Muslim names, instructing them in the religion, and composing a manuscript entirely in Arabic. In his will, he requested to be buried with his prayer rug and Quran. James Hamilton Couper, a plantation owner, recalled the piety of one of his slaves, Salih Bilali, who was a devout Muslim. "He is a strict Mahometan; abstains from spirituous liquors, and keeps the various fasts, particularly that of Rhamadan. He is singularly exempt from all feeling of superstition; and holds in great contempt the African belief in fetishes and evil spirits. He reads Arabic and has a Koran."[13] By the Civil War, the restrictiveness of slavery and the deaths of early practitioners of African Islam greatly inhibited the formation of Black Muslim

12. Georgia Bryan Conrad, *Reminiscences of a Southern Woman* (Hampton, VA: Hampton Institute, n.d.), 13.
13. Sylviane A. Diouf, *Servants of Allah: African Muslims Enslaved in the Americas* (New York: New York University Press, 2013), 94; Edward E. Curtis IV, *The Call of Bilal: Islam in the African Diaspora* (Chapel Hill: University of North Carolina Press, 2014).

institutions in America that would have formally instructed future generations in the tradition's tenets.

The autobiography of Omar ibn Said provides insights into African Muslim life. In his autobiography, Said writes,

> Before I came to the Christian country, my religion was the religion of Mohammed, the Apostle of God—may God have mercy upon him and give him peace! I walked to the mosque before day-break, washed my face and head and hands and feet. I prayed at noon, prayed in the afternoon, prayed at sunset, prayed in the evening. I gave alms every year. . . . I went on pilgrimage to Mecca. . . . When I left my country I was thirty-seven years old; I have been in the country of the Christians twenty-four years.[14]

Born around 1770 near the Senegal River at Senegal's border with Mauritania, Omar ibn Said was highly educated in Africa before being enslaved and brought to Charleston, South Carolina. Said escaped to Fayetteville, North Carolina, but was captured while praying in a church and jailed. Writing on prison walls in Arabic drew the attention of many, and he soon became the property of General James Owen of Bladen County. Said's conversion to Christianity and life story garnered the attention of several newspapers and periodicals. In his autobiography, Said writes,

> When I was a Mohammedan I prayed thus: "Thanks be to God, Lord of all worlds, the merciful the gracious, Lord of the day of Judgement, thee we serve, on thee we call for help. Direct us in the right way, the way of those on whom thou hast had mercy, with whom thou hast not been angry and who walk not in error. Amen."—But now I pray "Our Father" . . . in the words of our Lord Jesus the Messiah.[15]

His own characterization of his life story noted tensions between Christianity and slaveholding. However, many of his white Christian

---

14. Cornel West and Eddie S. Glaude, eds., *African American Religious Thought: An Anthology* (Louisville: Westminster John Knox, 2003), 242.
15. Ibid.

biographers celebrated his conversion. After Said was given a Bible translated into Arabic, the Philadelphia newspaper, *The Christian Advocate*, wrote that he "now reads the scriptures in his native language, and blesses Him who causes good to come out of evil by making him a slave."[16] It is said he died at the age of ninety-four.

The biography of Job Ben Solomon describes the lore surrounding his life. Ayuba Suleiman Ibrahima Diallo was born in the kingdom of Futa in Senegal around 1700. Around 1730, Mandingo slave traders captured Ayuba Suleiman Diallo near the Gambia River in Bundu in Senegal. From the shores of West Africa, Diallo was taken to Annapolis, Maryland, where he was sold to a tobacco farmer. In America, he became known as Job Ben Solomon or Job, the son of Solomon. According to his biography, he was mocked by white children as he said his Muslim prayers in the woods. He escaped but was eventually captured and imprisoned. In prison, Thomas Bluett an English minister observed, "He was brought into the tavern to us, but could not speak one word of English. Upon our talking and making signs to him, he wrote a line or two before us, and when he read it, pronounced the words Allah and Mohammed; by which and his refusing a glass of wine we offered him, we perceived he was a Mohametan. . . . For by his affable carriage, and the easy composure of his countenance, we could perceive he was no common slave." Seeking to escape bondage, Diallo wrote a letter to his father in Bundu hoping that he would secure his freedom. Like many educated Muslims of the Fulbe or Fulani ethnic groups, Job spoke not only Fula but could read and write Arabic and had memorized the Quran. Although his letter to his father never reached its destination, James Oglethorpe, a member of the British parliament, obtained the letter

16. *The Christian Advocate* (Philadelphia: July 1825) no. 3, 306–7; Omar ibn Said, "Autobiography of Omar ibn Said, Slave in North Carolina, 1831," *American Historical Review* 30, no. 4 (July 1925): 787–95.

and had it translated at Oxford. Drawn to his story and impressed by his educational accomplishments, Oglethorpe purchased his "bond." Two years after his arrival in Maryland, Job, with the support of Oglethorpe, traveled to England. During this voyage, observers noted that Job prayed regularly, prepared his meat according to Sharia Islamic law, and did not eat pork. Legend has it that Job handwrote three copies of the Quran from memory while in England. Job's biography, published in 1734 by Bluett, made him a celebrity in the eighteenth century.[17] His story is one of many examples of the rich history of African American Muslims in America.

Slaves, Masters, and Missionaries

The Great Awakenings, a series of revivals that swept across colonial America from 1720 to the 1740s, witnessed a dramatic shift in the ethos of the American religious landscape. Led by preachers such as George Whitefield, enormous religious meetings, some estimated at over 40,000, took the colonies by storm. Long before mass advertising, purveyors of this new revival format distributed flyers announcing the ministers' appearances and creating a buzz that drew audiences in droves. Fiery sermons exhorting sinners to turn to Jesus and urging backsliders to renew their faith created an urgency and imminence to salvation. The common view that a long discipleship must precede true piety gave way to the necessity of an immediate heartfelt conviction of one's sin and God's mercy and grace to gain admittance into the Christian community. High-flown theological treatises were displaced by an emphasis on "plain doctrine." If the revival preacher fell into old habits of lofty prose, exuberant audiences would shout "Make it plain!" to bring the orator back down to earth.

17. Thomas Bluett, *Some Memoirs of the Life of Job, the Son of Solomon, the High Priest of Boonda in Africa* (London: Printed for R. Ford, 1734).

The revival atmosphere leveled the socioeconomic, educational, and political status of participants united in their pursuit of the gospel message. The Great Awakenings also stood the requirements to enter the ministry on its head. While prior to the 1740s, preachers attended divinity schools and received formal instruction in Greek and biblical exegesis, the Great Awakenings prioritized a converted heart and a gifted tongue as the qualifications to preach. Those denominations that best adapted to this new emphasis on an emotional conversion, such as the Baptists and Methodists, saw the greatest increases in their membership over the latter half of the eighteenth century. From the earliest frontier camp meetings of the eighteenth century, slaves responded to the messages of preachers. The movement of the Holy Spirit led to shouting and dancing not only at outdoor revivals, but during regular church services. The ring shout, in which participants would move in a circular movement, shuffling steps, stamping, and gesturing, was a particularly prevalent form of religious expression among the slaves.

The late eighteenth and early nineteenth centuries would see greater growth of Christianity among African Americans slave and free. Denominations and conference gatherings made the evangelization of slaves a top priority, publishing pamphlets and forming missionary societies and associations. These efforts were impacted by the growing abolitionist movement in the North and sectional tensions within churches. The publication of literature such as David Walker's *Appeal* also increased southerner wariness of missionaries. Passages in Walker's pamphlet were seen as a cautionary tale about the perils of allowing missionaries to have contact with slaves. David Walker's *Appeal* included passages such as:

> I tell you Americans! That unless you speedily alter your course, you and your Country are gone!!!!!! For God Almighty will tear up the very face of the earth!!!! Will not that very remarkable passage of Scripture

be fulfilled on Christian Americans? Hear it Americans!!" and "O Americans! Americans!! I call God—I call angels—I call men, to witness, that your destruction is at hand, and will be speedily consummated unless you repent."[18]

Denominations began to split over the issue of slavery: The Methodist Episcopal Church, South in 1844 and the Southern Baptist Convention in 1845. To counter public concerns about the Vesey and Turner rebellions, plantation missionaries maintained that correct religious instruction would improve slave morale and reliability and that those slaves who rebelled were fanatics or the product of false teachings. Supporters of missions argued that Christianity was the ideal medium to regulate relations between slaves and masters. Some slaves rejected the message of docility preached by missionaries. Others learned the tenets of Christianity from fellow slaves. Some slaves were distrustful of the interpretation of the Bible by whites and sought to interpret the text for themselves. Because they were illiterate, some slaves believed God revealed his word to them directly. In many cases, the missionaries pressed the image of the planter-patriarch ruling over his happy slaves.

However, there were limits to Christian fellowship. White and black members of churches covenanted to together to practice personal behavior and engage in social relationships that were consistent with the Bible. They agreed to watch over each other's activities. When church doctrine was transgressed, disciplinary meetings were held to report un-Christian conduct. After testimony was given, members could be suspended or expelled from the congregation if found guilty or readmitted into church fellowship if they repented. However, slavery raised a range of issues not previously seen in the church. What was acceptable discipline of slaves by their masters and when did it become abuse? In 1796, the

18. David Walker, *Walker's Appeal* (Boston: D. Walker, 1830), 39–49.

Baptist Dover Association of Virginia raised the question, "Is there no restriction on believing masters in the chastisement of their servants?" The conclusion of the discussion was that "[t]here is no doubt but Masters may, and sometimes do exercise an unreasonable authority; but as it is very difficult, and perhaps impossible to fix a certain rule in these cases, we think the churches should take notice of such as they think improper and deal with the transgressor, as they would with offenders in other crimes."[19]

This emphasis on the condition of the Christian heart, relationships, and the ability to speak to present concerns and contexts meshed much more closely with the African traditional religious cosmology, which partly accounts for the rise in slave conversions, church membership, and black preachers. Since a converted heart and gifted tongue were the essential qualifications for a preacher and not formal educational training, many black men and women ascended to the pulpit, even, on certain occasions, speaking to crowds of both blacks and whites. Black preachers were charged with making the tenets of Christianity resonate with the experiential world of slaves. To do so, they drew upon an African oral tradition to deliver charismatic sermons, memorize entire biblical passages word-for-word, and convey the narratives in vivid detail, in many cases without being literate. Debates have raged about whether the black preacher served as a source of accommodation or resistance within the slave community. Under white supervision, the slave preacher was restricted in how strongly and directly they could press issues of social justice, yet even the presence of African Americans in authoritative positions presented a challenge to the oppressive institution that enslaved them. While the answer likely varies depending on the local congregation, city, or colony, the question of

19. Albert J. Raboteau, *Slave Religion: The "Invisible Insitution" in the Antebellum South* (New York: Oxford University Press, 2004), 181.

whether slave preachers were a voice for social control or the spark for resistance endures.

Slave preachers who got too close to suggesting equality between whites and blacks could be severely punished. Most slave preachers were illiterate at a time when the written word of the Bible was central. However, being unable to read did not mean that slave preachers were not eloquent. Slaves preferred their own preachers. Accounts attest to the vivid imagery and dramatic delivery of slave preacher sermons. The emergence of the folk sermon developed a familiar structure: phrases, verses, passages that the preacher knew by heart, repetition, dramatic use of voice and gesture, oratorical devices, and rhythmic cadence. The preacher was a consistent prominent public figure and authority in the community.

Roman Catholicism

While the majority of Christian slaves embraced a particular Protestant denomination, there is a rich African American heritage within Roman Catholicism. The oldest black Catholic community began in St. Augustine in Florida. Maryland had the largest community of black Catholics in colonial times and the antebellum period, and Louisiana had a substantial population as well. In 1785, 3,000 of the 16,000 Catholics in Maryland were black slaves. However, unless they were owned by a religious order, slaves usually received only cursory and sporadic religious instruction. Some Catholics such as Orestes Brownson questioned the ability of slaves to convert to Christianity.

> Why is it that you can rarely get a negro to embrace any thing of Christianity but its animality . . . or its exterior forms, and that after generations of Christian worship and instruction, he falls back to the worship of Obi? Why is it that you can scarcely get a single Christian thought into the negro's head, and that with him religion is almost sure

to lapse into a groveling superstition? Why, because he is a degenerate man, and superstition is degenerate religion, and the religion of the degenerate.

However, in New Orleans, French-speaking "free people of color," particularly after the infusion of refugees fleeing the Haitian Revolution after 1792, founded prosperous communities. African American women who were denied the opportunity to become women religious formed their own institutions. Black nuns established the Oblate Sisters of Providence in Baltimore in 1829 and the Sisters of the Holy Family in 1842 in New Orleans. The first black Americans ordained in the priesthood were James Augustine in 1854, who would become the chancellor of the diocese of Boston; Alexander Sherwood Healy in 1858; and Patrick Healy in 1864, who served as president of Georgetown University.[20]

Slavery raised a number of challenging issues for Christian doctrine, particularly regarding slave marriage. In 1839, Pope Gregory XVI condemned the slave trade in the apostolic letter *In Supremo Apostolatus Fastigio*. The Council of Trent had decreed that marriages were not valid unless vows were taken in front of a priest and two witnesses. However, would marriages performed in secret or slave marriages be canonically valid given the power of slaveholders to separate them at any time? While the church required that Christians maintain the marital tie, slaveholders were reticent to give up the right to sell their slaves as they saw fit. Lutherans opted to require married Christian slaves to be faithful to their partners as long as they were not separated by their masters. If they were separated, they could not be remarried without the permission of their master or

---

20. Cyprian Davis, "History of the African American Catholic Church in the United States: Evangelization and Indigenization," in *Directory of African American Religious Bodies* (Washington, DC: Howard University Press, 1991), 257–63; Cyprian Davis, *The History of Black Catholics in the United States* (New York: Crossroad, 1993).

minister; however, slaveholders could end a Christian marriage when they wanted even without the consent of the husband and wife.

Slave Religion

Dissatisfied with messages to obey their master and be docile, slaves held their own secret meetings outside of formal institutions such as churches. They sought preaching that resonated with their experiences. Slaves faced severe punishment if they were caught attending secret prayer meetings. They met in secluded locations such as the woods, ravines, and "hush harbors" to avoid detection. There are accounts of slaves overturning pots to cover the sound of meetings which may have been functional or for a more symbolic purpose.

There were a number of distinctive elements of slave Christianity. Africans, drawing on their traditional musical heritage, created an original musical form: the spontaneous, improvised slave spiritual. Religious terms such as freedom alluded to both physical and spiritual bondage. For many slaves, contact between God and humans occurred in worship and praise services and the singing of spirituals. Spirituals highlighted the stages in the Christian spiritual journey from conversion, repentance, and salvation. They exhorted the sinner to change their ways and "Go down into the lonesome valley" where the "mourner" felt their sin before "comin' through" to conversion. As for many figures in the Bible, the wilderness was where slaves waited for the Lord in the woods, marshes, and other isolated locations. At revivals and prayer meetings, Christians sang and prayed over "mourners," in some cases the entire night. The spirituals encouraged slaves to follow the example of those who walked the Christian road before them. The songs urged Christians to remain faithful and not revert to old ways. Although the spirituals warned against the snares of "Old Captain Satan," they rarely invoked hellfire and damnation and the devil was described more as a malevolent trickster than a fearful demon. The concern was less external spiritual warfare, but the internal troubled spirit. Slaves trusted God in the face of life's trials. These songs carried encoded meanings that were meant to be interpreted at a number of levels. The classic spiritual, "Steal Away," was at once an expression of longing for the next world and signaled the appointed time to escape to freedom in the North. Another song with a similar call to action was:

> O Canaan, sweet Canaan,
> I am bound for the land of Canaan,
> I thought I heard them say
> There were lions in the way;
> I don't expect to stay
> Much longer here.
> Run to Jesus, shun the danger.
> I don't expect to stay
> Much longer here.

Ancient narratives of the Hebrew Bible such as Jacob wrestling with an angel were reframed to have direct and relevant meaning in the present for a sinner struggling with their soul. From the African American perspective, Christ enduring suffering, persecution, and death on a cross made Jesus an ever-present friend and imbued him with a unique ability to empathize with the downtrodden and specifically the plight of a people enduring slavery. Black preachers repositioned Jesus as a second Moses who would deliver his people, the African slaves, from their bondage in America. The final deliverance from the troubles of the world came with death. Death was the passage to freedom that could come at any time; a well-prepared death then, was a blessing. For a people displaced from their own homeland, heaven became both a symbolic and literal final gathering place where families and friends who had been separated and sold away would be reunited forever. Spirituals were imbued with biblical images. The moods of the spirituals varied from sad, triumphant, future focused, intense, and light. Slaves also expressed their religious feelings in prayers and stories.

Conversion and public acknowledgment of spiritual experiences was central to the slave experience. The usual time frame was several days to weeks of anxiety over their salvation before conversion. The mourners' bench or anxious seat at prayer meetings and revivals is often where sinners became seekers. Conversion was usually an intense, internal, and individual experience. Conversion narratives most often described a feeling of the weight of sinfulness, a vision of damnation, and an experience of acceptance by God and being reborn and made new. Some experiences were accompanied by visions and trances. Public slave services on Sunday could last all day if allowed. White observers attest to the emotional impact of the worship. Baptism was a memorable occasion for slaves and the most dramatic event in the slave's religious life, which included song, shouting, and ecstatic behavior. Funeral services required permission from masters which was not always given.[21] While drawing on the same Christian lineage, as Frederick Douglass suggested, a strong case could be made that because they were built on separate moral grounds, honed in the crucible of slavery, and expressed by an African worldview, slave Christianities were fundamentally distinct from their European American counterparts.

21. Raboteau, *Slave Religion*, 247.

3

African American Religious Institutions

Concurrent with the creation of the "Invisible Institution" of slave religion, free blacks in urban centers in the North, such as Philadelphia, New York, and Baltimore, were experiencing racism and discrimination within historically white Christian congregations. Although the majority in many denominations, African Americans had to submit to the social practices and tenets of the traditions to which they now belonged. Many northern free blacks felt called to be in Christian community and endured very restrictive conditions to do so. They entered a dynamic in which many white congregants were uncomfortable with a black presence in their church but were even more concerned about unsupervised black gatherings. In many religious institutions, blacks were systematically excluded from leadership positions, ordination, voting, and having a voice in church polity. Some congregations allowed African Americans to receive communion only after all whites were extended the sacrament. Accounts abound of white pastors refusing to hold black infants to christen them. African Americans had little to no freedom to worship as they saw fit and faced stark restrictions on exuberant or emotional displays during services. Upon death, African Americans were buried in a separate cemetery away from departed white members of the churches. Many blacks were offended that slaveholders remained on church rosters and were allowed to assume ministerial positions. Like the "invisible institution" within slavery, northern black Christian denominations emerged as a protest against mistreatment, an affirmation of their faith, and a desire to worship in a manner that best expressed their devotion to God.

The Rise of Independent Black Churches

The origins of the African Methodist Episcopal Church demonstrate a dramatic exodus from a white denomination. In November 1787, St. George's Methodist Episcopal Church in Philadelphia was undergoing renovation. During the construction, the location of the segregated areas designated for African American congregants kept changing. On one particular morning, some black members inadvertently sat too close to the white section and were pulled up off of their knees during the worship service and prevented from even finishing their prayers before being escorted to the "Negro pews." This was the final indignation. This group of African Americans, led by Richard Allen, left St. George's determined to begin their own denomination. Allen describes the event in his autobiography:

> A number of us usually attended St. George's church in Fourth street; and when the colored people began to get numerous in attending the church, they moved us from the seats we usually sat on, and placed us around the wall, and on Sabbath morning we went to the church and the sexton stood at the door, and told us to go in the gallery. He told us to go, and we would see where to sit. We expected to take the seats over the ones we formerly occupied below, not knowing any better. We took those seats. Meeting had begun, and they were nearly done singing, and just as we got to the seats, the elder said, "Let us pray." We had not been long upon our knees before I heard considerable scuffling

and low talking. I raised my head up and saw one of the trustees, H—M—, having hold of the Rev. Absalom Jones, pulling him up off of his knees and saying, "You must get up—you must not kneel hear." Mr. Jones replied, "Wait until prayer is over." Mr. H— M— said "no, you must get up now, or I will call for aid and force you away." Mr. Jones said, "Wait until prayer is over, and I will get up and trouble you no more." With that he beckoned to one of the other trustees, Mr. L— S— to come to his assistance. He came, and went to William White to pull him up. By this time prayer was over, and we all went out of the church in a body, and they were no more plagued with us in the church.[1]

Founding an African American institution would not be a totally new experience. Years earlier, Allen and others formed the Free African Society, a mutual aid organization, whose proceeds went to support the less fortunate in the black community.

This account is based on Richard Allen's autobiography, discovered in 1831 in a trunk after his death. While there is some evidence that St. George's underwent construction a few years after the date mentioned in Allen's journal, the substance of the account provides one of the most compelling narratives in the history of the formation of independent African American churches and a window onto early African Methodism. In some instances, Allen provides only the initials rather than full names of the participants in certain events and incidents. This may have been just a shorthand, or it could have been done to protect the identity of those individuals and himself from any negative repercussions for his reflections and commentaries. In one entry in his journal, Allen attests to the veracity of his accounts and the limits of his methodology. He wrote, "A great part of this work having been written many years after events actually took place; and as my memory could not exactly point out the exact time of many occurrences; they are, however, (as many as I can recollect)

---

1. Milton C. Sernett, ed., *African American Religious History: A Documentary Witness* (Durham, NC: Duke University Press, 1999), 146; Richard Allen, *The Life Experience and Gospel Labors of the Rt. Rev. Richard Allen* (Philadelphia: Martin and Boston, 1833).

pointed out; some without day or date, which I presume, will be of no material consequence, so that they are confined to the truth."[2]

The formation of independent African American churches was not only about escaping white restrictions, but was centered around tensions and disagreements over belief, practice, and religious affiliation. For those displaced from St. George's Church, it was far from unanimous which denomination to organize under. While Richard Allen felt more strongly aligned with the Methodists because of their historical opposition to slavery and straightforward doctrine and preaching style, many black congregants, still stinging from the ill treatment, pushed for an Episcopalian affiliation. In the end, some followed Allen toward the goal of denominational independence and others, like Jones, chose to remain within the Protestant Episcopal tradition. Jones took over the pastorate of the newly established St. Thomas African Episcopal Church.

While race clearly played a role in the formation of independent African American churches, the importance of religious and denominational identity should not be downplayed. In his autobiography, Richard Allen consistently expressed a profound loyalty to the early Methodist missionaries who extended the gospel message to African Americans.

> We were in favor of being attached to the Methodist connection; for I was confident that there was no religious sect or denomination would suit the capacity of the colored people as well as the Methodist; for the plain and simple gospel suits best for any people; for the unlearned can understand, and the learned are sure to understand; and the reason that the Methodist is so successful in the awakening and conversion of the colored people, the plain doctrine and having a good discipline.[3]

In another entry, he reminisces,

---

2. Allen, *The Life Experience and Gospel Labors of the Rt. Rev. Richard Allen*, 139.
3. Ibid., 148–49.

> The Methodists were the first people that brought glad tidings to the colored people. I feel thankful that ever I heard a Methodist preach. We are beholden to the Methodists, under God, for the light of the Gospel we enjoy; for all other denominations preached so high-flown that we were not able to comprehend their doctrine.[4]

Racial and denominational identity were closely intertwined for Allen and drove his crusade for independence.

After the dramatic walk out of St. George's ME Church, the history of the AME denomination would be intricately interwoven with the ME Church for years to come. Despite disputes over property ownership, membership requirements, and access to leadership positions, Allen strove to fashion a working relationship within the broader Methodist community. The ME Church was often conflicted over the formation of independent black churches. While somewhat pleased to have a predominately white congregation, some ME members were troubled by the idea of autonomous black churches. White ME Church leaders and congregants filed lawsuits, opened an alternative African American church, and denied or demanded large sums of money to offer communion to AME members. Despite these tactics, Allen's Mother Bethel Church in Philadelphia had a membership in 1813 of over thirteen hundred. Two years later, the relationship had grown so testy that a white minister was physically prevented from speaking from Bethel's pulpit. The preacher filed a writ of mandamus, which reached the Philadelphia Supreme Court. In 1816, the judges found in favor of the black congregants and granted official independence to Mother Bethel Church.

At the time of its founding as an independent denomination in 1816, Richard Allen, the first AME Church bishop, and his fellow ministers made few adjustments to the Methodist Episcopal Church *Discipline*. Allen and the other leaders sought to align more closely

4. Ibid., 149.

with early Wesleyan Methodism. In the first *Doctrines and Discipline of the African Methodist Episcopal Church* of 1817, members issued a prohibition against wearing robes that had been omitted from ME Church doctrine and did away with the position of presiding elder, a step above elder but below the bishopric, which some felt was a remnant of Catholicism. Perhaps, most significantly, the new *Discipline* reestablished Wesley's ban against slaveholders holding church membership, which many white Methodist congregations had failed to enforce.

Like the AME Church, the AMEZ traces its origins to the 1790s, when a group of African Americans protested the racial prejudice and discrimination in an ME Church in New York and left to form their own congregation, gaining official denominational independence in the 1820s. James Varick took the reins as its first superintendent. The "Zion" in the title was added much later in 1848 to distinguish itself from the AME Church. Like other black churches, the AMEZ sent missionaries to the South after the Civil War to evangelize the newly freed slaves. Its membership increased from 5,000 before 1865 to over 700,000 in 1916. The AME Zion Church earned the epithet, "the Freedom Church," because so many prominent abolitionists such as Sojourner Truth, Harriet Tubman, and Frederick Douglass were associated with the denomination. Today, the AMEZ is the second-largest black Methodist denomination.

The Colored Methodist Episcopal Church emerged from the Methodist Episcopal Church, South, which separated from the larger Methodist Episcopal Church body in 1844 over a number of doctrinal issues, but the institution of slavery proved to be the most divisive. The missionary efforts of the AME, AMEZ, and Methodist Episcopal Church following emancipation secured significant portions of the membership of the Methodist Episcopal Church, South, lowering it to 40,000 in 1870. On December 15, 1870, a group of African

Americans left the ME Church, South and formed the Colored Methodist Episcopal Church. At the General Conference, William H. Miles and Richard H. Vanderhorst were elected the denomination's first bishops. Although it expanded at a more gradual pace than the other African Methodist traditions, by 1890, the CME had a membership of over 100,000 with three-quarters of that number residing in the South. In 1954, the denomination was renamed the Christian Methodist Episcopal Church. Because they most often abstained from venturing into the political issues of the day and the relative late date of their departure from the ME Church, South, the CME was strongly criticized by other nineteenth-century African Methodists and caricatured as a "bootlick" operation and "little slave church" by their sharpest critics. However, it is a matter of perspective whether remaining as a racial minority within a tradition or establishing one's own congregation constitutes the more radical form of action.

Not all black churches emerged out of dramatic racial conflicts. The earliest black Baptist churches formed organically as like-minded Christians sought a site of worship. Predating the rise of independent African American churches in the North, a number of black ministers founded Baptist congregations throughout the South in the eighteenth century. The location of the first black Baptist church is a matter of debate. The African Baptist or "Bluestone" Church organized on the William Bird plantation in Mecklenberg, Virginia, in 1758. The Silver Bluff Baptist Church was officially founded by George Liele between 1773 and 1775 near Silver Bluff, South Carolina, but some accounts place the first services as early as 1750. George Liele and David George founded another black Baptist church in 1777 at Yama Craw near Savannah, Georgia. One of the early converts in this congregation, Andrew Bryan, established the First African Church there in 1788.

Yet, the Baptist tradition was not immune from racial tensions. Throughout the nineteenth century, unequal treatment in white Baptist churches led to the formation of independent black Baptist congregations such as the African Baptist Church in 1805, the Absyssinian Baptist Church in 1808, and the First African Baptist Church in Philadelphia in 1809. The potential barriers blocking the formation of independent black Baptist churches were slightly less formidable than those facing their African Methodist counterparts, who required the sanction of the broader white Methodist community to keep their Episcopal lineage and structure intact. In contrast, Baptist polity provides for the absolute independence of each local church. However, this emphasis on congregational autonomy created additional challenges in the formation of a national denomination from 1815 to 1880. The first efforts to do so at the Consolidated American Baptist Missionary Convention ended almost before it got started, but its initial momentum led to the formation of three conventions: the Baptist Foreign Mission Convention of the United States of America in Montgomery, Alabama, on November 24, 1880; the American National Baptist Convention in St. Louis on August 25, 1886; and the National Baptist Educational Convention of the U.S.A. in Washington, D.C. in 1893. On September 28, 1895, the three organizations merged into the National Baptist Convention, U.S.A. However, this union did not endure, with the departure of the National Baptist Convention of America twenty years later and the creation of the Progressive National Baptist Convention in 1961. Today, the National Baptist Convention, U.S.A., Inc. remains the largest black denomination.[5]

It continues to be a matter of debate just how independent these early black churches were. Most of these early black churches relied

5. C. Eric Lincoln and Lawrence H. Mamiya, *The Black Church in the African American Experience* (Durham, NC: Duke University Press, 1990).

heavily on white philanthropy for spiritual and financial support. African Methodist preachers were initially commissioned by white ME bishops. Black Baptists were often required to be licensed by two white Baptist ministers in good standing. In the early nineteenth century, since there were relatively few ordained black preachers, white ministers regularly delivered the Sunday-morning sermons to black congregations. The land upon which many black churches stood was often held in trusteeship by whites. Yet, the psychological independence that came from African Americans being able to worship freely and in the manner they chose fit should not be underestimated. Race along with a panoply of other issues and concerns informed the development of independent black churches. Disputes over polity, organization, and personality clashes were just a few of the factors that informed the myriad of schisms that occurred in black Christendom.

Roman Catholicism

While they also wrestled with racism and discrimination within Roman Catholicism, black Catholics found the rituals of mass, sacraments, devotions, and reverence for the saints empowering in their experience of slavery. Yet, by 1891, only five black priests served in America: Charles Randolph Uncles, Patrick, James, and Sherwood Healy, and Augustus Tolton. James Augustine Healy entered the seminary in Montreal in 1849. After ordination to the subdiaconate in 1852, Healy transferred from the seminary in Montreal to the Sulpician Seminary at Issyles-Molineaux near Paris. James Augustine Healy was ordained a priest in the Cathedral of Notre Dame on June 10, 1854. From 1889 to 1894, black Catholic conferences across the country convened to discuss issues facing the community such as ending discrimination in the church. Having edited and published a black Catholic weekly newspaper, the *American Catholic Tribune*, Daniel A. Rudd was a central voice in these settings and took the lead in establishing the African American Catholic congresses. Rudd maintained that the future for African Americans both spiritually and racially lay in the universality of Roman Catholicism and not in the separatism of black Protestant "race churches." The first meeting of delegates from black parishes and Catholic organizations on the national stage was in January 1889 in Washington, D.C., followed by other gatherings in Cincinnati (1890), Philadelphia (1892), Chicago (1893), and Baltimore (1894). Rudd recognized that African American Catholics were at times seen as outsiders to the larger black community. He wrote in his newspaper that some "fancy even, that because a Negro is a Catholic, he is nigh a renegade to his race . . . every Colored Catholic must, at times, feel his Colored brethren look upon him as an alien." However, Rudd believed that black Catholics would play a distinct role in the uplift of the African American race. "The Catholics of the Colored race should be the leaven, which would raise up their people not only in the eye of God but before men."[6] These gatherings of black Catholics sought to articulate ways to advance all people of African descent.

Many black Catholics had to balance their trumpeting of the egalitarian nature of Roman Catholicism with their work to eliminate discriminatory practices within the church, such as the exclusion of black children from attending Catholic schools. This tension has continued through the history of black American Catholicism. The Federated Colored Catholics founded by Thomas Wyatt Turner in 1917 sought to connect black Catholics across the country, develop black leadership, and protest discrimination in America and the

---

6. Cyprian Davis, "Black Catholic Theology: A Historical Perspective," *Theological Studies* 61 (2000): 661; Cyprian Davis, *The History of Black Catholics in the United States* (New York: Crossroad, 1993).

Catholic Church. Initially supported by two white Jesuits, Father William Markoe and Father John La Farge, the mission of the organization became torn between a focus on empowering black Catholics and pushing for interracial cooperation. The organization's journal, the *Chronicle*, was changed to the *Interracial Review*, foreshadowing a schism in the group that saw Turner's community disband in the 1950s. As the Catholic Church expanded its missionary work into Africa, some black Catholics maintained that while racism might exist, in some cases, at the parish level, the sacraments worked *ex opere operato*, independent of the individual perspective of the priest. Others such as Father George Stallings protested the racism he saw in the Roman Catholic hierarchy and formed his own Imani (Swahili for "faith") Temple movement in 1989. As other temples emerged, Stallings supported the ordination of women, birth control and abortion, communion to divorced and remarried Catholics, and made celibacy optional for priests. Yet, while a wave of black churches emerged from white denominations, black Catholics, for the most part, chose the universalism of Catholicism over the formation of separate divisions.

The presence of saints of African descent root Roman Catholicism firmly within African American religious history. St. Moses the Black was one of the first black saints from the Coptic and Ethiopian traditions. In Palladius's compilation of monastic lives (365–425 CE) in the Lausiac History in the early fifth century, Moses is characterized as having a strong build and black skin. Stories abound of his exploits as an outlaw and possibly a murderer. While the specifics of his conversion are unknown, he most likely encountered ascetics in the Egyptian desert where fugitives often shared living spaces in their efforts to escape Roman laws. St. Moses the Black was a member of the first generation of desert ascetics after the death of St. Antony of Egypt in 356. One of the few ordained priests at the time, he led the hermits living in the desert of Scete near Alexandria. He was martyred around 407.

Saint Moses the Black is one of many Roman Catholic saints with African ancestry. In March 1998, Pope John Paul II beatified Cyprian Tansi who was a Trappist Nigerian monk. Beatification declares formally that a deceased person showed a heroic degree of holiness in his or her life and therefore is worthy of public veneration, which is the first step toward canonization. Born in 1903, Michael Iwene Tansi was one of the first ordained Nigerian priests and served twenty-three years as a diocesan priest. St. Benedict the Moor, also known as St. Benedict the Black, was born Benedetto Manassari in 1526 in Sicily. He was freed at the age of twenty-one and joined a hermetic group that followed the Rule of St. Francis. He was eventually made superior of the friary of Santa Maria di Gesu in Palermo. St. Benedict the Moor was renowned as a spiritual guide and became the object of popular devotion in Europe almost immediately after his death in 1589. In Sicily, he became known as the protector of the black race and patron of the city of Palermo. He was canonized by Pope Pius VII in 1807. There is widespread devotion of St. Martin de Porres throughout North and South America. Although he died in 1639, he was not canonized until 1962 by Pope John XXIII. Born in 1579, he entered the Dominican order at fifteen; however, Spanish law prohibited individuals who had black, Indian, or mixed ancestry from being ordained. Working at the Dominican convent of Our Lady of the Rosary, he became well known for his extensive charity work throughout Lima and his roles as a healer and mystic.

Black women have been central to Roman Catholicism. Victoria Rasoamanarivo was born in 1848 in Antananarivo, Madagascar. At fifteen, she was baptized a Catholic. As a relative of the royal family, she protected the Catholic tradition and appealed to the queen and prime minister and advocated for Catholic schools and churches to be kept open and was acclaimed for her works of charity among the poor, prisoners, and lepers. She died in 1894, and Pope John Paul II beatified her in 1989. Saint Josephine Bakhita was born in 1868 in Sudan. Around the age of ten she was kidnapped by Arab slave traders and given the name "Bakhita," which means "Lucky One." When her owners, the Michielis, took her to Venice where slavery was illegal, she was granted her freedom. At baptism she took the name Josephine, and in 1893 she entered the Institute of the Daughters of Charity, known as the Canossian Sisters. She was known for her kindness and quiet spirit. She died in 1947, was beatified in 1992, and canonized as a saint on October 1, 2000. Anuarite Nengapeta was born in 1941 in the Belgian Congo, baptized in the Catholic Church in 1943, joined the diocesan religious community the Sisters of the Holy Family, and made her vows in 1959 taking the name Marie Clementine. Captured during the movement for independence in the Belgian Congo, she chose to be put to death on December 1, 1964, rather than suffer abuse at the hands of her captors. Pope John Paul II, calling her a "witness of hope," beatified Anuarite in 1985 in the Republic of the Congo.[7]

The Black Presence in White Churches

African Americans have also had a strong presence in predominately white traditions. In the nineteenth century, many African Americans were drawn to the Episcopal Church. One attraction was the notion of being catholic or universal. The Episcopal tradition offered a church for all people that went beyond any historical moment, culture, or race. Given this notion of catholicity, Episcopalians could point toward a tradition that predated slavery and the social injustice

---

7. Davis, *The History of Black Catholics in the United States.*

that African Americans experienced on a daily basis in America. Many Episcopalians also asserted that many of the church fathers, such as Tertullian, Cyprian, Monica, Origen, and Augustine, were of African descent and therefore were black. There was also an expressed ideal of a spiritual fellowship based on racial equality symbolized in the taking of Holy Communion together. Many black churchmen had a great respect for all things English. England was widely regarded as less racist than America, acknowledging one's education and achievement regardless of race. For many, England and British institutions were seen as the pinnacle of western civilization. The Episcopalian emphasis on the intellect and the power of liturgy also appealed to many African Americans. Given this focus on reason and will, many black Episcopalians viewed the larger black denominations with their more expressive worship styles as overly emotional and not conducive to instilling the rationality that would allow humans to live up to their full potential. As one black man said to Bishop Quintard in Memphis in 1869, "I am tired of excitement and ranting noise of various meeting houses. I want Episcopal services! Why should you white folks have the nice Episcopal services all to yourselves?"[8] The sermons of black Episcopalians addressed racial themes and issues relevant to the black community.

The eighteenth century witnessed the first efforts of the Presbyterian and Lutheran churches to do missionary outreach to slaves in America. As early as 1774 Lutherans began baptizing slaves. The North Carolina Synod, which had representation from South Carolina, Tennessee, and Virginia, passed a series of resolutions in the early nineteenth century that addressed the denomination's

8. J. Carleton Hayden, "Black Episcopal Preaching in the Nineteenth Century: Intellect and Will," *The Journal of Religious Thought* 39 (Spring/Summer 1982): 15; George Freeman Bragg, *The History of the Afro-American Group of the Episcopal Church* (New York: Johnson Reprint Corp., 1968).

relationship to African Americans. The 1809 resolution allowed pastors, with the permission of the slaveowners, to baptize slaves. One year later, a resolution added the provision that the slave masters be committed to the religious instruction of their slaves. In 1814 the synod agreed "It is our duty to preach the Gospel to the Negroes, and after proper instruction to admit them to all the means of grace of the church, and for this purpose to make room for them in the churches. That masters are, in love, requested to grant liberty to their slaves for this purpose, and herewith it is placed on record that it is the duty of the master to have them instructed."[9] In 1817, the North Carolina Synod adopted a Five Point Plan for engaging African Americans. The plan included assertions that blacks slave and free should be "prepared and fitted for full acceptance in our church, according to their situation in society."[10] It also placed greater requirements on African Americans. While white members received instruction and were immediately extended Holy Communion, blacks were required to demonstrate a commitment to live a devout Christian life before gaining access to the Eucharist and then only at the same church as their master. Pastors could also deny communion if there was some question about the African American's lifestyle. Slave parents were responsible for having their children baptized, and blacks were granted the right to serve as sponsors at baptisms. In 1832, Lutherans began ordaining the first African Americans to the ministry, including Jehu Jones, Daniel Payne, and B. J. Drayton. Jones organized the first independent black Lutheran congregation, St. Paul's Colored Lutheran Church in Philadelphia. In 1866, the Lutheran synods of the South formally requested black members to

9. Jacob L. Morgan, ed., *History of the Lutheran Church in North Carolina 1803-1953* (United Evangelical Lutheran Synod of North Carolina, 1953), 114–15.
10. *Minutes of the German and English Lutheran Synod*, 19 October 1817, 59; Hugh George Anderson, *Lutheranism in the Southeastern States, 1860-1886: A Social History* (The Hague, Netherlands: Mouton, 1976).

form separate congregations and ecclesiastical structures. In 1889, Black Lutherans formed the Alpha Evangelical Lutheran Synod of Freedmen in America, the first separate black Lutheran ecclesiastical organization in the United States. Lutherans established the first institution of higher learning to train black ministers in Concord, North Carolina. In 1958, Nelson Trout was elected bishop of the American Lutheran Church. In the late 1960s, black caucuses were formed to articulate the concerns of African Americans within the Lutheran church. Reverend Samuel Davies led the first efforts to evangelize slaves in the Presbyterian Church in 1747. Davies's Hanover Presbytery consisted of all the Presbyterian churches south of the Potomac which, in 1757, reported that 150 slaves had been baptized. For many African Americans, the Presbyterian Church was perceived to be less active in removing slaveholders from the denomination and integrating slaves into their congregations than Methodist and Baptist churches. While Samuel Cornish is perhaps best known for editing the first black newspaper, the *Freedom's Journal*, he also founded the First Colored Presbyterian church of New York City in 1822.

Public discussions surrounding the impending Civil War had strong religious overtones. Both northerners and southerners believed that God was on their side and that divine favor rested upon them and their cause. Leading up to the military conflict, tensions within denominations abounded. By 1844, the Methodist Church had divided into a northern branch and the Methodist Episcopal Church, South. Southern Baptists formed the Southern Baptist Convention in 1845. Northern African Americans pushed for the right to be soldiers, black ministers served as chaplains to all-black divisions, and southern slaves prayed for a northern victory and deliverance from bondage.

The immediate elation of emancipation was followed by a

recognition that an uncertain future lay ahead for African Americans seeking to restore families that had been separated during the war, were impoverished, and had few solid prospects for the years ahead. Many wondered exactly what freedom would look like. The Freedmen's Bureau of the federal government, denominational agencies, and the American Missionary Association raised money, provided assistance, and sent teachers to the south to help educate the newly freed slaves. In addition to literacy, these instructors sought to instill moral values, temperance, a strong work ethic, and discipline. Out of these efforts, several historically black colleges were established. Some schools, such as Booker T. Washington's Tuskegee Institute in Alabama, emphasized industrial education and vocational instruction.

The end of the Civil War also opened up a whole new field of "unchurched" black Americans that both white and black northern missionaries sought to bring into the fold. This competition for members not only placed many black and white churches at odds, but also created tensions between black denominations. The success of this outreach effectively transformed many northeastern black churches into national denominations. Historians have estimated that in 1858, the membership of the AME Church was approximately 20,000 members, with virtually no members in the southern states. By 1896, the total membership of the church was over 450,000, with approximately 80 percent of the members residing in the south. The AME Zion membership rose from 27,000 in 1860 to 200,000 in 1870. Black Baptist congregations ballooned overnight from the exodus of thousands of African American members from Southern Baptist churches.

With the Reconstruction came unprecedented political opportunities for African Americans. The year 1865 witnessed the passage of the Thirteenth, Fourteenth, and Fifteenth Amendments, which banned slavery and granted African Americans full citizenship and enfranchisement. With the Union presence in the South, blacks organized and registered voters in record numbers. By 1867, there were 735,000 black registered voters to 635,000 white. The almost 80 percent black southern Republican party elected African American men to 15–20 percent of the publicly held offices including fourteen to the House of Representatives and two to the senate between 1868 and 1876. Reconstruction opened doors to occupations and societal roles that would have been unimaginable only a few years earlier. Ministers such as AME Bishop Henry McNeal Turner entered the United States Congress. Yet, post-Reconstruction would see each of these gains taken away as poll taxes, literacy tests, property requirements, and terrorist tactics were reinstated. In 1877, the removal of federal troops from the South left African Americans to fend for themselves in the face of violent white "redeemers" such as the Ku Klux Klan, who felt blacks had stepped out of their rightful subservient place. While countless lynchings have escaped the historical record, estimates suggest that between 1880 and 1930, 3,220 blacks and 720 whites were lynched in the South, with most taking place in Louisiana, Mississippi, Alabama, Georgia, and Texas. The rise of Jim Crow segregation meant that blacks were assigned to a second-class status, disenfranchised, and prevented from using white public facilities.[11]

The Experiences of Women

Having experienced restrictions placed on their own spiritual roles in white churches, one might expect the leadership roles in the newly formed black churches to be more fluid. However, the patriarchal structure that informed many white churches that they had left was

---

11. Stephen Ward Angell, *Bishop Henry McNeal Turner and African-American Religion in the South* (Nashville: University of Tennessee Press, 1992).

also reflected in the doctrine and polity of independent African American denominations. While from their inception roles were fairly malleable in the early nineteenth-century black churches, as the movements for independent religious expression transitioned into institutions, leadership roles were increasingly defined along gender lines. In 1830, Rebecca Cox Jackson sought to preach in black denominations, but was denied based on the church disciplines and eventually left the black church in favor of the Shaker tradition. Jarena Lee was sanctioned by Richard Allen and was one of the most powerful orators in the AME Church, experiencing little difficulty securing speaking appearances during the formative years of the church. However, by 1839, in Philadelphia, she experienced resistance to her presence in the pulpit and her requests to preach were denied. Other black female preachers such as Zilpha Elaw also faced obstacles in ascending the leadership ranks of black churches. Yet, potential female ministers faced additional obstacles than those of their male counterparts. Female preachers were often criticized for "abandoning" their families and children for the mission field. Despite their own ambitions, some black female preachers felt a tension between motherhood and the ministry. In her autobiography, Jarena Lee remembers leaving her sick son to preach for a week at a church that was thirty miles away and asking God to keep her son from her mind so that she could accomplish his will. Since her friends and family had taken good care of the child, she considered leaving domestic life to focus on missionary work. Throughout her autobiography, Lee recalled leaving her children, believing divine intervention lessened her maternal instincts. Similarly, Zilpha Elaw felt called to minister to others even as her daughter experienced conversion at a revival.

Prohibitions excluding women from speaking from the pulpit were a result of the dramatic change in requirements put in place for preachers in many black churches in the 1830s. From their inception many black churches made only subtle distinctions between the positions of exhorter and preacher, and women regularly spoke from the denominations' pulpits. The 1836 General Conference of the AME Church was one of the first to explicitly separate the callings of preacher and exhorter in its legislation. "It is not expected that an exhorter will attempt to preach formally, to read a text, announce a theme, and divide his subject; but he will sing, pray and then read a passage of Scripture, and make such remarks as he may feel disposed."[12] However, the imprecise phrasing that granted exhorters the opportunity to "make remarks" allowed for quite a bit of leeway in the interpretation of the line between exhorter and preacher. Consequently, the enforcement of the passage varied from church-to-church in the tradition. By the late 1830s, male AME Church leaders had sharpened the distinction between preachers and exhorters. Practically, this meant that female exhorters were increasingly denied access to the pulpit. By mid-century, often drawing on the disciplines of the white denominations that they had separated from, most black churches had official rules in place to limit formal preaching to licensed ministers. While, in the early nineteenth century, women had spoken at revivals, church meetings, and conferences of the major black denominations, the male leadership increasingly defined the roles of preacher and pastor as masculine endeavors.

Women used all means at their disposal within the church disciplines to make the case for female preachers. Female members aspiring to the ministry, as well as the Daughters of Zion, petitioned the AME General Conference calling for the denominational leadership to officially sanction female preachers in 1844, 1848, and

12. Alexander W. Wayman, *Manual, or Guide Book for the Administration of the Discipline of the African M.E. Church* (Philadelphia: AME Book Rooms, 1886), 16.

1852. In each case the request was refused by a large margin. Further pleas received little notice and, by 1864, the General Conference did not even call for a vote on the issue. Although unsuccessful in their motions, by petitioning the General Conference, these female members called for the right to lead and forced the question of gender into the public discourse of the AME Church and other black denominations. Female members of black congregations who felt called by God to preach and those who believed that women should not be denied the opportunity to lead in the church fought for equal rights.

While not going so far as ordination, black denominations sought compromises that would elevate the status of women but not upset what had become traditional gender roles in black churches. The 1868 AME General Conference created the first official positions specifically for women in the church, the offices of stewardess and female superintendent. Pastors had the ability to nominate a Board of Stewardesses, a position that did not require ordination, fell under the authority of the male leadership, and established women as "assistants" in the church. According to AME Church polity, stewardesses were a "collection of sisters, numbering not less than three nor more than nine, who assist the stewards, class leaders and pastor . . . but cannot always be recognized as a board, as they have no legislative or judicial discretion, but are merely assistants."[13] The legislation did not offer women the opportunity to become stewards in the church. Pastors and male stewards had the final say over potential candidates and the length of their time in the position. In contrast, AME Church legislation granted no power to allow stewardesses to remove stewards. The female superintendent was required to "assist" the male superintendent in "preserving order in the school, especially

13. Henry McNeal Turner, *The Genius and Theory of Methodist Polity, or the Machinery of Methodism* (Philadelphia: AME Church, 1885), 165–66.

among the females." In addition, the female superintendent oversaw female teachers and their classes.

Although the 1884 AME General Conference licensed female preachers, at the close of the nineteenth century, the AME Church still had not sanctioned female ordination. Instead, male AME Church leaders created the position of deaconess, to be held exclusively by women. In 1900, the denomination published *The Deaconess Manual of the African Methodist Episcopal Church,* defining "woman" as "pre-eminently the helper of man." It stated that in order to hold the office of deaconess women "should so know how to demean themselves as not to prejudice the work in the minds of their husbands. A woman who has not the confidence of her husband can do but little good in church work." A woman feeling called to the deaconess position still needed the approval of the pastor and agreed to be under his "general direction." The pastor could suspend a deaconess for impropriety, immorality, and disharmony. The manual stated that the deaconess should not argue with the pastor, but should instead "be quiet and let him have the right of way."[14] It further instructed women to use their spare time for cleaning. The position of deaconess was strikingly distinct from that of deacon, which came with ordination.

Controversy surrounded women's roles in the AME Zion Church as well. Bishop Charles Calvin Pettey ordained Mary J. Small to the order of elder in 1898. Prior to this, women had preaching licenses and could be ordained as deacons. However, Small's ordination to the eldership, the highest level of the ministry, gave her the authority to pastor churches, administer the sacraments, and potentially to become a bishop in the church, which marked a significant step during this era. Some demanded that the General Conference rescind

---

14. James T. Campbell, *Songs of Zion: The African Methodist Episcopal Church in the United States and South Africa* (Chapel Hill: University of North Carolina Press, 1998), 52.

the ordination. Part of the passionate response was due to concerns that this action was a slippery slope that would eventually grant women access to every position and sphere in the denomination. Others asserted that women should have equality in all aspects of church life. Defenders of Small's ordination found passages in the Bible that pointed toward gender equity and provided examples of female leaders. The universal application of scriptural verses that seemed to suggest the subordination of women were dismissed as written for specific historical contexts and sets of issues facing the early churches. They invoked "historical progressivism" and made the case that although gender equity may have not have been normative in the first century, the Bible unfolded greater truths and freedoms in later epochs. Practically, some argued, women needed to fill the roles that current black male ministers were failing to do. Still more fell somewhere in between questioning the religious basis for the ordination of women, but resigned to the fact that church law as written could not be used to deny Small the position. At the 1900 General Conference of the AME Zion Church, Reverend A. J. Rogers put forth a resolution against female ordination. The motion was defeated. According to the AMEZ General Conference, the ordination had been carried out in accordance with church laws and the candidates were fully qualified. The ordination stood after a sometimes contentious debate, and in 1900, Julia Foote was also ordained to elder just prior to her death. While women continued to face challenges in their ascension to roles in the church, this was an important step toward gender equity in black churches.

Historically, African American women have found slightly greater access to leadership roles in predominantly white churches. The expansion of women's roles in black churches often paralleled similar developments within white Protestant churches. The Women's Missionary Society in the ME Church was founded in 1869, while the AME Church's Women's Mite Missionary Society began in 1874. In 1880, the ME Church heard the first case for female ordination, and the AME General Conference faced the same issue in 1884. In 1888, the ME Church instituted the position of deaconess, which became an official position in the AME Church in 1900. In 1853, the Congregationalists—now known as the United Church of Christ—had trained female pastors, and the Universalists did the same as early as 1863. By 1900, the Disciples of Christ and the American Baptist Churches in the U.S.A. had also ordained women to pastorates. However, for other traditions change came more gradually. The Presbyterian Church ordained women in 1955 and the Methodist Church did so in 1956. Eight years later, the Southern Baptist Convention ordained a woman, but she did not receive official denominational sanction. The Church of God had women pastors from its inception in 1880. The United Methodists elected Leontine T. C. Kelly to the bishopric in 1984, and Barbara C. Harris was elected as the first African American bishop of the Episcopal Church four years later.

The American Baptist Home Mission Society and its women's auxiliaries in the Northeast and Midwest played a central role in the education of black leaders. In the 1880s, black churches in Atlanta and Richmond raised money for women's education. These efforts led to the founding of the Atlanta Baptist Female Seminary which would be renamed Spelman. Henry Morehouse, executive secretary of the ABHMS from 1879 to 1893 and from 1902 to 1917, envisioned a different kind of education for the "Talented Tenth" of African Americans. While industrial education was sufficient for 90 percent of blacks, Morehouse believed that the best and brightest should learn to value a liberal arts education, industriousness, piety, and refined manners. Developing a black elite would allow the chosen few to lead and uplift the rest of the community.

In the 1880s tensions arose between African Americans and the American Baptist Home Mission Society, which maintained policies that blacks felt were racist and paternalistic. They called for more black faculty and administrators at white-controlled schools. The rise of women's state conventions allowed black churches to acquire resources to sustain institutions. Women's associations within individual churches worked together to form state conventions. Conventions worked to represent women in every black Baptist church in a state. Women formed their own missionary organizations such as the Women's Baptist Home Mission Society, which focused on black family life and sent missionaries to the South to work within homes, churches, and industrial schools. Within the National Baptist Convention, the Women's Convention was founded in 1900. The Women's Convention focused on missionary work. By 1903, Nannie Burroughs reported that the Women's Convention had a membership of over a million and in 1907 she noted an increase of another half million. Black Baptist women made the church a site of self-help, built schools, and provided social welfare services to black communities.

Black Baptist women also fought for gender equality in black churches. Feminist theologians of black Baptist churches, such as Mary Cook, Lucy Wilmot Smith, and Virginia Broughton, challenged popular notions of women as fragile and impressionable and instead promoted their capacity to influence men. While none of the women was formally trained as a theologian, they closely read and analyzed the Bible and presented their interpretations in the public sphere with the fervency and thoughtful articulation of the most celebrated ministers of the era. Raised free in Tennessee, Broughton attended private school and graduated from Fisk University in 1875. She married John Broughton but continued to work as a missionary and teacher. In 1885, she challenged the appointment of a less-qualified black male teacher over herself and won the case. She drew upon biblical symbols to empower black women. She published her lectures and writings in a volume in 1904 titled *Women's Work, as Gleaned from the Women of the Bible*. Born a slave in 1862 in Kentucky, Cook graduated from the Normal Department of State University of Louisville in 1883 and taught literature and Latin there. She married the Reverend Charles H. Parrish in 1898 and was an active member of the National Association of Colored Women, black women's clubs, and the national convention of black Baptist women. Cook was an active writer and speaker, publishing articles in the black newspapers and an anthology and delivering speeches to large gatherings including the American National Baptist Convention. Cook worked diligently for gender equity in black churches and she viewed the Bible as an "iconoclastic weapon" to dispatch negative stereotypes of women. Smith was born into poverty in 1861. She graduated from the Normal Department of the State University of Louisville and subsequently taught there and worked as a journalist. She was a principal of the Model School at the State University of Louisville, served as Historian of the American National Baptist Convention, helped lead the Baptist Women's Educational Convention of Kentucky, and expressed her opinions in black newspapers on a variety of topics including articles in favor of woman's suffrage.

The efforts of Cook, Smith, and Broughton to expand women's roles in the black Baptist tradition exemplify the strategies employed by black women across denominational lines to achieve gender equity in black churches. Women found inspiration in the mothers of key figures in the Hebrew Bible such as Moses, Isaac, and Samson. They elevated Mary, the mother of Jesus, as the highest expression of womanhood. Although motherhood was a central image in the ideology of feminist theologians, their own lives were often not preoccupied with maternal responsibilities. They also addressed the importance of the roles of wives, sisters, and daughters in the home in their writings. Feminist theologians shifted the focus from the loyal wife supporting her husband unconditionally to woman's relationship with Jesus that by implication extended female duties outside the home since her primary obligation was to God, not her mate. They drew upon female leaders in the Bible to make the case for more aggressive church work. Feminist theologians found biblical examples that illustrated that God used women in every capacity. They noted Huldah, wife of Shallum, who studied the law and interpreted it for audiences who sought her advice, including priests. Feminist theologians drew upon the example of Deborah in the Book of Judges who became a prophet, judge, and warrior appointed by God to lead Israel. Although a married woman, they emphasized her independent spirit from her husband. These are just a few examples of the ways black Protestant women made the case for the expansion of their roles and gender equity in the church.

The prospect of female preaching illumined how much black men had at stake in their roles as the leaders of black churches at mid-century. From 1840 to the late 1860s, the discourse in the public literature of many black churches centered around the achievement of manhood. By mid-nineteenth century a new understanding of manhood emerged that defined manhood based on individual entrepreneurship, success in competition, and exerting power over others. Unlike earlier notions of manhood, these traits were understood to be attainable by all men. Because the ideology presumed a level playing field, if men failed to demonstrate their prowess in each of these areas, they had only themselves to blame. One's manhood had to be perpetually proven, inducing a pervasive insecurity among many men. In addition, physical strength and public authority rounded out the contours of the cultural expectations of true manhood. Manliness was not bestowed upon birth but was a criterion to be reached and achieved. In the nineteenth century, facing both de jure and de facto racial discrimination in America, African Americans had access to few societal outlets and professions that would allow them to demonstrate their acumen in the public spheres and arenas of power that were presupposed in popular notions of masculinity. Because becoming a preacher was one of the few careers available for talented and educated African Americans, often the best and the brightest entered the ministry. This historical trend coupled with the ambiguity of nineteenth-century conceptions of manhood raised the stakes regarding access to the pulpit.

For a brief period, the interests of uneducated men meshed with those of female preachers. Many male ministers continued to argue that a converted heart and a gift for preaching were more important than a formal education. Uneducated African American church leaders faced the real possibility that additional requirements for preachers might cost them their ministerial positions. In their autobiographies, female preachers in the early black churches downplayed the importance of an educated ministry. Zilpha Elaw felt the "wise and learned" often did not embrace "the heavenly discipline of God's Holy Spirit." Similarly, Jarena Lee believed that in many cases the uneducated had a unique sensitivity to the "operations of the Holy Spirit." While early female preachers made similar arguments, downplaying the necessity of education, most male black church leaders viewed them as the competition for ministerial positions, rather than as potential allies.

Throughout the nineteenth century, the emphasis that black churches placed on an educated ministry increased. Not surprisingly it was often the well-educated ministers who advocated for the necessity of formal instruction as a prerequisite for effective preaching. Ministers increasingly linked education and manhood to the role of preacher. Some suggested that women could support the minister by helping men in their efforts to achieve their education through prayer and financial support. Access to pastoral positions increasingly fell along gender lines. In their public literature, leaders regularly defined ministerial positions and education as masculine endeavors.

Despite emphasizing the "natural nurturing" ability of mothers in the home, the central AME church text on domesticity was written by Daniel Payne. Payne's *Treatise on Domestic Education* (1885) appeared at an opportune historical moment. Published only one year after the licensing of female preachers, Payne's work was readily received by an eclectic audience that was critical of mothers who "abandoned" their families for the pulpit and what appeared to some observers as a devaluing of the contributions of women in the church and the home. In the midst of the turmoil surrounding the licensing of female preachers, Payne offered his notion of mothers as "domestic educators" as a means of uniting the divided constituency of the AME Church. Payne was one in a long line of ministers who viewed the licensing of female preachers as a threat, not only to the family, but to a sense of male authority as well. The ambiguity of the duties of fatherhood only increased the importance of the pulpit as a site to demonstrate true manhood.

Not all black male ministers were opponents of female preachers. Born on April 17, 1843, Theophilus Gould Steward often clashed with the conservative stances taken the many of the elder statesmen in black churches. In April 1862, the AME Church licensed Steward to exhort and on September 26, 1863, he earned his preaching license. Although he had received little formal education, Steward proved to be an effective preacher and was appointed to the Macedonia AME Church in South Camden, New Jersey. Steward pastored there until early in 1865, when Daniel Payne assigned him to be a missionary in South Carolina.

Steward became one of the most outspoken advocates for the expansion of women's roles in black churches. In his effort to sway public opinion in black newspapers, Steward challenged the patriarchal structure that had become entrenched in the denomination. Steward questioned why the public roles of the church—preaching from the pulpit, receiving ordination, and voting at Quarterly and General Conferences—were understood as exclusively male pursuits, while women were expected to support the church at the local level by raising funds and supporting church programs. Although his stance was very unpopular in many circles, Steward made a case for the expansion of women's roles across denominations.

Some male ministers encouraged women to use their voting power in churches to enact change. While men held the highest leadership positions in the church, women constituted the majority of most black churches' membership. According to the AME Church *Discipline*, any person seeking to be a licensed preacher or an exhorter had to be nominated by members of his congregation. An individual aspiring to rise in the ranks of the church needed the recommendation of his local congregation. Because of this approval process, some black leaders made the case that women should be able to vote in all church meetings, including the election of the trustees. If female members voted throughout a minister's career, some argued, they should not be restricted in other instances.

Despite obstacles to formal leadership positions, black women banded together in their own organizations to press forward the work of the churches to which they belonged. African American women were essential to the missionary efforts of black churches. The AME Church's Women's Mite Missionary Society formed in

1874. From 1874 to 1878, Mary A. Campbell, the first president of the organization, raised money for local societies and missionary work in Haiti, Santo Domingo, and West Africa, as well as domestically in the South. In less than two years, the WMMS had raised over six hundred dollars to support missionary work in Haiti. By far, the WMMS raised most of the money for the late nineteenth-century missionary efforts of the AME Church. Many wives of bishops and pastors in black churches served as unofficial leaders in the church. They formed women's missionary organizations and "Mite Missionary Societies" in their husbands' churches. The women hoped that by gathering small "mites" from members of the church, the collective effort would result in a substantial amount of money to put toward missionary work. In the AME Church, the founders of the organization were seven bishop's wives: Mary Quinn, Eliza Payne, Harriet A. E. Wayman, Mary A. Campbell, Maria Shorter, Mary L. Brown, and Mrs. Bishop Ward. Officially, the WMMS fell under the authority of the missionary department and therefore served as a "helper" to the AME Church. Although women's missionary societies were headed by women, male leaders often asserted their authority over the organization, and played a large official role in the proceedings of the meetings. The presumption that women were the assistants to the male leaders impeded the early efforts of organizations like the WMMS, particularly their attempts to form separate branches of organization. Women who expressed interest in forming a women's missionary society needed the support of the elders, trustees, and stewards of the church. The leadership of black churches, at times, posed a real power barrier to the involvement of women in the missionary efforts of the denominations.

Despite the desire of the male leaders to have a hand in the organization, the female leaders made the missionary societies their own. Female-led organizations raised money for local societies and missionary work around the world. While many male black church leaders referred to Africa as the "fatherland" that they would "conquer" with the gospel, many women viewed Africa as the "motherland" that needed support in the nurture of her children. While women's missionary societies often raised most of the money for the late nineteenth-century missionary efforts of black churches, male leaders still sought to define the boundaries of the group and maintained final authority on the group's decisions. Many black churches limited female participation to the role of "helper" in the missionary process as well.

Other women, such as Amanda Smith, found the limitations placed upon female missionaries in black churches too restrictive. In April 1865, Amanda Smith joined the Mother Bethel AME Church in Philadelphia. In November 1870, at the Fleet Street AME Church in Brooklyn, Smith felt called to preach. Smith gained renown speaking before white and black audiences at "holiness" revivals. Because the AME Church would not sponsor female missionaries traveling abroad unless their husbands accompanied them, some women within black churches worked with white denominations that had fewer prohibitions against female missionaries. In 1878, in conjunction with the white Methodist Episcopal Church, Smith engaged in missionary efforts across the globe and eventually traveled to London, India, and Africa. In 1890, she returned to the United States and became involved with the Women's Christian Temperance Union in Chicago. She published her autobiography in 1893.

A number of scholars have examined the varied experiences of African American women and wrestled with the challenges sometimes presented by the power dynamics within black denominations. As previously mentioned, the AME Zion Church was one of the first black denominations to ordain women as elders to the pulpit ministry. Bishop Charles Calvin Pettey ordained Mary J. Small to the position in 1898, which was officially acknowledged by the denomination in 1900. Bishop James Walker Hood of the AME Zion Church ordained Julia A. J. Foote as deacon in 1894 and itinerant elder in 1900. Women would not be granted ordination in the AME Church until 1948, and in the Christian Methodist Episcopal Church in 1954. Historically, the Church of God in Christ did not allow for female pastors, but it did permit women to serve as missionaries and evangelists. Of the national black Baptist bodies, the Progressive National Baptist Convention has been most open to female ordination. The 1884 AME General Conference passed a motion to license female preachers, but the denomination would not elect its first female bishop, Vashti Murphy McKenzie, until the year 2000. As we have seen, positions were fairly malleable in the burgeoning independent black church movement in the early nineteenth century, exemplified by women such as Jarena Lee delivering sermons at Mother Bethel Church in Philadelphia.[15] Yet, as the independent African American church movement transitioned into institutions, male leaders formalized rules, raised educational requirements to head congregations, and more rigidly mapped the

15. Stephen Ward Angell, "The Controversy over Women's Ministry in the African Methodist Episcopal Church During the 1880s: The Case of Sarah Anne Hughes," in Judith Weisenfeld and Richard Newman, *This Far by Faith: Readings in African-American Women's Biography* (New York: Routledge, 1995); Sandy D. Martin, *Black Baptists and African Missions: The Origins of a Movement, 1880-1915* (Macon, GA: Mercer University Press, 1998) and *For God and Race: The Religious and Political Leadership of AMEZ Bishop James Walker Hood* (Columbia: University of South Carolina Press, 1999); Anthea Butler, *Women in the Church of God in Christ: Making a Sanctified World* (Chapel Hill: University of North Carolina Press, 2007); William H. Becker, "The Black Church: Manhood and Mission," in the *Journal of the American Academy of Religion* 40 (Spring 1972): 316–33; Julius H. Bailey, *Around the Family Altar: Domesticity in the African Methodist Episcopal Church, 1865-1900* (Gainesville: University of Press of Florida, 2005); James T. Campbell, *Songs of Zion: The African Methodist Episcopal Church in the United States and South Africa* (New York: Oxford University Press, 1995).

boundaries of gender roles in the church, which increasingly limited opportunities for women to assume leadership.

4

Enduring Themes in Nineteenth-Century African American Religious Life

As African Americans organized the first independent African American churches, they united around not only the shared experience of being discriminated against in white congregations, but a drive to worship and have autonomy over their own church homes and sacred spaces. These emergent churches were not free from the politics of the congregations that they had left. Who would lead these new congregations? Who was the appropriate face for these unprecedented "African" denominations? While certainly not an exhaustive list, there are certain themes and historical epochs that students should be aware of as they consider the development of nineteenth-century African American religious traditions. These include the development of print culture, which was employed to shape public opinion about a range of issues impacting African Americans and the religious communities to which they belonged, as well as the black responses to social Darwinism, efforts to merge Christian denominations, and the religious meanings of Africa for missionaries, emigrants, and those who remained in America.

Denominational Leadership

How to understand denominationalism is an ongoing challenge in the study of African American religions. On the one hand, some traditions such as the Baptists emphasize the local autonomy and independence of their congregations. Yet, on the other hand the National Baptist Convention, USA, Inc. is the largest black Baptist convention and organization. Similarly, African Methodist Episcopal traditions are known for their hierarchical structure, but the actual day-to-day practices of African Methodist churches can vary pretty widely. These examples illustrate just how difficult it can be to make sweeping judgments and proclamations about black denominationalism. Seemingly each decision made and put forward by these nascent black churches in the eighteenth and nineteenth centuries was subject to the scrutiny of diverse African American religious perspectives and an often skeptical white American public.

These dynamics are highlighted by the choice of the first leaders of the black traditions. In the African Methodist Episcopal Church, Richard Allen, having been among those to be pulled from their knees during the worship service at St. George's Methodist Episcopal Church for praying in the wrong section of the church, was a fairly straightforward candidate to be the denomination's first bishop and leader. However, Daniel Coker, a former slave, and now deacon and a key leader in the African Methodist movement in Baltimore, arguably had the larger national following. While Richard Allen was likely the best-known black preacher in the northeast, Daniel Coker's speeches and writings, such as his "A Dialogue between a Virginian and an African Minister" (1810), had dealt with issues such as abolition that had engaged an American audience.[1]

---

1. Daniel Coker, "A Dialogue between a Virginian and an African Minister," in *Negro Protest Pamphlets: A Compendium*, ed. Dorothy Porter (New York: Arno Press, 1969), 39–40.

Despite the heated competition, on April 9, 1816, at the First General Conference of the AME Church, constituents from Delaware, Pennsylvania, New Jersey, and Maryland elected Coker the denomination's first bishop. However, he was only in the position briefly. The historical record is unclear whether Coker had the title stripped from him or if he voluntarily left office. The next day, Richard Allen was installed as the denomination's first bishop. While the details around the event remain murky, one delegate to the conference, David Smith, would later write that some in attendance felt that Coker was "too light to lead" the new denomination. Ongoing personality conflicts with Allen resulted in Coker being reprimanded in 1818, and limitations on his preaching and speaking opportunities ultimately led to Coker's departure to Africa. While there were likely a myriad of reasons for Allen ascending to the central leadership role, Smith's remark and Coker's ministerial career point to the intradenominational tensions that are often overlooked in African American religious history.[2]

Print Culture

Print culture—such as tracts, pamphlets, and newspapers—has been essential to the development of African American religion. While other racial and ethnic groups have also employed print culture to change Americans' perceptions of their communities and religions, African Americans, brought to America by the Atlantic slave trade, have had to consistently challenge negative assumptions about their abilities, skills, and potential. Written materials were particularly effective because they could be printed at relatively low cost, could be distributed widely, and could concretely challenge negative stereotypes of the race and religious practices either directly or

---

2. David Smith, *Biography of Rev. David Smith of the AME Church* (Xenia, OH: Xenia Gazette Office, 1881), 31-33.

implicitly in the publication of intellectually refined prose, powerfully articulated arguments, heartfelt poetry, literature, and the cultural arts. Pamphlets were a particularly effective medium because they could engage major issues such as abolition, racism, equity in education, and social justice but in efficient, cost-effective, often thin brochures that could be widely circulated and passed on to a variety of communities and constituencies. Print culture is one of the central media to emerge for African Americans to shape American public discussion about key issues facing the race and African American religious traditions.[3]

One of the best examples of African American religious traditions employing print culture to shape public opinion occurred in 1793. A Yellow Fever epidemic had broken out in Philadelphia, and several white newspapers had emphasized that African Americans had capitalized on the situation by robbing the sick and weak and burglarizing their homes. Absalom Jones and Richard Allen, who we remember from the incident in the white St. George's Episcopal Church, produced a pamphlet to counter the negative narrative about black Philadelphians and provide an account that was truer to what actually happened. Jones and Allen published the brochure, *A Narrative of the Proceedings of the Black People During the Late Awful Calamity in Philadelphia*, to provide a correction to the slanderous account that had been produced by the white press. Jones and Allen highlighted not only the fiction of suggesting that black thieves were on the loose during the epidemic, but placed a spotlight on the selfless acts of many African Americans who rendered aid and offered their resources to others at the risk of their own health during the crisis.[4]

---

3. Dorothy Porter, ed., *Negro Protest Pamphlets: A Compendium* (New York: Arno Press, 1969), iii–vii.
4. Richard S. Newman, ed., *Pamphlets of Protest: An Anthology of Early African American Protest Literature, 1790–1860* (New York: Routledge, 2001), 33, 38.

In addition to local crises and misrepresentations, pamphlets could also be used to address national issues. Daniel Coker published his abolitionist work, "A Dialogue between a Virginian and an African Minister" (1810), in the South. But the nineteenth century was an era in which African Americans articulating clear and persuasive informative opinions and perspectives could be threatening to a white public holding firmly to notions of white supremacy and superiority. A straightforward intellectual position piece on the problems and impact of slavery on the nation could alienate the precise constituency that Coker and others sought for support for their causes. Many African American writers would have to seek mediums that did not offend white sensibilities in order to effectively convey their messages to a broader audience. This dynamic was often magnified for black women, who faced both racial and gender prejudice and discrimination. Maria W. Stewart's "Productions" (1835) exemplifies this approach in her advocacy for women's reform movements and activism. In Coker's "Dialogue," this meant couching nuanced and subtle arguments against slavery in the form of a conversation between a slaveholder and African American minister. Consistent with the literary form, the African minister is passionate at the outset and his arguments increase in breadth and depth as the pamphlet unfolds. Similarly, while not portrayed as a buffoon, it soon becomes clear that the white Virginian will be no match for his counterpart in the debate. By the conclusion of the brochure, the white Virginian has totally reversed his position on slavery and agreed to emancipate all of his slaves. Yet, deference was just one of many strategies and tropes employed by African Americans in the varied literary genres of the nineteenth century.[5]

In the nineteenth century, many African Americans traveled to

---

5. Daniel Coker, "A Dialogue between a Virginian and an African Minister," in *Negro Protest Pamphlets: A Compendium*, ed. Dorothy Porter (New York: Arno Press, 1969), 39-40.

Africa to repatriate, as missionaries, and in some cases to connect with a part of their past and culture that they were forcibly separated from. On January 31, 1820, Coker made that journey, leaving from New York for the shores of West Africa. Once again Coker used the pamphlet format to share his experiences during his voyage across the Atlantic and to spur other African Americans to make a similar step. Coker did not hold back on the challenges and travails that he faced during the journey, including health issues, rocky seas, loneliness, and uncertainty about the future. Coker's writings highlight the varied dynamics facing those African Americans who chose to venture to Africa as well as those who opted to remain in America. Some African Americans romanticized Africa while harboring reservations about Africans themselves. An African continent that seemingly held such a prominent role in the African American past and potential for the black future was also the home of indigenous people who, in some cases, had not accepted the Christian message that had also become a part of the identity of many nineteenth-century African Americans. One way of reconciling these seemingly competing views was to hope for the imminent conversion of Africans, a hope that brought solace to Coker on his journey. As with other forms of writing, how one described the nature of settlement in Africa had far-reaching implications for the American public. The experiences of repatriates who failed to successfully "return" to Africa could be read as confirmation that blacks belonged in America, were incapable of self-sufficiency, and were inherently inferior to other races. For Coker, this meant only allowing the best and the brightest to come to Africa because the obstacles and stakes were so high. However, like other literature at the time, these pamphlets operated at a number of levels. On the one hand, they were seemingly straightforward advertisements calling for African Americans to leave the oppression of America for the greener pastures of Africa. On the other, the realistic challenges that one would face in such a relocation had to be honestly conveyed. Poverty, competing Muslim missionaries, and the potential impact on the perception of the entire black race were all real elements of migration and missionary work in Africa. Strategically Coker depicted these aspects while calling for the elite of the race to join him on the continent of their ancestors.[6]

African American Periodicals

Many of the writers and supporters of protest pamphlets also contributed to and edited denominational newspapers and periodicals to disseminate information, assert their civil rights, and engage in public debate about the best future course for the black community. The African Methodist Episcopal Church created the *African Methodist Episcopal Church Magazine* in 1841, and its official denominational newspaper, the *Christian Recorder*, in 1852. Other African American newspapers such as the *Freedom's Journal*, the *Colored American*, the *National Watchman*, the *Weekly Anglo-African*, the *Mirror of Liberty*, and Frederick Douglass's the *North Star* all began in the first half of the nineteenth century. The AME Church's *Repository of Religion and Literature and of Science and of Art* ran from 1858 to 1863. *The AME Church Review* was founded in 1884; the Protestant Episcopal Church began the *Afro-American Churchman* in 1886 and the *Church Advocate* in 1894. The *AME Zion Quarterly Review* was established in 1890, the *National Baptist Magazine* in 1894, and the *Colored Catholic* in 1909.

The post-Civil War period witnessed concerns that the work of important people during key moments in the denomination's past might be lost, so black churches recorded their histories to an

---

6. Daniel Coker, *Journal of Daniel Coker, a Descendant of Africa* (Baltimore: Edward J. Coale, 1820), 9–47.

unprecedented degree. The fifty-year anniversary of the founding of the AME Church was commemorated by Daniel Alexander Payne's *The Semi-Centenary and the Retrospection of the African Methodist Episcopal Church* (1866), and in 1867, Benjamin T. Tanner published his *Apology for African Methodism* (1867). One hundred years after leaving St. George's Methodist Episcopal Church, Payne published his *Recollections of Seventy Years*. In 1891, he too wrote a *History of the African Methodist Episcopal Church*. Alexander Wayman published *My Recollections of African M. E. Ministers or Forty Years Experience in the African Methodist Episcopal Church* in 1881 and the *Cyclopaedia of African Methodism* in 1882. Regional histories and theological works were also popular. In 1885, H. T. Kealing wrote the *History of African Methodism in Texas* and Henry McNeal Turner published *The Genius and Theory of Methodist Polity*, and in 1891, Wesley J. Gaines penned his *African Methodism in the South*. The AME Zion Church also produced a wide range of histories, such as John H. Acornley's *The Colored Lady Evangelist—Being the Life, Labors, and Experiences of Mrs. Harriet A. Baker* (1892), James Walker Hood's *One Hundred Years of the African Methodist Episcopal Zion Church* (1895), and *Sketch of the Early History of the African Methodist Episcopal Zion Church* (1914). In 1884, Bishop John Moore published the *History of the AME Zion Church in America* and even earlier Christopher Rush wrote *The Rise and the Progress of the African Methodist Episcopal Zion Church in America* (1843). The Baptist tradition also published its fair share of histories. In 1913, Samuel William Bacote published *Who's Who among the Colored Baptists of the United States*. In 1895, Charles Octavius Boothe published *The Cyclopedia of the Colored Baptists of Alabama*, and in 1888, E. R. Carter wrote *Biographical Sketches of Our Pulpit*. In 1887, Richard B. Cook's *The Story of the Baptists in All Ages and Countries* appeared, and in 1911 N. H. Pius published his

An Outline of Baptist History. While these histories may have looked similar to other white Protestant literature at the time, in the face of charges that African Americans had no history, these denominational narratives sought to demonstrate that the black past was just as rich and divinely guided as any other race or religious tradition.[7]

Racial and Religious Identity

Racial and religious identities were fluid in the nineteenth century, which was reflected in the varied terms applied to people of African descent. At different times, "African," "people of color," "colored people," "Colored American," and "Negro" were all options to signify African Americans in nineteenth-century America. In the early nineteenth century, "African" was prominently included in the titles of various organizations, from schools and benevolent societies to churches including the AME and AMEZ churches. As with most elements of nineteenth-century African American religious life, it is difficult to come to sweeping conclusions about this naming process. The prevalence of the term "African" could reflect a continued connection and identification with Africa. It could have just been the common nomenclature of the time. White Americans were also major contributors to many of these nascent black organizations and may have also had a say in what these institutions were ultimately named. The founding of the American Colonization Society in 1816 and their efforts to involuntarily repatriate blacks to Africa gave the term "African" parallel connotations of being non-American and outsiders to America. At other historical moments terms such as "Colored" were understood as conveying more respectability, and other terms such as "Negro" were seen as problematic in some moments and rehabilitated as positive in others.[8]

---

7. Penelope L. Bullock, *The Afro-American Periodical Press, 1838-1909* (Baton Rouge: Louisiana State University Press, 1981), 39–43.

Black religious congregations were often front and center in these debates over names since many had the word "African" featured prominently in their denominational titles. A seemingly straightforward solution would be to simply change the church's name. Yet, in many cases, racial and sacred histories of peoples became melded together in numerous African American Christian traditions. In many ways, Richard Allen, Absalom Jones, and Daniel Coker were not only important actors in the AME Church's history, but were key figures in a sacred drama that was being carried out according to God's will. When times in the present became difficult, congregations remembered the courage and strength displayed by their forefathers and mothers for models of how to overcome racism and discrimination and other potential roadblocks to success. If the "African" in the denominational title lent strength to those who came before, removing that term also risked losing yet another connection to that sacred past. Even the departures from white churches presented challenges since it seemed to undercut the idea of Christians living together in harmony. While independent black churches were a milestone, they also potentially represented the irreconcilability of race relations in the nineteenth century. These issues would become even more complicated with the rise of Social Darwinism as terms such as "survival of the fittest" and "natural selection" made their way into the common vernacular.

As Social Darwinism increasingly came to prominence and applied Darwin's scientific notions of evolution to peoples, institutions, and societies, African Americans had to sort through these suggestions that they had an "organic" connection to one another and their denominations. As ecumenical movements moved through white congregations, black Christian communities were also considering

8. Patrick Rael, *Black Identity and Black Protest in the Antebellum North* (Chapel Hill: University of North Carolina Press, 2002), 82–117.

uniting the varied black denominations. In the early 1880s, the AME Church and the black National Baptist Convention were both vying to become the largest black denomination in America. Plans for unifying black church traditions highlighted how distinctive black denominations had grown over time.

Social Darwinism

While Darwinism captured the scientific world in the late nineteenth century, Social Darwinism emerged as a persuasive framework for understanding a wide range of social behaviors from the rise and fall of civilizations, why some people groups seemed to succeed and others fail, as well as why some religions thrived and others disappeared over time. The rise of the ideology of manifest destiny made the case for the expansion of "civilization" through the colonization of the societies around the world. The "dark continent" of Africa exemplified the kinds of cultures that needed the civilizing white influence. If one's race determined their prospects in life, then those who excelled as well as those who did not were believed to be in their rightful social status. This perception also held true for entire countries and continents such as Africa.[9]

Responses to Darwinism

The harsh post-Reconstruction political climate in America made emigration to Africa by African Americans an increasingly viable option. Black nationalist leaders such as Martin Delany, Alexander Crummell, and Henry McNeal Turner eloquently made the case that the brightest possible future for African Americans lay in Africa, not in America. By "redeeming" Africa, they argued, all people of African

9. Tunde Adeleke, *UnAfrican Americans: Nineteenth-Century Black Nationalists and the Civilizing Mission* (Lexington: University of Kentucky Press, 1998), 13–19.

descent would likewise be elevated. The unrealized America dream in the United States could be manifested in Africa. This alignment of African American self-fullment with a self-sufficient Africa ran directly counter to many of the growing understandings of Social Darwinism.

African American church leaders discussed and analyzed the details of the leading works and theories of Social Darwinism. As Darwinism became one of the central scientific theoretical systems, African Americans became increasingly concerned about its implications for their Christian faith. Yet, unlike their white Protestant counterparts, African Americans were not seen as at the top of the racial Social Darwinian hierarchy. Instead, recognizing the growing influence of Darwin, African American leaders and laity sought to reconcile theories that seemed to disparage both their racial and religious identities.[10]

Science and the Bible

Many African Americans distinguished between scientific theory, which could be changed and updated over time, and what they believed to be the inerrant and unchanging word of God as divinely expressed in the Bible. For many it was an either/or proposition. Either evolution was true or the Bible was true. There was no middle position. Many questioned why evolution had been deemed the ultimate authority about the creation of the world. While the truth of the Bible could withstand any potential critique, some suggested that the veracity of Darwin's theories would be thrown into doubt over time. Like other theories that were widely embraced by scientists and were later disproved, so too would evolutionary theories run their

10. Ronald L. Numbers and John Stenhouse, eds., *Disseminating Darwinism: The Role of Place, Race, Religion, and Gender* (Cambridge: Cambridge University Press, 1999), 145-46.

course. Many African American Christians took issue with those who refused to take a stand in the evolution and biblical creation debate.

African American ministers questioned scientific methods that seemed to embrace the "facts" that supported their hypotheses and ignored those that challenged them. Some African American Christians challenged Thomas H. Huxley's arguments against creation as a gradual process, by questioning the credibility of the newly founded scientific field of geology, which they felt was inconclusive at best in its efforts to disprove the creation narrative. In his book *Genesis Re-Read*, Theophilus G. Steward exemplified the efforts of those trying to find some middle ground between the scientific method and notions of biblical inerrancy. Because no human had been present for the creation of the world, Steward argued that it was pointless to make the case for a literal twenty-fou-hour day in the creation story. By finding commonalities between the Genesis account and Darwin's theories, Steward sought to downplay the implications of Darwin on Christianity.

Other aspects of the science versus religion discussion were theories of racial origins and polygenesis. The theory of polygenesis suggested that the two accounts of the creation of humans in Genesis were not stories of the beginning of one human race, but in fact separate races. From this perspective, Gen. 1:26-27 describes the creation of the white race and Gen. 2:7, in which God creates man out of "dust from the ground," is understood to be the creation of the "mud people" or the "darker" races. These theories were particularly challenging since they wedded scientific theories with biblical scripture to argue for separate origins of the races. One of the common counterpoints to these theories was the understanding that almost every culture had some sort of flood narrative in their history. If that was the case, then all people groups emerged after a flood and not as the result of the creation of two different races as some interpreted the creation stories in Genesis. Herbert Spencer's theory suggested that different races passed on certain traits to their progeny. This notion posed challenges for African Americans, many of whom had an interracial ancestry. Because the racial and ethnic heritage of African Americans came from several different cultures and traditions, some argued that black organizations were destined for tension and disunity because of the warring factions in their bloodstream. It would be an ongoing challenge for many African American Christians to reconcile competing theories of race into a coherent understanding of the racialization process in the United States.[11]

The Word "African" and Denominational Titles

The priority placed on the redemption of Africa would continue to play a large role in discussions about the retention of the term "African" in the denominational titles of black churches. For his part, Martin Delany framed the question of denominational nomenclature as a moral problem, advocating strongly for the retention of the "African" in the AME tradition and encouraging every race to maintain their identity. Delany was surprised that the question was even an issue. From his perspective the term "African" had historically been used to differentiate the activities and institutions of people of African descent and those of white Americans. The tragedy and cruelty of a slave system put in place by Europeans, the beating and killing of slaves, questioning the religious sensibilities of blacks, and proclaiming them the inferior race all framed the choice of the word "African" by these early African American institutions as a means of activism against whites at the time, according to Delany. Delany

11. Albert G. Miller, *Elevating the Race: Theophilus G. Steward, Black Theology, and the Making of an African American Civil Society, 1865-1924* (Knoxville: University of Tennessee Press, 2003), 58-69.

had led the way on the creation of all-black military regiments and believed that retaining the word "African" in their denominational titles would similarly guide African American churches to a successful future.[12]

Continued discussions about merging denominations within Methodism and other Christian traditions kept the issue of the term "African" in the headlines of black newspapers. For his part, Henry McNeal Turner refused to make the question of denominational merger solely about African American Methodism, but rather saw the issue as impacting Methodism as a whole. Plans for merger between the AME and AME Zion churches met with little success. In 1864, one effort to unite fell apart over which governance structures and church disciplines would be embraced by the new denomination. Whose doctrine would prevail? How long did individuals serve in leadership positions? Which bishops from which denomination ordained the bishops of the other? If all of the bishops of the various denominations continued to be recognized, would that dilute the power of individual denominations? These were just a few of the many questions that held up the potential mergers. Perceptions of the Colored ME Church as a puppet for white southern politicians framed the denomination as an infiltrator for the other side. All of these factors made the prospects of one united black Methodist denomination pretty slim in the nineteenth century. Further movements for union between black denominations failed to gain traction in the final decades of the nineteenth century.

The "African" question in African American churches persisted throughout the nineteenth century. Some maintained that the term African emphasized racial distinction from other Christian churches. Others felt the term enhanced race pride. Still more made the case

12. Martin Delany, "An Indisputable Moral Problem," *Christian Recorder* 28 (April 1880).

that the term marked an ecclesiastical distinction rather than a racial one. Leaders and laity on both sides of the issue tried to interpret what the founders of the denominations meant when they put "African" in the denominational title in the first place. These were only a few of the many voices weighing in on the issue. Some black ministers argued that all black Methodist denominations should organize under the title the Second M. E. Church. Others sought to recover Richard Allen's original intent when naming the church. A sizable contingent remained firm in their call for the removal of "African" from the denominational title. Others made the case that simply because white Americans used the term in a derogatory way, that was no reason to change the name of the church. Many ME ministers wrote letters to black newspapers voicing support for maintaining the AME title. Still more appealed to practicality, citing that the church property had been deeded under the name AME Church. Others felt that a name change would undo all the hard work of Allen and his legacy. Even further, the term was interwoven in history and to remove it would create irrevocable harm.

While for some observers arguments over denominational titles seemed to involve mere semantics, the weight of the debates held important implications for understanding an American past and shaping the perceptions of the race into the future. For many, even a seemingly slight adjustment in the denominational title marked a sharp departure from a shared history and the legacy of revered founders. As much as African American ministers trumpeted their independence, the lack of Christian unity symbolized by the schisms within African American Protestantism remained troubling to some. Some African American leaders and laity embraced Social Darwinian notions of race, but challenged the theories on religious grounds.[13]

13. Rev. R. H. Cain, "The Bishop Question," *Christian Recorder*, 1 January 1880, 1; A. W. Wayman, "The Union of All the Colored Methodism," *Christian Recorder*, 1 January 1880, 1; Benjamin

African American Missionaries to Africa

The "Nadir" in black history led to an abundance of theological writing about the meaning of that suffering for African Americans. For some African Americans the spiritual revitalization of Africa was the silver lining that would emerge from the historical cloud of the oppression hanging over African Americans in the United States. However, Africa has maintained a complicated place and role in African American religious cosmology. At times, it has been understood as holding the racial and religious heritage of black people and representing a potential refuge from social and political persecution in the United States. In this way, it inspired various Back-to-Africa movements in the nineteenth century. At other moments, the continent and its culture has been something to be distanced from as western ways and viewpoints were preferred to an African past. Yet, whether one embraced one perspective over the other, Africa figured prominently in understanding the meaning of slavery in the black experience.

The story of black evangelical efforts in Africa stretch back to the early nineteenth century. The American Colonization Society funded a number of missionary efforts including Lott Carey from the Baptist tradition. Liberia in West Africa, founded in 1822 as a colony for emancipated American slaves, was a popular location for black missionaries. The American Colonization Society initially established the colony as a solution to the "Negro problem" in America with the hopes of spurring a large-scale exodus of African Americans. After the independence of Liberia in 1847, the need for black missionaries only increased. Independent African American churches were active

---

T. Tanner, "African Methodist Union," 5 August 1880, 2; Edward Wilmot Blyden, *Christianity, Islam, and the Negro Race* (Baltimore: Black Classic Press, 1994); Alexander Crummell, *Civilization: The Primal Need of the Race*, Occasional Papers, no. 3 (Washington, DC: American Negro Academy).

in missionary work in Africa, and many white denominations sent black Americans as their representatives on the continent.

One of the most influential of these missionaries to Liberia was Alexander Crummell. Born free in New York City in 1819, Crummell was ordained as a clergy in the Episcopal Church in 1844. After graduating from Queen's College of Cambridge University in 1853, he was sent on behalf of the missionary department of the British Anglican Church to Liberia. Shortly after his arrival, Crummell established himself as one of the central intellectuals in Liberia and his speeches and writings were widely disseminated around the globe. Crummell was a staunch believer that Africa needed both the gospel and "civilization" and that African Americans, given their compatibility with the climate and experiences in slavery, were divinely prepared to undertake this important work. In a speech titled "The Regeneration of Africa," delivered at the Pennsylvania Colonization Society in 1865, Crummell stated, "The black Christian emigrant, on the other hand, is indigenous, in blood, constitution, and adaptability. Two centuries absence from the continent of Africa, has not destroyed his physical adaptation to the land of his ancestors. There is a tropical fitness, which inheres in our constitution, whereby we are enabled, when we leave this country, to sit down under an African sun; and soon, and with comparative ease, feel ourselves at home, and move about in the land as though we had always lived there. Children, too, are born to us in our adopted country, who have as much strength and vitality as native children; and soon we find ourselves establishing families right beside those of our heathen kinfolk." Crummell's stature only increased after his return to America in 1873.

Another prominent missionary to Africa was Edward Wilmot Blyden. Blyden, Liberian educator and statesman, who many have deemed the father of West African Nationalism and Pan-Africanism, was a prolific writer who penned several volumes: *A Voice from Bleeding Africa* (1856), *Liberia's Offering* (1862), *The Negro in Ancient History* (1869), *The West African University* (1872), *From West Africa to Palestine* (1873), *Christianity, Islam and the Negro Race* (1887), and *The Jewish Question* (1898). While Blyden nuanced his arguments over time, in general, he advocated for the proper recognition of the history and culture of Africa, rejected notions of black inferiority, detailed the contributions of Africans and African Americans to humanity, and found Islam to be the most appropriate religion to uplift the black race. Born free in 1832 in the West Indies, Blyden grew up in the Presbyterian Church, which sent him to the United States to receive his theological training. After being denied admission to Rutgers University because of his race, the church sponsored his relocation to Liberia in 1851. After earning his degree, in 1861, Blyden accepted a position as professor of Greek and Latin at the newly established Liberia College. He soon became internationally known for his work in classical studies. Blyden grew increasingly frustrated by the seeming lack of interest in Africa expressed by most people of African descent. In his 1862 work, *Liberia's Offering*, Blyden wrote,

> All other people feel a pride in their ancestral land, and do everything in their power to create for it, if not already, an honorable name. But many of the descendants of Africa, on the contrary, speak disparagingly of their country; are ashamed to acknowledge any connection with the land, and would turn indignantly upon any who would bid them go up and take possession of the land of their fathers.[14]

As Blyden became more familiar with the teachings of Islam and

14. Howard Brotz, ed., *African-American Social and Political Thought, 1850-1920* (Transaction Publishers, 1991), 112. Edward Wilmot Blyden, *Christianity, Islam, and the Negro Race* (Baltimore: Black Classic Press, 1994); Alexander Crummell, *Civilization: The Primal Need of the Race*, Occasional Papers, no. 3 (Washington, DC: American Negro Academy).

had direct contact with members of the faith, he became increasingly empathetic in his writings about the tradition. Over time, this approach created tensions with his Presbyterian sponsors who felt he had strayed too far from his allegiance to Christianity. In the early 1860s, the Liberian government sent both Blyden and Crummell to America to recruit more black emigrants.

African Americans had a number of motivations to become missionaries in Africa. In addition to a concern for Africa's soul, black Americans hoped that their own denominations would experience growth on the continent. Becoming a missionary raised the social status of an individual within both white and black religious circles, clearly establishing their superior character to the rest of their race. Demonstrating their own attainment of "civilization" provided a stark contrast between themselves and the "heathens" they sought to convert. There was also a belief that the enlightenment of Africa would benefit African Americans as well by fulfilling their divine destiny to bring their lineage of sisters and brothers into the Christian fold. There was also an understanding that by elevating the glory of Africa, European Americans would come to truly appreciate the abilities of people of African descent, leading to newfound respect and social equity.

Like European American missionaries, many African American Christians sought to go abroad not only to spread the gospel, but to introduce western culture. While identifying with Africa, some African Americans also accepted white stereotypes of the "dark" continent and viewed Africans as "savages." Drawing on notions of "survival of the fittest" in social Darwinism, many observers presumed that Africa would either one day be civilized or fall into extinction like other inferior cultures of the past. Having embraced Victorian ideals, missionaries took issue with the lack of clothing in many

African communities, which they understood as a lack of modesty, a result of polygamy, or the influence of Islam.

White churches, like their black counterparts, hoped to spread the gospel to Africa and in the process increase the presence of their own denominations. The relatively lower costs necessary to support black missionaries and the power of the belief that blacks were "naturally suited" for the African climate also contributed to the growth of African missions. The sickness and disease that impeded the work of the earliest nineteenth-century white preachers on the continent, many speculated, would have little to no effect on black Americans because of their racial descent. A number of organizations, including the American Board of Commissioners for Foreign Missions, supported African missions. White denominations purchased space in black newspapers and ministers spoke at historically black colleges and white-sponsored schools such as Fisk University in Tennessee and the Freedmen's Aid School to urge African Americans to "redeem" Africa.

However, the majority of African Americans did not venture to Africa or feel called to do missionary work there. Some identified more strongly as Americans than with an African ancestry. Even further, some African American leaders asserted that identifying with Africa would weaken the cause for civil rights in America. Blyden and other black nationalists made the case that this reticence to identify with Africa was a byproduct of the negative literature and stereotypes that had been circulated in the American public discourse. Others, such as Daniel A. Payne of the AME Church, made the case that African American missionaries seeking to extinguish African culture in the name of the gospel were no better than whites who sought to do the very same thing. Some felt there were more fertile grounds for evangelization in locations other than Africa.

Pragmatically, few black denominations had the resources to fund large-scale overseas missionary work.

Emigration to Africa

Others returned to Africa not for missionary work but to reconnect with their previously lost heritage. Depending on how one frames the phenomenon, the first Back-to-Africa movements occurred with the various forms of resistance to avoid capture on the west coast of Africa and revolts aboard slave ships bound for the new world that were turned around and pointed eastward toward their homeland following African uprisings. However, the first official rumblings of a return to Africa by African Americans occurred shortly after the American Revolution. Prince Hall, a prominent free black in Boston, led a group who petitioned the support of the General Court of Massachusetts for a plan to resettle African Americans to Africa because of the "disagreeable and disadvantageous circumstances" facing blacks in the United States.

One of the organizations at the forefront of the African emigration movements was the American Society for Colonizing the Free People of Color of the United States, established on December 28, 1816. As its title indicated, the central concern of the organization was the relocation of free blacks to Africa. In 1817, at the inaugural meeting, Henry Clay, the Speaker of the House, suggested that this mass emigration would be a key element in solving the "Negro problem." "Can there be a nobler cause than that which, whilst it proposes to rid our country of a useless and pernicious, if not dangerous portion of its population, contemplates the spreading of the arts of civilized life, and the possible redemption from ignorance and barbarism of a benighted quarter of the globe?"[15] While there had

---

15. Henry Clay, *The Papers of Henry Clay: The Rising Statesman, 1815-1820*, Volume II, (Lexington: University Press of Kentucky, 2014), 264.

been some support for emigration to Africa in the black community, these statements marked a sharp reversal in course. Led by Richard Allen, James Forten, and Absalom Jones, a large group of African Americans met at Bethel Church in Philadelphia to discuss Clay's remarks and the goals of the ACS. Forten later wrote, "Three thousand at least attended, and there was not one sole [sic] that was in favor of going to Africa. They think that the slaveholders want to get rid of them so as to make their property more secure."[16] Yet, others would later accept the support of the ACS, such as John Russwurm, founder of the black newspaper *Freedom's Journal*, who immigrated to Africa in 1829. Despite the controversy the society engendered, the ACS resettled 4,000 blacks to West Africa between 1820 and 1843.

A number of African Americans opposed African immigration. In 1830, the American Society of Free Persons of Color was against African immigration but supported relocation to Canada. David Walker's *Appeal to the Coloured Citizens* contained a section entitled "Our Wretchedness in Consequence of the Colonization Plan." Some African Americans were skeptical about the long-term economic and social viability of Liberia. The 1848 Colored National Convention issued an official resolution condemning the ACS and criticizing its tactics as "deceptive and hypocritical."

For some African Americans, missionary work and emigration to Africa went hand in hand. In 1815, Paul Cuffe, a sea captain by trade, financed and transported thirty-eight African Americans, some of whom were missionaries, to Sierra Leone as one of the earliest efforts to support the evangelization of Africa and the relocation of blacks. In 1891, Bishop Henry McNeal Turner of the AME Church established AME churches in Sierra Leone and later in Liberia and South Africa. In 1862, as an elder in the AME Church, Turner took

---

16. Patrick Rael et al., *Eighty-Eight Years: The Long Death of Slavery in the United States, 1777-1865* (Athens: University of Georgia Press, 2015), 140.

the lead in the church's missionary efforts to the South. Turner was adamant that the education and uplift of southern African Americans should not be done by whites. He proclaimed, "Every man of us now, who has a speck of grace or bit of sympathy for the race that we are inseparably identified with, is called upon by force of surrounding circumstances, to extend a hand of mercy to bone of our bone and flesh of our flesh."[17] Disillusioned by the mistreatment of African Americans and his own expulsion from the legislature by the white majority in 1870, Turner became one of the strongest advocates for African American emigration to Africa. The dire situation of post-Reconstruction sparked a similar renewed interest in Africa among many black Americans. By establishing communities in Africa that fully lived up to the American ideals of democracy and Christian values, many Back-to-Africa proponents argued, African Americans could finally realize self-governance, which would serve as a shining example of their progress, abilities, and self-sufficiency. For others, the "promised land" lay not across the Atlantic, but the northern and western United States.

In the late nineteenth century, black churches formed a number of denominational committees to investigate the issue of African emigration, presumably to put the question to rest once and for all. From their position the high poverty rate, the black "inexperience" with citizenship and leadership, the lack of a military, the previous colonization of the continent, and the greater opportunities in America all argued against emigration. Others maintained that African Americans were just as American as any in society, having fought in wars and built the country with their slave labor.

Perhaps more so than any contemporary issue, the African emigration movement revealed how varied black experiences were

---

17. William E. Montgomery, *Under Their Own Vine and Fig Tree: The African American Church in the South, 1865-1900* (Baton Rouge: Louisiana State University Press, 1994), 60.

in the post-bellum era, particularly around socioeconomic standing. In the 1870s, grassroots emigrationist movements utilized communication networks that connected plantations and farms spread across the countryside to voice ideas and spread their message to poorer laborers. Emigrationist sentiment increasingly resonated with rural blacks as the possibility of a unified African American community outside of the United States started to be seen as a real possibility. Print culture played a large role in disseminating emigrationist thought through such mediums as handbills and pamphlets, particularly the *African Repository*, the journal of the ACS. The growing literacy rates and interest of rural blacks can be seen in the hundreds of correspondences to the American Colonization Society inquiring about their programs.

Facing the potential disintegration of their own churches if congregants left for Africa in large numbers, many African American church leaders again turned to print culture to make their case to stem this groundswell of emigrationist sentiment. In the late nineteenth century, the press had become firmly established as the medium through which national debates could be discussed and presumably settled through public discourse. Yet, even the pages of black newspapers were not level ground. Editors, ministers, and the educated elite disproportionately contributed to almost every conversation in black religious newspapers.

Advocates and Opponents of Emigration

Those against emigration to Africa employed a number of strategies to sway public opinion, one of which was to paint Back-to-Africa movements as the pawns of whites seeking to rid the country of the black race. African Americans expressed concerns about the organization of certain companies and saved its most strongly worded rebukes for white-run groups looking to deport black Americans. Opponents noted the failure of past efforts of mass relocation to the West Indies, Central and South America, and Canada and framed the formation of Liberia as an effort of whites to relieve themselves of guilt over slavery. Others viewed white colonization societies as seeking to rid America of people of African descent. The committee made an exception regarding the *Azor* project, which will be expanded upon later in this chapter.

Black churches across the country met regularly to discuss the emigration question. Some, such as the AME's Committee on African Emigration of the Philadelphia Annual Conference, passed sweeping legislation against emigration and prohibited leaders and laity from encouraging African Americans to leave the country. Ministers expressed concerns over the viability of the climate of Africa for African Americans to live in. Emigration movements, some argued, discouraged African Americans from putting their talents and energy toward being socially and economically successful in America. Opponents of emigration suggested that while the leaders of the movement spoke loudly in favor of relocation to Africa, very few actually took those steps themselves. Those against a return to Africa questioned the viability of particular sites to hold the future of the race. They placed the mortality rate of those who went to Liberia at more than 70 percent due primarily to the climate, limited availability of clean water, food, and proper housing as well as the illnesses present in Africa.

Rather than arising naturally from within African American communities, some made the case that it was "outsiders" who were constantly stirring up the question and taking advantage of the gullible. They took issue with the recently formed Liberian Exodus Association or a Liberian Joint Stock Steamship Company in South Carolina for proposing to transport African Americans to Liberia.

They suggested that field agents were marketing the movement to African Americans and compelling people to sell their possessions at below market value for the pipedream of investing in the company, which claimed to issue 30,000 shares of stock at ten dollars per share. Those who invested in shares received transportation to Africa provided that they were able to support themselves in Liberia for six months without assistance. These types of schemes, the conference lamented, did irreparable harm to black communities. Rather than cultivating farms and making a life for themselves in America, the poorest, most uneducated, and least ready to make a move to Africa were being preyed upon by leaders who should have had their best interests at heart.

Given their progress in America, some African Americans saw no need for blacks to emigrate. To emigrate was to lose the fruits of past hardships and struggles and allow other immigrant groups to reap the benefits fought for by African Americans. Most conferences had no problem with the leaders of the Liberian Exodus Association emigrating if that was their choice, since they were mostly educated and professional men who could make an informed decision about the emigration question and could contribute to the prosperity of Africa. They felt the tropical climate, sickness, lack of food, proper schools, and military protection were all deterrents. In addition, the leadership felt that African Americans would come up short in the competition with the indigenous Africans, who were stronger and more familiar with the climate and therefore would secure most of the manual-labor jobs.

While many African American ministers denounced African emigration, for many "ordinary" black Americans the American dream had not been realized and starting a new life abroad was appealing. Prominent white and African Americans heralded black progress in America, particularly in the realm of education. However, improving conditions in America were a matter of perspective. Many African Americans in the nineteenth century had yet to realize the promised American dream and even the uncertainty of Africa outweighed the racial discrimination and prejudice that limited the opportunities for African Americans in America. This disconnect between the viewpoint of the elite based in hypotheticals and abstract moral stands continued, in stark contrast with the survival-driven practicality of many working-class African Americans. By the end of the nineteenth century, the "masses" were still pressing the issue of African emigration, particularly in the South.

The varied understandings of emigration to Africa can been seen in the coverage of ship launchings in black newspapers. In the spring of 1878, 206 emigrants left from Charleston, South Carolina on board the *Azor*, which would carry them across the Atlantic to Liberia. Ultimately, twenty-three died on the voyage to Liberia, several more died after arrival, but of those who remained some went on to become successful in business and farming, and a small group established a mission church. On the one hand, the journey of two hundred emigrants to Liberia in 1878 barely registers on the larger African American historical record in the second half of the nineteenth century. Yet, the coverage of the event in the black press linked the fate of the African emigration movement to that of those passengers who boarded the *Azor* venturing to the shores of Africa. So too did opponents and advocates of the Back-to-Africa efforts. Other newspaper accounts emphasized the dangers of the voyage to Africa, focusing on the mortality rate of those aboard the *Azor* and accounts of disease and sickness as well as the profound disappointment experienced by those who resettled in Liberia. The not-so-subtle moral was that African emigration was foolhardy, doomed to failure, and would only be entertained by the simpleminded and the easily manipulated. For others, the growth of industry and the spiritual progress made in Liberia were harbingers of a brighter future for blacks in Africa. Their example, then, could be held up to inspire the mass migration that Martin Delany and others hoped to catalyze.

African American churches played a major role in the *Azor* endeavor from its inception. The Liberian Exodus Joint Stock Steamship Company which sponsored the voyage was the initial vision of B. F. Porter, a local AME pastor who became the company's first president. R. H. Cain, a future bishop in the AME Church, was the strongest political ally for the movement, having served in both the U.S. Senate and the House of Representatives. At least thirty of the first 206 emigrants who embarked on the initial voyage were African Methodists. The *Christian Recorder* was instrumental in gathering funds for the *Azor*. Martin Delany, another officer in the steamship company, purchased advertising space and wrote letters encouraging African Americans to purchase stock at ten dollars per share to buy a steamship, a price that included transport to Africa. Through these individual investors, Delany and others were able to cobble together enough funds to build the *Azor* and charter the Liberian Exodus Joint Stock Steamship Company. However, overwhelmed with debt, the *Azor* was auctioned off after this one inaugural trip to Africa.

Reconstruction

During Reconstruction, African American literature was, for the most part, sharply against emigration to Africa. Letters forecast a brighter future for the race in America with the end of slavery and with prejudice and discrimination seeming to lessen and African Americans empowered to take hold of their own destiny. While emigrationists held out Africa as the site of true freedom, others held on to an optimistic attitude about the political climate in America. Just as immigrants had worked to overcome the Know-Nothing Party, so too could blacks live up to their potential once they gave up the notion of running away to Africa. Any effort that would be expended to adapt to African culture would be better spent assimilating to America. Many lay the success or failure of the race squarely at the feet of African Americans. They suggested that members of the race derailed their own progress. Others were against the best and the brightest African Americans leaving America to go across the Atlantic. Some urged blacks to use their political and voting power to influence the U.S. government's relationship with Africa. Others rejected romantic notions of a nostalgic connection between African Americans and Africa. Rather than a land of their ancestry, some African American Christians viewed Africa as another land that needed the Christian gospel, nothing more, nothing less. Many made the case that blacks were first and foremost Americans. The first step would be to seek to overcome the tensions that had historically divided segments of the black community, particularly in the South, and to band together to advance the race through education and economic advancement. Some argued that African Americans needed to realize that they have a strong and continuing interest in America and its government, which was built on the backs of slave labor. Others made the case that given the state of European colonization in Africa, the continent could hardly be considered a refuge from white oppression or white influence. Some made the case that the time would likely come but did not lie in the immediate future. Many African American churches at the time did not have the resources for widespread missionary work abroad. Some cast emigration as an attempt for a few elite black leaders to regain the power and influence they had lost after Reconstruction.

The general optimism of Reconstruction was followed by the

Compromise of 1876 and President Hayes's removal of federal troops from the South, which once again restricted the rights of African Americans and left them vulnerable to the southern "redeemers" who terrorized and killed black southerners at will. The lines of racial and social separation between African Americans and whites stiffened. Rather than seeking support from white America, many called for African Americans to rely on their own organizations for self-improvement and the elevation of the race. By improving their condition, African Americans could take their place among the other great races of the world and contribute to the progress of American society. This turning inward to racial self-reliance catalyzed the fledgling Back-to-Africa movements. The political climate of post-Reconstruction America signaled to some that the time to return to Africa was at hand.

This stark change in political climate reverberated through discussions of African emigration. Some felt that the experiences of a few disgruntled and unprepared emigrants were being projected upon the entire emigrationist enterprise. Rather than an uncivilized and barren wasteland, emigrationists portrayed western Africa as a metropolitan place with permanent settlements, commercial relations, stable government, several thousand English speakers, and ever-increasing numbers of churches, schools, and farms. Pro-emigrationists portrayed Africa as an inviting place in which all who came would receive a free home, land, and full citizenship upon declaring loyalty to Liberia. Africa was depicted as a utopia free from prejudice and discrimination where enterprising people faced no limits to the prosperity they could achieve. It was not the conditions in Africa that limited emigrants but their own lack of ambition that would lead to failure. If Europeans could consistently make money on the continent, so too could African Americans, unless, as some white observers asserted, slavery had destroyed the morality, intellect, and potential for greatness in African Americans. While the first generation of emigrants might not prosper, their legacy, some argued, would pave the way for increasingly prosperous subsequent generations in Africa. Observers marveled at Africa's mineral resources and agricultural potential. Those who wrote negatively about Liberia and Africa generally had no knowledge of the continent, emigrationists asserted. Global trade with Africa would open up unprecedented opportunities for those bold enough to relocate to the continent of their ancestors.

Some black intellectuals framed African emigration as running away from a problem rather than overcoming it, as had been true for many obstacles facing the race over its history. The passage of legislation such as the Louisiana Separate Car Act of 1890, the precursor to *Plessy v. Ferguson* (1896), codifying the notion of "equal but separate" accommodations, sparked outrage in the pages of the black press. Readers parsed the wording of the law which stated, "We consider the underlying fallacy of the plaintiff's argument to consist in the assumption that the enforced separation of the two races stamps the colored race with a badge of inferiority. If this be so, it is not by reason of anything found in the act, but solely because the colored race chooses to put that construction upon it." As the efforts of the American Colonization Society gained increased renown, many prominent blacks framed the emigration less in terms of "pull" factors that drew them to Africa and more toward the ramifications of allowing themselves to be pushed out of the country. If African Americans were perceived to be an inferior race that could not survive in America, the last thing that should be done, some asserted, would be to leave the country, confirming their lack of self-sufficiency and exhibiting cowardice in the face of adversity.[18]

18. Eric Foner, *Reconstruction: America's Unfinished Revolution, 1863-1877* (New York: Harper &

"Back to Africa" Movements

The final decade of the nineteenth century saw an increasing downturn in the prospects for a return to Africa. African Americans took issue with the idea that they were being forcibly removed to Africa. If African Americans could not be successful in America, they likely could not do so in Africa. Some politicians suggested that there existed a natural animosity between whites and blacks and therefore a return of blacks to Africa was the only solution to the American race problem. This sentiment was regularly responded to fervently by African Americans. It was one thing for African Americans to plan a return to Africa, but it was quite another to have whites try to rid the country of blacks. Others felt more planning and preparation were needed before further emigration took place. Some maintained that not enough information had been provided about the conditions in Africa to allow African Americans to make an informed decision about whether to venture to Africa or not. Demographic data on African countries including facts on soil, climate, industry, and agriculture were not widely accessible, some argued. For others, the solution to the "Negro Problem" rested with an eventual realization among whites that the participation of all races in all aspects of society would uplift the nation as a whole. Still others maintained that blacks were the quintessential Americans, drawing comparisons between the current African American experience with the travails of the early founders of the country.

Folklore about naïve victims who had fallen into the hands of preying charlatans also served to deter African emigration. Stories abounded of midwesterners and southerners selling their land and all of their possessions to secure passage to Africa from New York

Row, 1988); Frederick Douglass, *Narrative of the Life of Frederick Douglass, An American Slave* (Boston: Anti-Slavery Office, 1845).

only to arrive on the East Coast to find that the ship had already left or had never existed. African Americans criticized groups such as the International Migration Society, which seemed to only have the goal of separating southern black people who were often illiterate from their life savings. Ministers called upon each other to warn their congregants about the dangers of the practice.

Whether the stories were primarily real or imagined, African American churches took steps to try to prevent their congregants from losing their money. Black church conferences encouraged ministers in the church to visit congregations across the country and inform them about potential fraud involving emigration schemes. They encouraged those who were able to purchase land and could employ African Americans to farm it, to do so and create a mutually beneficial business arrangement. Editorials in black newspapers warned that those advocating for emigration should be considered with suspicion since they often sought out the less educated. Schemes in Arkansas, Georgia, and Mississippi charged between one and three dollars for passage to Africa and provided a certificate granting membership into "transportation organizations." In some cases, emigration companies placed the names of politicians and prominent African Americans on their literature to give the appearance of legitimacy. The key to these schemes was to get the potential emigrants so excited about Africa that they would sell their possessions for a fraction of what they were worth. These cautions were expressed not only toward white-run emigration societies, but also for black-based organizations that purportedly did the bidding of scurrilous white men. While the warnings seem to be delivered from a sincere concern for the race, the cautions also revealed strong northern stereotypes and biases toward southerners that portrayed them as uneducated country bumpkins who were easily manipulated and could not think for themselves.

During Reconstruction, when the future for African Americans in America seemed brightest, emigration to Africa appeared to be an unnecessary risk, and a strong contingent countered even the hint that Africa held the future for blacks. However, in the aftermath of the end of Reconstruction, calls for emigration to Africa grew louder, hailing a bright future in the land of their ancestors, predicting the imminent civilization and evangelization of the continent, and framing those who chose to remain in America as the ones disloyal to the race. While advocates and opponents alike framed the debates along a series of binaries, positing that one was either African or American, loyal to ancestry or nationality, and for or against emigration, the relationship of African Americans to Africa was never as dichotomous as either side sought to make it.[19]

19. Stephen Ward Angell, *Bishop Henry McNeal Turner and African-American Religion in the South* (Nashville: University of Tennessee Press, 1992); William E. Montgomery, *Under Their Own Vine and Fig Tree: The African American Church in the South, 1865-1900* (Baton Rouge: Louisiana State University Press, 1994); Eric Foner, *Reconstruction: America's Unfinished Revolution, 1863-1877* (New York: Harper & Row, 1988); James T. Campbell, *Songs of Zion: The African Methodist Episcopal Church in the United States and South Africa* (New York: Oxford University Press, 1995).

5

African American New Religious Movements

In his autobiography, Malcolm X poignantly describes why he chose the symbol "X" to replace his birth name of Little. Because he did not know the precise region and tribe in Africa from whence he was descended, Malcolm chose the "X" to represent his lost heritage and unknown personal history. Malcolm X was one of many African Americans who have sought to recover their personal African heritage. Indeed, the Atlantic slave trade has left a lasting void for many African Americans. Today, DNA tests seek to trace African American ancestry to particular areas and people groups in Africa. While the relationship between immigrant groups and their homelands may vary by generation—embracing or distancing themselves, at times, from their cultural past during the process of acculturation—the attempts to strip away all remnants of African culture from colonial slaves have made the African American search for identity distinctive in America. As the United States entered World War I, African Americans faced a choice that they seemingly have had to make in every military effort in American history: whether or not to fight for a freedom for their country that they themselves continued to be denied. As in the other armed conflicts, African Americans answered in the affirmative. In the wake of their service, the "New Negro" of the Harlem Renaissance emerged. The racial and ethnic pride demonstrated in the literature and arts of the period would be matched by the proliferation of creative expressions within black new religious movements (NRMs).

As the hostile racial and political climate of post-Reconstruction America questioned the ability of the race to survive outside the bonds of slavery, African Americans countered this dominant ideology by embracing identities that they found empowering and instilled hope. For some, this inspiration came from within "mainstream" religions such as Christianity or Islam. For others, new religious movements spoke most clearly to their present situation. The Great Migration of the late nineteenth and early twentieth centuries witnessed a rise of contemporary black religious communities that offered at once new and ancient answers for the question of African American identity.

The Great Migration

Before the Great Migration, 90 percent of African Americans lived in the South, with 80 percent of those residing in rural areas. In the 1910s, lower cotton prices, a bollweevil epidemic that inflicted widespread damage on crops, and severe floods all contributed to an economic depression and trying social conditions in the South. The few blacks who owned land were reduced to sharecropping. The rampant violence perpetrated by white "redeemers" (operating unchecked by federal authorities in the post-Reconstruction South) led to the lynching of blacks in unprecedented numbers. This hostile climate also contributed to the massive migration northward as African Americans fled the onslaught. From 1915 to 1920, between five hundred thousand to a million African Americans left the rural

South for the urban North and West. In the 1920s, those numbers doubled. There was also a simultaneous smaller-scale migration from rural towns to larger southern cities. The black population of Detroit was estimated at 6,000 in 1917 and was over 120,000 by the late 1920s. In 1910, Chicago had 40,000 African American residents, but over 240,000 by the 1930s. New York City's black population rose from 100,000 to 330,000 during the same time period. By any standards, this was an unprecedented shift in the African American population and demographics.

Challenging conditions in the South were coupled with a number of "pull" factors that drew African Americans northward. Prominent black newspapers such as the *Chicago Defender* described the North as the "Promised Land" that beckoned to southern African Americans. Through the encouragement of letters from friends and family touting the lands of "milk and honey" awaiting them in urban centers such as New York, Detroit, and Chicago in the early 1900s, an unprecedented number of African Americans responded to the call. However, the jobs, freedoms, and racially harmonious environment that the migrants were promised in the North did not come to fruition. In most cases, blacks exchanged a rural poverty and overtly racist society for an urban, de facto segregation that left many feeling disillusioned and disenfranchised.

Those migrants looking to find a home within the established northern African American religious traditions also faced obstacles. For the most part, the exuberant and emotional worship services of the South were a rarity in the north. Most middle-class black churches were larger and more formal in their Sunday services than those found in the South. Some recently relocated African Americans found these religious sites colder and less familiar than the traditions they had left behind. These dynamics created an atmosphere in which a large, denominationally uncommitted black population was struggling to locate a spiritual "home" and becoming increasingly open to religious alternatives. Black new religious movements thrived partly because of this transplanted population as the twentieth century witnessed an unprecedented creativity and variety in African American religious expressions, institutions, experiences, beliefs, and practices.[1]

The Moorish Science Temple

One of the first black new religious movements to come to prominence during this period was the Moorish Science Temple. In 1913, the Noble Drew Ali founded the new community in Newark, New Jersey. From his reading of history, African Americans were descended from the Moorish empires and glorious, advanced civilizations that had conquered Europe. Ali articulated clearly what many inherently felt, that the referents employed to identify a racial or ethnic group mattered and had a direct impact on how individuals felt about themselves, how they were understood by the broader society, and ultimately how they were treated. Ali asserted that by identifying as "Negroes," African Americans were undermining their true Moorish heritage. For him, this meant renouncing his Christian name, Timothy, and taking the name, the Noble Drew Ali, which he felt was more consistent with his Islamic heritage.

As slaves did in the close confines of their cabins and in brush harbors throughout the South, many African Americans in the twentieth century questioned why a just God would have allowed the institution of slavery and all of the cruelty and devastation that accompanied it. The Noble Drew Ali attributed the current plight of the African American race to their denial of Allah. This shunning of the one true God led to the Atlantic slave trade, being torn from their

1. Eric Arnesen, *Black Protest and the Great Migration* (Boston: Bedford Press, 2002).

homeland, and their misplaced glorification of European American culture and the religion of their masters, Christianity. Having lost touch with their real identity, African Americans needed to regain a deep understanding of their true self. Proslavery advocates advanced biblical justifications to substantiate their belief in black inferiority and the enslavement of Africans. However, Ali laid the impetus for the negative connotations surrounding people of African descent squarely at the feet of Caucasians and not to any divine directive. The moment of spiritual renewal could only occur, Ali preached, when blacks made stark improvements in their health and social and economic status. Only when black self-identity matched their material condition could the final Armageddon commence. This process would happen most expediently if African Americans removed themselves from the cultural context that reinforced their negative self-esteem, namely living among Caucasians. Ali saw himself as fulfilling the role of prophet who would inaugurate this period of enlightenment for blacks. Like other millennial groups in American religious history, the Moorish Science Temple did not put forth specific dates of the Messiah's return, but rather pointed toward an imminent final judgment.

Ali's teachings were a combination of eastern philosophy and Islam. His *Holy Koran*, the sacred scripture of the community, was published in 1927. Written for the Moorish community in America, sixty-four pages long, the introduction advises readers to "know yourself and Your Father God-Allah that you may learn to love instead of hate." The *Holy Koran* states that Allah has been known by many names. "You Brahmans call Him Parabrahm, in Egypt He is Thoth, and Zeus is His name in Greece, Jehovah is His Hebrew name, but everywhere His is the causeless cause, the rootless root from which all things have grown." Although the community was open to all who self-identify as Asiatics, almost all of the members were African Americans. Once a member, Moorish Americans added either "El" or "Bey" after their names to signify their true heritage as Asiatics. Traditionally men wear fezzes and turbans and women wear head coverings and long dresses, especially in the temple. Members were prohibited from using alcohol or drugs. Some chose not to drink anything with caffeine and abstained from eating meat and eggs. The physical and spiritual well-being of individuals was believed to be closely related.[2]

Marcus Garvey and the UNIA

Only a few miles away, in New York City, Marcus Garvey was harnessing the momentum of his Universal Negro Improvement Association that was becoming a global movement in 1917. Garvey sought to unite all people of African descent in an African republic. Through his weekly newspaper, the *Negro World*, and devoted members, Garvey's philosophy spread and was embraced by countless black Americans and people around the world. Although officially a secular organization, part of the power of the movement was its use of religious symbols and rituals during meetings, including singing hymns, performing the UNIA creed and catechism, as well as baptismal ceremonies to initiate new members.

Born in St. Ann's Bay, Jamaica, in 1887, Garvey had a profound recognition about race in his childhood. Garvey recalled:

At fourteen my little white play mate and I parted. Her parents thought the time had come to separate us and draw the color line. They sent her and another sister to Edinburgh, Scotland, and told her that she was never to write or try to get in touch with me, for I was a "nigger." It was then that I found for the first time that there was some difference in humanity, and that there were different races, each having its own

2. Arthur Huff Fauset, *Black Gods of the Metropolis: Negro Religious Cults of the Urban North* (Philadelphia: University of Pennsylvania Press, 2014).

separate and distinct social life. I did not care about the separation after I was told about it, because I never thought all during our childhood association that the girl and the rest of the children of her race were better than I was; in fact, they used to look up to me. So I simply had no regrets. After my first lesson in race distinction, I never thought of playing with white girls any more, even if they might be next-door neighbors.[3]

Garvey apprenticed as a printer before moving to Kingston in 1904. As a young man, Garvey traveled throughout the Caribbean and Central America in search of work and regularly encountered the economic oppression of people of color. In 1912, Garvey relocated to London where his pan-African ideology that encouraged the creation of schools, businesses, newspapers, and nations governed, owned, and operated by people of African descent began to take shape. Garvey founded the UNIA upon his return to Jamaica in 1914 and relocated the organization's headquarters to New York three years later. Beginning by addressing small church groups and street gatherings, Garvey's message of racial pride resonated with many African Americans in New York. He soon gained an enormous following that has been estimated at its height at around two million. His survival of an assassination attempt on October 14, 1919, elevated his status even further.

Garvey was convinced that every great nation possessed power through shipping lines and engaging in trade. In May 1919, Garvey announced plans to create a Black Star Line shipping company to rival the White Star Line that had produced massive ships including the *Titanic*. Unable to completely finance the venture through the UNIA, he turned to public funding, selling five-dollar shares to African Americans across the country. In October 1919, Garvey

3. Milton C. Sernett, ed., *African American Religious History: A Documentary Witness* (Durham, NC: Duke University Press, 1999), 454–55; Amy Jacques-Garvey, ed., *Philosophy and Opinions of Marcus Garvey*, vol. 2 (New York: Atheneum, 1925), 124–34.

purchased his first ship, and by August 1920 had three in his fleet. In 1920, he organized and led the First Annual Convention of Negro Peoples of the World in New York City. In 1921, he sent an UNIA delegation to Liberia to establish a branch there. Only a few years into the venture, the Black Star Line was in severe financial straits. In 1922, Garvey began his controversial speaking tour to known white racist organizations, asserting that such groups were the most open and honest about the true American sentiment toward blacks. In one such meeting with Edward Clarke, head of the Ku Klux Klan, Garvey discussed their shared support of Jim Crow segregation in the South and suggested that his organization and theirs had common goals. His criticism of the federal government's treatment of black Americans made him a popular culture hero in the African American community, but also, some have asserted, a large target for the IRS, which indicted him on mail fraud charges in 1922. The central evidence was a Black Star Line flyer that the FBI argued made a deceptive claim that the company owned and operated a ship that could travel to Africa when in fact the organization was only attempting to purchase one. Garvey was found guilty in 1923 and sentenced to five years in prison. After an unsuccessful appeal, Garvey was deported to Jamaica in 1927. Acting as his own lawyer after the conviction raised awareness about the UNIA, but the decision did not necessarily help his legal defense. Despite efforts to revive the organization outside of the United States, Garvey was unable to recapture the glory of the 1920s. Without his presence the movement lost momentum and membership, but his ideas can be seen in later movements such as the Nation of Islam and among pan-Africanists around the world.[4]

---

4. Colin Grant, *Negro with a Hat: The Rise and Fall of Marcus Garvey* (New York: Oxford University Press, 2010).

The Rastafarian Movement

Garveyism had a strong influence upon the Rastafarian movement, which emerged in the late 1920s in the midst of the Great Depression. Garvey, who titled the anthem of his UNIA "Ethiopia, Thou Land of Our Fathers," sought to correct the broad misconceptions about Africa that had been circulated so widely throughout history. Garvey informed the world about the great civilizations of Africa and the restoration of the glory of the continent that had been ravished by slavery and colonialism. Early Rastafarians embraced this ideology, understanding themselves as one of the twelve tribes of Israel. The burgeoning group turned into a movement following the accession of Ras ("prince") Tafari ("creator") Makonnen to the throne of Ethiopia in the 1930s upon which he took the name Haile Selassie. Selassie, represented by the symbol of the lion, became viewed within the African diaspora as the literal fulfillment of Ps. 68:31, "Princes shall come out of Egypt; Ethiopia shall soon stretch out her hands to God." This renewal, many followers believed, had been prophesied in the Hebrew Bible. Within this cosmology, Selassie served as the Messiah who would deliver all peoples of African descent from white oppression ("Babylon") and return them to their African homeland. Over time, this return transformed from a literal emigration to a mental enlightenment about the true meaning of being African, having a relationship with the homeland, and living an African lifestyle.

The beliefs, rituals, and practices of Rastafarianism center on the discovery of the divine within each individual. Rastafarians believe that Jah ("God") had a special purpose and destiny in mind for the African race. "I and I" is a central expression that recognizes the divine in all people and the unity of all humanity. Ethiopia and Africa are seen as heaven on earth. The colors of the religion are red, symbolizing the blood of martyrs; yellow, the wealth of the homeland; green, the beauty and vegetation of Ethiopia; and black for their African heritage. One of the more controversial practices is taking the chalice or the smoking of ganja (marijuana) for religious and medicinal purposes and meditation. Orthodox Rastas only eat "I-tal" food that contains no chemicals and is completely natural. Rastas often wear their hair in "dreads," representing the power that lies within every person and the hair of the Lion of Judah. This practice later became a rebellion against societal norms about the appropriate length of one's hair. All of these practices are designed to rid the psyche of the inferiority and self-doubt left by slavery and colonialism.

Rastafarianism has undergone a number of transformations over the years. One pivotal moment was the overwhelming popularity of the music of Bob Marley in the 1970s, which brought the movement squarely into the public consciousness. Rasta traditions emerged in Brazil, Latin America, Australia, New Zealand, North America, and eventually around the globe. This growth attracted members of non-African descent around the world, which transformed the movement. Some navigated around the origins of the tradition by asserting an African ancestry from a previous life. This race-based requirement eventually gave way to having the appropriate African spirit. A movement that emerged from racial and socioeconomic oppression now has members of all races, economic status, and walks of life. Feminist theorists have questioned whether women in the movement have truly been embraced in the same way and received the same support and empowerment as men. Leonard Howell, one of the first Jamaicans to deify Haile Selassie, espoused principles for Rastafarianism that included anger toward whites, black racial superiority, and retribution for historic white mistreatment of the black race.

These racialized positions are still a part of the movement, yet, unlike other black religious communities such as the Nation of Islam, there is little public outcry about the ideology. Instead, Rastafarianism has been successfully positioned as a nonthreatening "lifestyle" rather than a dangerous "hate group."

The Nation of Islam

In the summer of 1930, a mysterious peddler appeared in an impoverished area of Detroit called "Paradise Valley." While he sold clothing, silks, and other products, he also dispensed advice about physical and spiritual health. He described the "true religion of Black Men" and their real heritage dating back to Asia and Africa. Employing both the Quran and the Bible, he taught first in the homes of followers and later rented a building which he named the Temple of Islam. He called himself alternately, Wali Farrad, Farrad Mohammed, and W. D. Fard. Fard understood the power differential between whites and blacks in the early twentieth century as a temporary historical occurrence that would be rectified as African Americans gained "knowledge of self" and dethroned what he called the "blue-eyed devils." He wrote guidelines for the movement, *The Secret Ritual of the Nation of Islam*, which was passed down orally, and the *Teaching for the Lost-Found Nation of Islam in a Mathematical Way*, which was written in a special code that can only be interpreted by the most devoted members.

An early follower of Fard and one of his chief assistants was Elijah Poole, who took the Muslim name Elijah Muhammad. The son of a Baptist minister and sharecropper in the rural town of Sandersville, Georgia, Poole moved with his family to Detroit in 1923. He and his brothers joined the Nation of Islam in 1931 and rose rapidly in the ranks of the organization. In 1934, Fard unexpectedly disappeared, which instituted a heated battle over the leadership of the community. Muhammad took the helm of one faction and relocated to Chicago in 1936, establishing Temple of Islam No. 2. In the 1940s, as the movement transitioned into an institution, Fard's status ascended from a profound teacher to "Allah," God incarnate, and Elijah Muhammad was viewed as his "messenger." The Nation of Islam brought a distinctive interpretation of the Shahada, the Profession of Faith in Islam: "There is no God but Allah (incarnate in Fard) and (Elijah) Muhammad is his Messenger." Muhammad promoted economic independence and a rallying cry of "Do For Self," which scholars have characterized as "Black Puritanism" because of its emphasis on hard work, productivity, and a simple lifestyle. Under Muhammad's leadership, the Nation of Islam established over a hundred temples across the United States, several grocery stores, restaurants, and other businesses. Strict dietary codes forbid alcohol, drugs, pork, and unhealthy foods as outlined in Muhammad's *How to Eat to Live* (1972). Muhammad's message resonated strongly with blacks in poor neighborhoods and prisons. In his *Message to the Black Man* (1965), Muhammad suggested that the African American psyche and self-confidence had been damaged by white racism, resulting in a confused identity and self-hatred. Complete separation from whites through the formation of an independent black nation was the only remedy to restore the dignity of the black race and inaugurate the final Armageddon, in which the "evil whites" would finally be banished and African Americans would assume their rightful place and rule with Allah.

One of the more controversial teachings of the Nation of Islam is "Yacub's History," which offers a distinctive account of the origins of the white race. According to the narrative, as described in the *Autobiography of Malcolm X*, after the moon separated from the earth, God placed black people, "the Original Man," in Mecca. In the holy city, there were twenty-four brilliant scientists, but one of them, "Mr. Yacub," created an "especially strong black tribe of Shabazz," who were the ancestors of present-day African Americans. Between 5000 and 4500 BCE, Yacub, born with an abnormally large head as well as a superior intellect, fulfilled his destiny to wreak havoc on society. An effective orator, Yacub gathered so many converts that the established religious authorities banished him (along with his 59,000 followers) to the island of Patmos, the location where John received the message that would become the Book of Revelation in the New Testament. Upset about being exiled, Yacub sought revenge against Allah by creating a "devil race—a bleached-out white race of people." Possessing scientific knowledge of recessive and dominate genes, Yacub set about breeding a progressively lighter-complexioned and physically and mentally weak people. To facilitate the process, Yacub allowed only lighter-skinned blacks to marry and reproduce, while those children that were deemed to be too dark were killed. According to the narrative, it took over eight hundred years to proceed from black, brown, red, and yellow to finally arrive at a pure white race.

These "blond, pale-skinned, cold blue-eyed devils," in the Nation of Islam tradition, were hairy "savages" that, like animals, walked on all fours, and lacked the ability to cover themselves with clothes. After six hundred years, this white race made their way from the island to the mainland and within six months of their arrival began to deceive black people and stir up intraracial tensions that turned an Edenic existence into conflict-filled hell. Recognizing that the whites were the source of their problems, blacks captured them, placed them in chains, "generously" covered their nakedness, and led them across the Arabian desert to the "caves of Europe." After two thousand years, God raised up Moses to lead this people. The first to respond to his message were the Jews. According to the prophecy, it was

God's will that white people would rise up and rule the world for six thousand years. Slavery was necessary then, to bring Africans to the New World to learn the "white devil's true nature" firsthand. It was prophesied that this white reign would continue until the chosen one, Fard, would come to the black race and instruct them about their true history and destiny. Because Fard was of African and European American descent, he was able to be both a member of the black race and move undetected among white people.[5]

This narrative provides a striking reversal of the use of religious scripture to advance notions of black inferiority. Within many nineteenth-century white Christian circles, the Bible was widely interpreted to justify African enslavement. Genesis 9:20–27 chronicles an episode in which Noah, drunk from wine, lies naked within his tent. Ham, the father of Canaan, sees Noah naked and tells Shem and Japheth, who walk backward into the tent, placing a blanket on their father while averting their eyes. When Noah awoke and found out what happened he said, "Cursed be Canaan! The lowest of slaves will he be to his brothers. . . . May God extend the territory of Japheth; may Japheth live in the tents of Shem, and may Canaan be his slave." Many contemporary biblical scholars contextualize the story within the tenth-century BCE Israelite enslavement of the "Canaanites." However, in the second century CE, the church fathers began to employ the passage to connect blackness with evil. Origen (185–254) wrote that by "quickly sink[ing] to slavery of the vices," Ham's "discolored posterity imitate the ignobility of the race" he fathered. Augustine (354–430) saw the origins of slavery in Ham's transgression, and Ambrose of Milan (339–397) wrote that Noah's chastisement only applied to the darker descendants of Ham. However, it was not until the fifteenth century

---

5. Malcolm X, *The Autobiography of Malcolm X* (New York: Ballantine Books, 1993), 167–71.

and the Spanish and Portuguese enslavement of people of color that the narrative became cemented as a justification for racial slavery. Early proslavery literature cited the "curse of Ham" and the "mark of Cain" among other biblical passages as a rationale for the Atlantic slave trade.

One of those who responded to the Nation of Islam's theology was Malcolm X. In one revealing passage in his autobiography, Malcolm X, having heard Yacub's story, ruminates on all of the white people he had encountered in his life to evaluate the NOI's assertion that Caucasians were all devils. From the state workers who institutionalized his mother in the Kalamazoo asylum to the judge who separated him from his brothers and sisters to the eighth-grade teacher who told him to be a carpenter when Malcolm expressed interest in being a lawyer, the actions of every white American that he encountered in his life seemed to confirm their innate ill will toward African Americans. That an individual could hear a narrative describing all white people as the devil and have it resonate with his life experience speaks not only to the tragedy of Malcolm X's early death, but reveals just how pervasive racism and discrimination were in America in the 1950s and 1960s.

Equally revealing is the way Malcolm X was introduced to the Nation of Islam. While Malcolm was incarcerated for robbery, his brother told him during one visit to the prison, "Malcolm, don't eat any more pork, and don't smoke any more cigarettes. I'll show you how to get out of prison." Later, as the inmates passed the plate of pork to Malcolm X during lunch and he said "I don't eat pork," the surprise and shock of the white inmates when he declined the meat, coupled with the subsequent shockwaves it sent through the jailhouse, instilled a sense of pride in Malcolm. His seemingly small gesture undermined a deeply ingrained stereotype about black people's eating habits and allowed Malcolm X to take on a new identity. The Nation of Islam's beliefs, emphasis on distinctive dress, eating habits, piety, and physical health, along with his own religious experience, all attracted Malcolm X to the movement.

During the years following Malcolm X's release from prison, 1952–1965, the Nation of Islam's membership increased exponentially. Malcolm X brought new life to the organization, establishing a newspaper, *Muhammad Speaks*, and requiring members to sell an ambitious quota of copies. He rapidly ascended the leadership ranks to lead Boston Temple No. 11, and later took the helm of Temple No. 7 in Harlem, the second-largest and most prestigious temple. Malcolm X's work ethic, oratorical skill, and devotion to Elijah Muhammad led to his appointment as the national representative of the Nation of Islam in 1963, which at the time had a membership of over half a million. Malcolm X was unwaveringly devoted to Muhammad until he learned of his extramarital affairs, some of which produced children. As his image of his father figure and spiritual mentor was shaken, Malcolm X began to hear murmurs that the Nation of Islam's leadership was plotting to have him assassinated partially because of his rise to national prominence. Malcolm X referred to the assassination of President John F. Kennedy as "the chickens coming home to roost," which resulted in Muhammad silencing him for ninety days.

During this time, Malcolm chose to go on the Hajj to Mecca where he would have a profound experience. All Muslims who have the ability, health, and financial means are expected to make the pilgrimage to the holy city as a part of the five pillars of Islam. During the eleven-day pilgrimage, he ate, slept, and prayed with fellow Muslims—some of whom were blond and blue eyed, yet worshiped with the same sincerity as he and other people of African descent. Malcolm X wrote, "We were truly the same (brothers)—because their belief in one God had removed the 'white' from their minds, the 'white' from their behavior, and the 'white' from their attitude." He returned to America with a hopefulness that Islam could bring about more harmonious race relations and took the orthodox Islamic name, El-Hajj Malik El-Shabazz. He also continued to espouse the importance of pan-Africanism, founding Muslim Mosque, Inc. as well as a secular group, the Organization for Afro-American Unity, to establish continuing connections between all peoples of African descent. Malcolm X was assassinated before the final editing of his *Autobiography of Malcolm X*, so it is unclear if this is where he would have concluded his own narrative. As Manning Marable has pointed out, the book was a joint writing project between Alex Haley, who served for twenty years in the U.S. Coast Guard, and Malcolm X. According to Marable's analysis, Haley, a liberal Republican, disliked the racial teachings of the Nation of Islam and framed Malcolm X's life as a cautionary tale of the problematic nature of self-segregation.[6] It remains an ongoing challenge to determine how much of the "real" Malcolm X one can glimpse in the book.

Father Divine

While the Nation of Islam advocated strict racial separatism, Father Divine (1877?–1965), born George Baker, founded an interracial religious community called the International Peace Mission Movement that came to prominence in America in the 1930s. Many of the details of George Baker's life before becoming Father Divine are disputed. Most sources cite his birthplace as Savannah, Georgia, in 1877, or Rockville, Maryland in 1879, but legal documents state that he was born in Providence, Rhode Island in 1880. As a child, he attended Jerusalem Methodist Church with his mother and his

---

6. Manning Marable, *Malcolm X: A Life of Reinvention* (New York: Penguin Books, 2011); Malcolm X, *The Autobiography of Malcolm X*.

siblings. After his mother died in May 1897, Baker's whereabouts are largely unknown until 1899 when he attended a series of storefront churches in Baltimore and, in 1902, did missionary work in the South.

Divine was influenced by a number of religious thinkers and events, including Charles Fillmore's Unity School of Christianity and the Azusa Street Revival in 1906. In 1907, he joined a Baptist storefront in Baltimore, whose leader, Samuel Morris, referred to himself as Father Jehovia. Shortly after, Baker became known as the Messenger. As Baker's oratorical skills grew and the number of his followers swelled, he began to assert that he was the incarnation of the divine. By 1912, Baker had formed his own ministry, leaving Baltimore for Georgia. Baker clashed often with the local ministers and was arrested several times for vagrancy and "lunacy" based on the observations of outsiders that his religious services were too enthusiastic and practiced *glossolalia* or speaking in tongues. After traveling around the country, in 1917, Baker settled in New York in a mostly white community, Sayville, in Suffolk County, Long Island, taking the name the Reverend Major Jealous Divine. In addition to Divine's teachings and writings, which were considered sacred, members followed the *International Modest Code* that prohibited tobacco, alcohol, drugs, gambling, and profanity and promoted dress codes for men and women, celibacy, economic self-sufficiency, and a commitment to living a peaceful and pacifist lifestyle. Divine had a diverse following that included both African Americans and whites and members of the upper and lower class. At the height of the movement the community had about 50,000 members.

On November 15, 1931, responding to a disturbing the peace complaint, officers arrested eighty members attending Divine's service. Fifty-five pleaded guilty and paid a five-dollar fine. Father Divine and others pleaded not guilty and stood trial. Most were found guilty and were forced to pay the fine. Justice Lewis J. Smith sentenced Divine to a year in jail and a five-hundred-dollar fine. Two days later, an apparently healthy Smith died of cardiac arrest. For many of Divine's followers the event confirmed his divinity. A new trial was ordered, but never took place. After thirty-three days, Divine was released from jail.

Divine's Peace Mission Movement opened hotels, restaurants, stores, and many other businesses, while providing jobs, housing, and free meals during the Great Depression. Divine became famous for his elaborate "Love Feasts," communion banquets, and services. In the mid-1930s, Divine moved his community to Harlem. In January 1936, Divine issued his "Righteous Government Platform," which called for the elimination of racial segregation, lynching, and capital punishment and advocated for additional government funds to end unemployment and poverty. In 1940, the movement petitioned for more stringent federal prosecution of lynching. Throughout his ministry, Divine had a number of accusations leveled against him, including racketeering charges. However, the movement grew steadily in the 1930s, with over a hundred and fifty communities across the country.

Following the death of his first wife, Divine married Edna Rose Ritchings, also known as Sweet Angel, on April 29, 1946. After the wedding, she assumed the title of Mother Divine. In 1947, the community moved to Woodmount, a suburb in Philadelphia. While the community held a variety of beliefs and practices, they emphasized racial and gender equity, patriotism to the United States, economic independence, and celibacy, which was required of each member. After Father Divine's death on September 10, 1965, the community was able to continue under the direction of Mother Divine. As his health declined, Father Divine put institutional structures in place for the continuation of the movement, developing new orders with their own codes of conduct such as the "Rosebuds" for young girls, "Lily-buds" for women, and "Crusaders" for men. Their newspaper the *New Day*, which appeared weekly during the 1930s, suspended publication in 1992. However, Father Divine's teachings and writings remain sacred to his followers.

Father Divine's influence remains strong in the Peace Mission Movement. Years after his death, followers still attest to feeling his presence during meetings and services. Believed to be the Mount of the House of the Lord mentioned in Mic. 4:1–2 and Isa. 2:2–3, from which Hebraic law would be spread to all nations. Today, pilgrims still journey to his burial spot in Woodmont, which they view as a sacred site. Followers have a distinctive reading of the Bible, understanding the miracles and events of the New Testament to have been performed by Father Divine, since he and Jesus are synonymous. Because Father Divine is viewed as God, all of his sayings and sermons are elevated to the status of ultimate truth. One of these central tenets was a mandate to treat all people equally regardless of race, ethnicity, or gender. Race, Divine preached, was merely a social construction that denied the sacred beauty of all human beings, the divine presence in all, and the responsibility to accord everyone with respect and dignity. As such, Divine discouraged his followers from even acknowledging race or gender as a category or noting racial, ethnic, or sexual distinctions among his congregations. Divine was also a staunch American patriot, consistently maintaining that the guide for true social equity lay within the frameworks of the country's founding documents, especially the U.S. Constitution. There are currently several hundred members of the Peace Mission Movement, with the largest communities in Philadelphia and Newark, but there are followers across the United States and around the world.[7]

Sweet Daddy Grace

One of Father Divine's chief competitors for new members was Sweet Daddy Grace. Born Marcelino Manoel de Graca on January 25, 1881, in Brava, Cape Verde Islands, he changed his name to Emmanuel Grace after migrating to New Bedford, Massachusetts, around 1900. In 1921, he established the United House of Prayer for All People. As with so many new religious movements, history primarily recalls the more dramatic beliefs and practices of the tradition. Grace's charismatic and engaging personality quickly attracted a substantial following in Southern California. Known for his long hair, three-inch-long fingernails that were often painted red, white, and blue, and adorning himself with large amounts of jewelry and expensive clothes, Grace became a larger-than-life character living in an eighty-four-room mansion in Los Angeles, and owning a twenty-acre estate in Havana as well as several other residences. Although most of his followers were poor, they apparently expressed few concerns about their leader's extravagant lifestyle.

During meetings, Grace usually sat upon a large, elaborately decorated throne on an elevated platform. One ritual involved a kind of monetary musical chairs in which members dropped money into collection plates while a band played. The individual who gave the most money before the music stopped was declared the winner. The services were characterized by ecstatic worship and strict pronouncements against smoking, drinking, dancing, and other forms of inappropriate entertainments. There were many similarities between the tenets of the United House of Prayer for All People and Holiness-Pentecostalism; however, a major divergence was Grace's belief that the Holy Spirit was made manifest in himself. Yet, Grace

7. Jill Watts, *God, Harlem U.S.A.: The Father Divine Story* (Berkeley: University of California Press, 1995).

never requested that his followers choose between his movement and Christianity. In fact, many members maintained a dual affiliation with another denomination.

Unlike Divine, Grace never asserted that he was God. Yet, the belief that he had special healing powers and the regular invocation of his name during worship services and prayers significantly blurred the boundaries between his human and divine status. The group attracted public attention with its mass ceremonies, such as "fire hose baptisms" in which hundreds of initiates became new members by being sprayed with a powerful firehouse hose. Grace had his own line of products, from soap, toothpaste, and other toiletries to periodicals and food products, and owned real estate, insurance companies, and funeral homes. Grace and Divine were direct competitors for black Harlemites seeking a new spiritual home. These tensions were magnified when Grace bought the house that Divine was renting to hold his meetings. For a brief time, Divine had to pay rent to Grace, which the latter used to his advantage to attract new members. IRS audits of Grace's tax records and a contentious divorce led him to leave the country in the mid-1930s, which effectively ended his rivalry with Divine. He returned to the United States in his later years and died in Los Angeles on January 12, 1960.[8]

Black Judaism

Dating back to slavery, African American Christians have identified with the Israelites of the Hebrew Bible and found parallels and inspiration in the deliverance of the Jews from the bondage of Pharaoh and African American liberation from slavery. In the late nineteenth century, a number of black Jewish movements emerged that extended those connections and transformed elements of Judaism

---

8. Marie W. Dallam, *Daddy Grace: A Celebrity Preacher and His House of Prayer* (New York: New York University Press, 2009).

to address the specific concerns in the African American community. The earliest such community was founded by F. S. Cherry, called the Church of the Living God, the Pillar Ground of Truth for All Nations, in Chattanooga, Tennessee, in 1886. Having gradually gained a larger membership over time, in the early 1940s the community relocated to Philadelphia. Cherry spoke Yiddish and Hebrew and viewed African Americans as the true descendants of the Biblical Hebrews. This created tension with American Jewish communities, which felt that this was not orthodox belief. Cherry brought an afrocentric approach to Judaism, preaching that God, Jesus, and all of those written about in the Hebrew Bible were of African descent. From his interpretation of the Bible, Caucasians were descended from the servant Gehazi, described in 2 Kgs. 5:27, who was cursed by the prophet Elisha with skin "as white as snow." The Atlantic slave trade and white historians, he argued, had obscured this glorious history and heritage of African Americans. Like other black Jewish communities of the time, the group maintained stringent rules against the consumption of alcohol, dancing, displaying self-portraits, embracing popular culture, smoking, swearing, and divorce.

Several other black new religious movements sought to enlighten African Americans about their true Jewish heritage. The Church of God and Saints of Christ was founded by William S. Crowdy in Lawrence, Kansas, in 1896, and relocated several times, first to Philadelphia in 1900, and then to Belleville, Virginia, five years later. For Crowdy, African Americans were the descendants of the ten lost tribes of Israel and therefore promoted several Jewish rituals including circumcision, following the Jewish calendar, wearing yarmulkes, the observance of the Saturday Sabbath, and celebrating Passover. He also interwove Christian elements such as baptism, communion, and ritual foot-washing. In the 1920s, Bishop Derks Field founded a smaller community with similar beliefs and practices called the Church of God in David in Alabama, which was later renamed the Spiritual Israel Church and Its Army after they relocated to Detroit. Like other black Jewish groups, they viewed themselves as the descendants of the ancient Israelites and their church as a restoration of the Hebraic tradition. Adam and Eve, according to their theology, were created in Africa and therefore all of the patriarchs and prophets were black.

Warren Roberson led the Gospel of the Kingdom in Virginia, which was both a church and social justice organization. The community practiced aspects of Orthodox Judaism, spoke Yiddish, and embraced Jewish culture. In 1917, they moved their headquarters to Harlem and established several houses of worship that they referred to as communal "kingdoms." At the height of the movement, there were over one hundred and fifty meeting places. One kingdom in Atlantic City received a large amount of media attention for being an alleged "baby farm" in which female members were compelled to bear Roberson's offspring. This was an especially critical charge since celibacy was a central tenet of the community. Authorities charged Roberson with transporting women across state lines for "immoral purposes" under the Mann Act in 1926. He pleaded guilty and received an eighteen-month prison sentence. The community would soon dissolve in Roberson's absence.

Rabbi Wentworth A. Matthew (1892–1973) established the Commandment Keepers Congregation of the Living God in 1930. Like other black Jewish communities, the Commandment Keepers believed that they were the descendants of the Ethiopian Jews and the ancient Hebrews. Matthew prophesied that white supremacy was temporary and that the true Israelites would ascend to power after World War III in the year 2000. The Commandment Keepers embraced their Jewish identity and, for the most part, had good relations with Jewish communities in New York City. They kept kosher, studied Hebrew, held meetings on Saturday, wore yarmulkes and prayer shawls, observed Jewish holy days, and had elaborate Passover celebrations.

Hulon Mitchell Jr., later to be known to followers as Yahweh ben Yahweh ("God, son of God"), founded the Temple of Love in Miami, Florida, in 1979. Raised in the Pentecostal tradition, Mitchell believed that God, the Bible, and himself constituted the "Great Light and rule and guide for faith." By 1982, Mitchell preached that God and Jesus were black and that he, God's son, Yahweh ben Yahweh, was sent as the savior to African Americans, the lost tribe of Israel, to free them from the four hundred years of white oppression, racial prejudice and discrimination, and abuse at the hands of authorities. As in the Nation of Islam, Mitchell referred to Caucasians as "white devils" and prophesied that "white America" would be punished by God. The group also did community outreach, pushing for better education, employment opportunities, housing, and health care for African Americans. Having condemned the secular world, Yahweh called for his most devout followers to live on the premises of the Temple and wear white robes and turbans reflective of their African heritage. Members relinquished their "slave names" and were bestowed new Hebrew ones with Israel as their surname. As the community came under increased public scrutiny, Yahweh formed the "Circle of Ten," an armed security force, to protect the entrance to the Temple. By 1985, the Nation of Yahweh had five communities across the country.

Yahweh won thousands of followers nationwide but made inner-city Miami the community's headquarters for a business empire that included supermarkets, hotels, restaurants, and beauty parlors. During their peak in the 1980s, they turned poverty-stricken inner-city areas and drug-infested neighborhoods into renovated neighborhoods. By

1989, they had temples in most major U.S. cities, assets of about $50 million, and the support of many of Miami's political leaders. Between April and October 1986, Yahweh allegedly sent his "death angels" into the Miami community on multiple occasions to kill white people randomly and to commit acts of retribution against blacks who interfered with the community's sales of products and the collection of donations. In May 1986, followers of Yahweh were accused of entering a predominantly African American neighborhood in Delray Beach and tossing Molotov cocktails through the windows of six homes, where two days earlier, local youths had beaten up several community members who were preaching door-to-door. Yahweh allegedly ordered the arsonists to stand in front of the residences and use their swords and machetes to murder anyone who tried to exit the burning homes. As early as the 1980s, connections were being suggested between the community and the deaths of individuals who had spoken out against the tradition. By 1993, the Yahweh empire was in bankruptcy, the members dispersed, and Yahweh Ben Yahweh and six of his closest followers were in federal prison for conspiring to commit murder.[9]

Religious violence and alleged scandal complicate the efforts of the student of religious studies to empathize with the groups that they study. While many new religious movements start off with the best of intentions, sometimes leaders or members of the community take actions that harm themselves or others. In some cases, one can attempt to separate the actions of the few that create a bad perception for the entirety of the religious community. Yet, accusations leveled against smaller and in many cases already marginalized new religious movements are generally accepted as truth by a largely skeptical American public. While larger and well-established religious

9. Tudor Parfitt, *Black Jews in Africa and the Americas* (Cambridge, MA: Harvard University Press, 2013).

institutions such as the Roman Catholic Church can weather concerns about alleged abuses, newer emergent traditions usually do not have that same power. Theoretically, the guarantees of religious freedom in America should extend the benefit of the doubt to nascent religious groups, but in practice this is rarely the case, particularly in the post-Jonestown era.

The People's Temple

Although not always categorized as a black new religious movement, at its height, African Americans made up between 70 and 80 percent of the membership of the People's Temple. On November 18, 1978, Congressman Leo Ryan flew to Guyana to investigate claims that Jonestown was a "cult." The visit resulted in not only his own murder, but over 900 members of the People's Temple taking their own lives. According to audio-tapes of the final moments of the group, it was the anticipation that the community would be destroyed by outsiders and Jim Jones's prophecy that the U.S. Government would torture surviving community members that precipitated the "revolutionary suicide."

There was little in the group's founding to suggest its ultimate end. The People's Temple became a member of the Disciples of Christ denomination in Indianapolis in 1960. From the outset it was an interracial community, with 20 percent of its membership being black. This relatively high number was an anomaly in the largely segregated state of Indiana. From all accounts, Jim Jones was a pillar of the community and a strong advocate for racial equality, ascending to chair the Indianapolis Human Rights Commission in 1961. Discouraged by the racism the church encountered, in 1965, eighty members, about half of whom were African American, relocated to Redwood Valley in Northern California. There, in addition to working-class families, a sizable number of young, college-educated whites, attracted to its commitment to peace and social justice, joined the movement.

In 1974, still greatly dissatisfied with the racial and political climate in the United States, the People's Temple leased four thousand acres in Guyana, South America, in hopes of establishing their own "promised land." The People's Temple Agricultural Project initially grew slowly, with only fifty residents in 1977. However, external factors would accelerate the exodus from the U.S. The IRS began challenging the church's tax-exempt status, and former members and families created a group called the "Concerned Relatives," claiming that members were being kept in the group against their will, which attracted additional media attention. Jones encouraged members to leave America for Guyana, a call that over nine hundred responded to in the summer and fall of 1977.

The letter-writing campaign of the Concerned Relatives reached the desk of Congressman Leo Ryan who agreed to go on a fact-finding mission to Guyana. On November 18, 1978, during the visit, a current member secretly gave Ryan a note asking for his help to escape the community. By the end of that morning, sixteen others requested to leave. When Ryan, his party, and those members who decided to leave reached the airstrip, they were gunned down by People's Temple members. Expecting outside persecution, for months Jones regularly held "white night" practice suicide drills with his followers. In anticipation of a strong U.S. governmental response, Jones told his followers that this was the real thing: families would be torn apart and children and seniors tortured for information unless they engaged in "revolutionary suicide." A large vat of purple "Flav-R-Aid" was prepared with cyanide and a variety of sedatives and tranquilizers. Lines were formed and parents were instructed to give the drink first to children and infants and then to take the poison themselves. Those unable to ingest the poison would receive injections. Afterwards, Jones was found with a gunshot wound to the head. In all, over 900 people died on November 18, 1978. At Jonestown, seventy of the members were five years old or younger, eighty-two were between the ages of six and eleven, 181 were between twelve and nineteen, 229 were between twenty and thirty-five, eighty-nine were between thirty-six and fifty, 104 were between fifty-one and sixty-five, and 146 were over sixty-six years of age.[10]

News coverage of the event, showing images of piles of bodies lying in the central pavilion of Jonestown, changed the landscape of religion in America. The terms "cult" and "brainwashing" gained new prominence in the American vernacular. Fear that maniacal leaders could manipulate the naïve and weak-willed entered the public discourse. Years later, in 1993, the Branch Davidians at Waco, Texas, were defined as a dangerous "cult," and after a fifty-one-day standoff, the federal authorities forcefully entered the Davidian complex. Although accounts of subsequent events vary, the siege resulted in the deaths of over eighty Branch Davidians. In March 1997, in Rancho Santa Fe, California, thirty-nine members of Heaven's Gate committed suicide. Unlike the previous examples of the People's Temple and the Branch Davidians, there was no impending threat of outside intervention, but, as evidenced in videotaped farewells, the members of Heaven's Gate calmly took their own lives in expectation of the appearance of the Hale-Bopp comet.

These tragedies have shaped the perception of contemporary African American religious movements. While several previous nineteenth-century new religious movements such as the Latter-Day

10. David Chidester, *Salvation and Suicide: An Interpretation of Jim Jones, the People's Temple, and Jonestown* (Bloomington: Indiana University Press, 2003); Mary Maaga, *Hearing the Voices of Jonestown: Putting a Human Face on an American Tragedy* (Syracuse, NY: Syracuse University Press, 1998).

Saints, Christian Science, and the Shakers experienced various forms of persecution, Jonestown's legacy casts a large shadow of suspicion upon all burgeoning religious communities that embrace distinctive religious beliefs and practices. Despite the publicity and stereotyping that so often accompanies the word "cult," many sociologists have sought to separate and sculpt a functional definition that discards the many pejorative popular-culture characterizations of the term. Yet, the challenge remains to construct categories that are not so unwieldy or esoteric as to include or exclude religious expressions that might otherwise be appropriately classified under the rubric. Rodney Stark and William Bainbridge coined the classical definitions of a church as a "conventional religious organization," a sect as "a deviant religious organization with traditional beliefs and practices," and a cult as "a deviant religious organization with novel beliefs and practices." The primary difference that marks a cult from a sect turns on whether the group emerged from within a larger umbrella tradition (sect) or spontaneously emerged from total religious innovation (cult).[11] Yet, as one may quickly observe, the terms in the definitions are not value neutral, but themselves offer and require interpretation. Which portrays a group more favorably, the word "conventional" or "deviant"? Similarly, what counts as a "traditional" belief or practice might lie squarely on who is making their case, the insider to the community or the outsider. Whether one receives the protections extended to religions under the First Amendment of the United States Constitution often turns on matters of outside perception, power, and having significant numbers to resist negative external labels and being able to define one's own place in the American religious scene.

---

11. Rodney Stark and William Sims Bainbridge, *The Future of Religion: Secularization, Revival, and Cult Formation* (Berkeley: University of California Press, 1985).

Case Study: The United Nuwaubian Nation of Moors

There are a variety of contemporary African American religious communities that confound the boundaries of clear-cut identification with one tradition or category over another. The United Nuwaubian Nation of Moors, led by Malachi Z. York, in Eatonton, Georgia, began in New York in the 1930s. Born in New York in 1935, York's religious vision emerged from the rich context of black movements that emphasized black power, self-determination, and pan-Africanism, including the Nation of Islam, black Jewish groups like the Commandment Keepers, the Five Percenters, and Marcus Garvey's Universal Negro Improvement Association (UNIA). In many ways York's views spanned the gamut of beliefs espoused by these groups. From the mid-1960s, during their time in Sullivan County, they integrated aspects of Islam in their theology and were known as the Ansaru Allah (Helpers of Allah) and Ansaru Pure Sufi, focusing on the mystic aspects of Sufism. In 1969, the community embraced a Jewish identity, referring to the group alternately as the Nubian Islamic Hebrews, Ancient Holy Tabernacle of the Most High, the Children of Abraham, and the Mystic Order of Melchizedek, all of which blended elements of Judaism and Christianity and, like many previous traditions, declared themselves a "chosen people." By the end of the 1980s, the tradition included writings on physics and extraterrestrials. Increasingly, York referred to the community as "Unarius." By 1993, when they relocated to Georgia, the community had embraced Neteru, an ancient Egyptian deity, in their worship services and emphasized the glorious history of African Americans in Egypt. This innovation in theological emphasis is demonstrated by the forty-foot-high black pyramid, eight-foot-high statues of ancient Egyptian gods and goddesses, columns with hieroglyphics, a sphinx, and smaller twenty-four-foot pyramids that had been built on their 476 acres of land in the town of Eatonton. Although distinct in its range of views, there is little "new" about this NRM. From William Miller's changing predictions of Jesus' return to the Nation of Islam's glorification of the African American race to Noble Drew Ali's repositioning of blacks as "Asiatics," adaptability in racial and religious identity has been the mainstay in a number of NRMs. However, privacy, although historically a weapon of self-defense for minority religions, becomes even more complicated in post-Jonestown America.

According to their sacred text, the *Holy Tabernacle Ministries*, the ancestors of the UNNM crossed from the Nile Valley to the Americas before continental drift. From their perspective, they were the original Native Americans. Given this self-identity, the Nuwaubians declared themselves a sovereign nation, built structures that defied local zoning ordinances, began issuing their own passports, and organized armed security units to protect their property; all of which led to conflict with the broader community. For the Nuwaubians, their community was Tama-Re or "The Land," at once a sacred site and their native homeland. In contrast, the media and local law enforcement commonly referred to the location as a "compound," invoking images of the Branch Davidians in Waco.

The UNNM eschatology included a prophecy that a spaceship from the planet Rizq would return on May 5, 2003, to ransom the 144,000 true believers before the coming judgment of those remaining on earth. Upon initial consideration, the Nuwaubian invocation of extraterrestrials seems an unlikely choice for a group seeking credibility as a minority in a small town, particularly the notion that York was an extraterrestrial being from the galaxy Illyuwn. However, extending their history beyond Egypt and the earliest civilizations to a time before the formation of the earth allowed the community to be at once new and ancient, uniquely

American and transcending humankind, and racially distinctive and supernatural.

Although some observers were incredulous about the community's reworking of the 2003 prediction in the fall of the same year, calculating dates for an imminent supernatural return is nothing new in American religious history. From William Miller's recalculations in the 1840s to the *Left Behind* series of books, Americans have speculated about and predicted the nature and date of the return of Jesus Christ. Although the parallels seem apparent, for most of the American public, a clear difference exists between the return of a UFO and the Christ. It is the underlying similarities between many "mainstream" and marginalized apocalyptic conceptions that make it so essential for observers to draw sharp lines of demarcation between the "deviant" actions of "cults" and the normalized practices of traditional religions.

The Nuwaubians have traveled a path that many previous new religious movements have previously taken. Privacy, although seemingly crucial to connecting and maintaining bonds within fledgling traditions, often raises the suspicion of the "mainstream," which quickly labels the group a "cult" and creatively fills in the remaining descriptive spaces with all the stereotypical elements associated with such groups: "brainwashing," a controlling charismatic leader, manipulation, and so on. The UNNM is perhaps the best example of a group that mediated its public perception in the press, while continually reworking its own "secret" and evolving communal identity. Although employing the survival strategies used by previous NRMs, in the information age of the twenty-first century, the ability to maintain privacy was never completely under the control of the UNNM.

Almost from the outset, the UNNM was described as the next Jonestown, Waco, or Heaven's Gate community. It is precisely this desire to conflate a small, predominantly African American religious community into definable and knowable categories that makes this group such a helpful illustration for analyzing not only the dynamics in Eatonton but also the broader interplay between race, religion, and privacy in the last decade of the twentieth century. Spanning the landscape of the nineteenth- and twentieth-century NRMs, one would be hard-pressed to find a group with more diverse beliefs over its relatively brief history: prophetic dates of Armageddon, notions of black racial superiority, elements of UFO religion, and religious narratives establishing Native American and Egyptian ancestry.

York's views indicate a complicated mapping of identity that emphasized different elements at different historical moments. As much as possible, York synchronized his own identity with the malleable narrative that undergirded and resonated with the community. In the 1960s, leading Ansaru Allah, he understood himself as the al Hajj al Imam Isa Abdallah Muhammad al Mahdi. As the leader of the Nubian Islamic Hebrews in 1969, his title was Rabboni Yeshua Bar el Haady. In the early 1980s, York self-identified as Christian, claimed to be the Messiah, and referred to himself as the Lamb. As his fascination with extraterrestrials increased, he was known as the Qutb ("Axis of the Universe"). Before journeying to Eatonton, Georgia, he was referred to by his Egyptian name, Neter A'aferti Atum Re.

Upon initial consideration, Eatonton, Georgia, seems an odd choice for an almost entirely African American community that had a consistent membership estimated at approximately four hundred from the early 1970s. The relocation of the UNNM from the North to a rural town in the South is one of the many anomalies embodied by the group's beliefs and practices when compared with other African American religious communities. In fact, their southern movement reverses the narrative surrounding the emergence of

African American NRMs in northern urban centers after the Great Migration in the first half of the twentieth century. Although the Nation of Islam called for a separate African American nation, economic independence, and land within the United States, no African American NRM has asserted sovereignty over an entire geographic region based almost solely on their religious narrative. According to their sacred text, *The Holy Tabernacle Ministries*, the "time was right" for the "Prepared Saviour" to "set up" their community in New York called Jazzir Abba in preparation for their eventual pilgrimage to the "Mecca of Nubians" in Georgia, which was the home of their ancestors, the Yamassee Native American Moors of the Creek Nation. Although economically land in Georgia was less expensive than in New York, there is some evidence that the choice was not entirely voluntary. Even in the more culturally diverse landscape of Brooklyn, the community had rocky relationships with their neighbors because of their practice of self-segregation. The group's use of the words "Islamic" and "Allah" in their previous titles and distinct interpretations of the Quran also stirred tensions with the local mosques. FBI reports around the time of their departure alleged that the Nuwaubians had committed a number of crimes such as arson, welfare fraud, and extortion. The origins of the group, their rationale for moving, and their claim to the land in Eatonton, Georgia, exemplify the relationship between the UNNM and their critics. Material used by the UNNM to engender sympathy toward the group was the very evidence invoked in the delegitimation process by those skeptical of the tradition.

The various interested parties also disagreed about the nature of the tensions in Eatonton. Despite their high profile in the community, by all accounts the Nuwaubians kept to themselves. However, in 1999, their request to rezone part of their property from agricultural to commercial was denied by Putnam County. Specifically, the

100-by-50–foot building that they hoped to use as the "Ramses Social Club," which was originally zoned for storage, became the central source of tension with the local authorities. Citing several violations, housing officials shut down what they referred to as a "nightclub." On June 15, 1999, local authorities padlocked five buildings, including two pyramids that Nuwaubians call their church and holy temple, over additional zoning violations. African American city officials bore the brunt of UNNM suspicions about outsiders. From the eschatological perspective of the Nuwaubians, good and evil were clearly identified in the conflict. Local law enforcement quickly took shape as the villain who was persecuting the community, but York, the spiritual leader of the Nuwaubians, who had served three years in prison for resisting arrest, assault, and possession of a dangerous weapon in the 1960s, raised concerns for the sheriff's department. The Nuwaubians claimed they never had a chance to correct the citations before the buildings were padlocked to prevent their entry. Thus began the conflict that would have the Nuwaubians claim racial and religious persecution and the local residents and sheriff's department of Eatonton maintain that they were protecting the town from a dangerous "cult."

While their beliefs and practices are sometimes seen as contradictory, the UNNM seemed comfortable with the apparent tensions. The group at once espoused patriotism and remained suspicious of the intentions of the government. The *Little Guide Book for Nuwaubians* contains the entire U.S. Constitution and prohibits disorderly conduct and urges cooperation with authorities. However, the community regularly turned away deputies with court orders regarding the zoning violations. From the perspective of the Nuwaubians, they have been unfairly targeted and harassed since their arrival in Eatonton. They feel their treatment is indicative of a lack of tolerance. At times the group has claimed racism but has consistently felt that their religion has been at the heart of their treatment. Although the exact racial demographics of the community are not available, some of the members were white, Asian, or various other ethnicities.

York also at once sought privacy and the public stage. On the one hand, he refused to appear for court appointments and regularly declined interviews. On the other hand, he was a prolific writer, penning over two hundred tracts that are used in prayer by many of the members as they circle the small labyrinth surrounding the main pyramid. He created his own language, Nuwabic, which is a blend of Arabic and English. At the same time that York failed to appear for court, the Nuwaubians held their annual Savior's Day Festival to mark York's birthday on June 26. Because local law enforcement had padlocked many of the buildings, the ceremony was held outdoors in a driving rainstorm. Although mostly a reclusive figure, York is often out front during key moments. When negotiations were going well with the Department of Justice mediators on June 30, 1999, he declared, "Peace is made" to his followers outside of the courthouse. His statement that "We're going to change the color of politics in Putnam County" also created unease among the white residents. Although on the one hand he courted controversy, on the other hand he seemed ultimately concerned about his public image. In the summer of 2001, York created another organization, Al Mahdi Shrine Temple No. 19, and described himself as "imperial grand potentate of the International Supreme Council of Shriners." York also held a very public New Year's Eve celebration in the downtown Athens Classic Center.

The legal cases illumined just how contentious the dynamics in Eatonton had become. In the summer of 1999, York was arrested for failing to appear for a court date. After the Nuwaubians called for 30,000 protesters to descend on York's hearing, the sheriff's office responded by mustering two hundred officers, a helicopter, and an armored personnel carrier. When the Nuwaubian turnout was less than expected, both sides defended their positions, and the conflict escalated. Nuwaubian supporters, operating as a group called the Concerned Citizens of Eatonton and People Against Violence in Eatonton, used flyers offering five hundred dollars for incriminating information on Sheriff Sills. In response, Robert Lee, a Putnam County minister, published an anti-Nuwaubian newsletter and led protests outside of the Nuwaubian community. With York in jail, the community struggled. On February 4, 2000, a sign, "Land for Sale" appeared on the property. The media latched onto any exciting tidbits, including rumors that Wesley Snipes's production company was interested in the property as a facility to train security officers, or even further that Snipes was an active Nuwaubian.

As the narrative increasingly framed the dispute as between a small town and a dangerous cult, the conflict soon came to the attention of the national media. The Macon *Telegraph* obtained copies of the applications to both the Holy Tabernacle Ministries and the Ancient Mystic Order of Melchizedek. According to them, the Mystic Order required a twenty-five-dollar membership fee and a vow of silence from discussing information about the community. The church application also asked for a medical history, HIV test, and copies of birth certificates and social security cards. Members were given passports and license plates that allowed them easy access to the community through the main gate.

During this hostile dispute, the UNNM continued to seek acceptance from the local community. There were plans for a theme park, the land was open daily to visitors during certain hours, and there were classes at 4 p.m. on Sundays about the Nuwaubian beliefs. Ironically, many of the structures that were under construction or were padlocked were inherently public facilities such as a health food store, bar, recording studio, and a taxi company. In the midst of their perceived persecution, the group kept a very public profile. Several Nuwaubians were removed from voter rolls in the summer of 2000 because of the large number of people listed as living at particular addresses. That same summer, the Nuwaubians had their annual festival that combined family films, volleyball tournaments, beach parties, puppet shows, and fishing tournaments, with political activities to support the group's legal battles. On June 28, an estimated six to eight hundred Nuwaubians protested outside of the Putnam County Courthouse. They chanted "AMUNMa-at," which they said meant "hidden justice" in ancient Egyptian. The group was also active in statewide politics and was strongly represented in the movement to remove the Confederate Stars and Bars from the Georgia state flag.

Throughout the court battles, each side gained victories and suffered defeats. In October 2000, the Nuwaubians' request to make the Ramses Social Club into a hunting lodge was denied. On October 25, 2000, the group won a small victory when the court ruled that Putnam County could not sue members of the Nuwaubians for damages in the ongoing zoning and building permit lawsuits. In April 2001, the Nuwaubians' suit that challenged the removal of 196 members from the voting rolls was dismissed. In 2001, a number of high-profile leaders visited the community, including Jesse Jackson and members of Rainbow/PUSH Coalition, Al Sharpton, Macon Mayor Jack Ellis, and former state senator Leroy Johnson, who acted as York's attorney.

The legal conflict shifted dramatically in May 2002 when York and his wife Kathy Johnson pleaded not guilty to charges of transporting minors across state lines for sex. Following the arrests, federal agents raided the community and confiscated potential evidence. In May of 2002, the Putnam County Department of Family and Children

Services took five children into protective custody. The FBI suspected that the Nuwaubians would attempt to retake the village, so Sheriff Sills set up a roadblock. Two women claimed that York failed to pay child support for three children. In 1998 and 1999, a person claiming to be a former member of the Nuwaubians sent anonymous letters to various Putnam County officials alleging York had committed child molestation. The numbers of children alleged to have been molested continued to grow in the summer of 2002. Allegations estimated that since 2000 York abused children on fifteen to twenty trips to Disney World in Florida. In addition to York and his wife, three other members (Chaundra Lampkin, Kadijah Merritt, and Esther Cole) faced charges of child molestation. Children as young as four, six, and eight years old were allegedly abused, as well as photographed and videotaped engaged in sexual acts, which led the judge to deny York bail.

As the legal proceedings continued, new revelations seemed to come to light daily. York had a $528,000 home in Athens, where officials found $125,000 in cash. York was charged with seventy-four counts of child molestation, twenty-nine counts of aggravated child molestation and related charges, and one count of rape. For each federal count involving the sexual exploitation of minors, York faced a maximum penalty of fifteen years in prison and a $250,000 fine. One teen girl testified that York, "the Lamb," told her that sex with him would lead to salvation. Her father sued York for one billion dollars in punitive damages on behalf of his daughter. In the summer of 2002, Putnam County again denied the Nuwaubians, petition to have the building be zoned as a "private hunting lodge."

A key "insider" source on the practices of the UNNM came from York's son who had information about York's Camp Jazzir Abba in Sullivan County, which had also experienced issues with building code and land-use violations. York's son claimed that the Savior's Day weeklong celebration drew four thousand people from around the world and earned $500,000 a year. The son attributed the popularity of the event to being the only time loved ones could see members of the group and readily paid the fifty-dollar entry fee in addition to other charges for amenities, such as food and housing. Many members remained in the community despite York's arrest. Even with York in jail, the Nuwaubians proceeded with plans to start a bookstore in Athens. In October 2002, the Putnam County Grand Jury raised the number of counts to 208 in the indictment, and York pleaded not guilty to all of the charges. After the trial was moved to Newton County, Nuwaubian members distributed flyers hoping that York would get a fair trial.

As the court proceedings took a downturn, York refused to let the court officials say his name during the trial. York said he was "secured" and would not give permission. Nuwaubians gave members of the media a "copyright notice" (stamped with "Received, Jan. 08, 2003" by the "Clerk of Federal Moorish Cherokee Consular Court, USA") that York's name and aliases could not be used without permission and stated that there would be financial penalties for "unauthorized" use of his name. The judge denied a series of motions from York to move and postpone the trial and to allow defense psychiatrists to interview the prosecution's witnesses. York's seeming retreat to secrecy regarding his name, rather than silencing the movement, allowed his followers to once again lay claim to the land based on their ancestry.

As York pleaded guilty to some of the charges as a part of a plea agreement in 2003, the UNNM seemed to be in its last days of existence. However, by mediating their relationship with the government, as they had with the media and other critics, the UNNM transformed the guilty plea into a larger eschatological battle between good and evil. The history of racial discrimination in

America coupled with their own sacred narrative claiming sovereignty allowed the UNNM to once again position York as the victim of a larger conspiracy. Even after his guilty plea, York is estimated to have received twenty to thirty letters a day. In June 2003, after U.S. District Judge Hugh Lawson denied his plea agreement, York claimed immunity as a sovereign Indian chief and held that he was not subject to federal law. He self-identified as "Chief Black Eagle" of the "Yamassee" tribe. In July 2003, York argued that he was under duress when he pleaded guilty to charges in January.

As the legal maneuvering continued, the UNNM refused to go away quietly. After a request by the defense attorney, Judge Lawson recused himself during intense plea negotiations and jousting over the need for a psychological evaluation of York and was replaced by U.S. District Court Judge C. Ashley Royal. The U.S. Attorney's office in Macon filed a civil suit seeking the forfeiture of money and property from York. Former members described the years of abuse they experienced. Although three members were linked to a fraudulent check scheme to buy two homes to relocate the community, the UNNM filed a billion-dollar common law suit over the mistreatment of York, leading to the withdrawal of his guilty plea. After the trial was moved to Brunswick, York filed a lawsuit alleging that he had been kidnapped and tortured since his arrest in 2002, including the denial of medication and "coercive sexual conduct." Judge Royal closed the courtroom to everyone but the media and the parties involved in the case, and he prohibited York's supporters from demonstrating outside of the courthouse. Throughout the trial in 2004, testimony by prosecution witnesses described the alleged abuse, while York's defense consistently claimed bias by the judge.

At the conclusion of the trial many "outsiders" to the community claimed victory and some UNNM members took to the defense of

York. One theory that had been circulated was that Judge Royal "hates" Nuwaubians, because his great-great-great-grandfather was a Confederate soldier who fought the Creek Indians. Some members defended York. Five women denied that York abused them. A mother and brother testified that they doubted the girls' testimonies. Testimony revealed that York made $850,000 from 1996 to 2001. Children testified that they sometimes worked twelve-hour days, packing soap and incense without pay. Leah Mabry, the daughter of York, testified that her brother made up the story to frame York. York was found guilty of ten of eleven child molestation and racketeering charges. Testimony alleged that if the girls pleased York, they would get rewards like diamond rings from Walmart or trips to restaurants. If they displeased him, they would be forced to live on rationed food and denied necessities like doctors' visits. In their defense of the community, Nuwaubians distributed flyers that compared the raid by federal agents to the situation in Waco, but stated, "We don't give interviews."

After York's conviction and sentencing to 135 years, the group underwent another transformation. The identity as the Yamassee Native American Moors of the Creek Nation became prominent, and they continued to claim the right to issue their own official documents. York is currently known as Chief Black Eagle. The dress of the group has also embraced Native American traditions. At the time of the initial conflicts in 1999, many members wore clerical robes and ancient Egyptian headdresses. Some women shaved their heads and had a single braid on the right side in respect for Mother Nature.

In the midst of crisis, followers looked for any signs of hope. Some pointed to a videotape in which an accuser seemed to recant her testimony and admit that she was coerced by York's son. Seven Macon police officers, an officer in training, and a firefighter, who supported York, resigned their positions in protest shortly after the conviction. One woman recanted her testimony, which prompted York's attorney to seek a new trial. Two people associated with the Nuwaubians were disqualified for running for sheriff of Putnam County. Initially, the Nuwaubians were allowed to maintain control of the land, until the court decided whether to grant York a new trial. Seven people sued Sheriff Sills, saying that he was slow to act to save their children from molestation.

By July 2004, things truly looked bleak. Judge Royal issued an order that allowed federal officials to seize the $1.7 million in property, which led to most of the Nuwaubians leaving the village. The government put the property up for sale. The witness who recanted her testimony said she had only done so out of concern for York. Judge Royal denied York's request for a new trial. The presence of the Nuwaubians in Eatonton has clearly declined, but the website remains vigilant, posting notices defending the community. Two hundred supporters rallied outside the courthouse in Atlanta because York's attorney filed the appeal.[12] From their arrival in Eatonton, the Nuwaubians have spent enormous effort and resources attempting to correct the record—a process, it seems, that has no clear end.

For some observers, the allegations and apparent downfall of the Nuwaubians confirm that it was a "cult" and, but for the efforts of the authorities, would have assumed its rightful place in the lineage of troublesome movements that ended in tragedy. Indeed, to make the case for a fair and unbiased approach to NRMs, the Nuwaubians seem one of the least likely communities to invoke to make the case. In their ideology, the Nuwaubians demonstrated both a malleability

---

12. Gary Tanner, "Judge Oks Seizure of Nuwaubian Property," *Macon Telegraph*, 14 July, 2004; Susan Palmer, *The Nuwaubian Nation: Black Spirituality and State Control* (Burlington, VT: Ashgate, 2010).

of beliefs and practices that allowed them to attract different constituencies and provide a sense of distinctiveness when compared with the "world." This strategy that worked to greater and lesser extents with the nineteenth-century movements, such as the Latter-Day Saints, the Oneida Community, and the Shakers, faced additional obstacles in the information age.

The positions of the people involved were also fluid. At any particular moment, the participants in the conflict laid claim to the role of victim, labeled the "other" as persecutor, and read evidence through a lens that supported their stance. Both the residents of Eatonton and the Nuwaubians argued that their rights were being infringed upon and felt they were demonized in the press. Although resisting the categorization as a "cult," the Nuwaubians compared their treatment by the authorities to the federal action at Waco. York espoused patriotism to America and simultaneously speculated about governmental conspiracies against the community. It is in the interplay between the charges of residents, officials, and the defense of the Nuwaubians that we glimpse something of how each imagined the contours of normative religion in America. It is in the vehemence with which each party denounced the other in the media that we learn, not so much about the Nuwaubians' beliefs and practices, but the outlines and paradoxes of the Americanization process in the early twenty-first century that places newer communities in a no-win situation. Although privacy can cause suspicion, as the Nuwaubians demonstrate, having a public presence can be equally agitating to the larger community.

In their struggle to remain in Eatonton, the Nuwaubians navigated the challenging position between maintaining distinctiveness and embracing assimilation. If they had abandoned the Egyptian motif, allowed local law enforcement to exercise authority, or made their private knowledge public, they would have lost the sense of specialness that bound them together. Privacy was their best weapon to combat public misunderstandings. Portrayed as invaders, they focused on their persecuted status; defined as "outsiders," they said they were the original Americans; and concerned about their racial and religious identity, they looked to an ancient supernatural past. In the study of religion there is the cliché that teachers should strive to "make the strange familiar, and the familiar strange." Although the veracity of the charges and future of the group remain in doubt, the Nuwaubians present perhaps the most compelling contemporary example of an NRM that embraced its "strangeness" and sought to make it "familiar."

Contemporary New Religious Movements

Other groups eschewed the label of an official religion and instead understood themselves as "spiritual" communities. Your Black Muslim Bakery was founded by Yusuf Bey in 1968. Born Joseph Stephens, influenced by the Moorish Science Temple and the Nation of Islam, he took the name Yusuf Ali Bey. Through his bakery, Bey sought to give African Americans in northern California moral responsibility and provide healthy food to the community. Over time, Your Black Muslim Bakery became the most visible black Muslim institution. Bey took the teachings of Nation of Islam leader Elijah Muhammad and melded them into a message that resonated with African Americans in the San Francisco Bay Area. YBMB advocated a strict dietary code, offered spiritual guidance courses and lectures, and sponsored natural healing centers. In addition, Your Black Muslim Bakery established a number of businesses, as well as community programs focusing on spreading an anti-drug message, creating work programs for recently released prisoners, and providing economic assistance for the poor. At its height, Your Black Muslim Bakery was a multi-million dollar business and a major religious and political power in Oakland. Bey won contracts to sell his preservative-free pies and goods at many venues, and his enterprise eventually grew into an empire that included several stores, a security company, dry cleaners, a school, and other properties.

Yet, as with other new religious movements, accusations of wrongdoing were alleged. Toward the end of his life, Bey was accused of relationships with young girls associated with the bakery that resulted in pregnancies. In 2002, Bey was arrested on twenty-seven counts of abusing children. After Yusuf Ali Bey's death, Yusuf Bey IV emerged from a series of power struggles to take the leadership of the organization. Bey IV was accused of ordering his followers to vandalize two Oakland stores for selling liquor. On August 2, 2007, Chauncey Bailey, the editor of the *Oakland Post* (a small weekly newspaper in Oakland, California) who had been working on a story on the community, was shot and killed on his way to work. Yusuf Bey IV was convicted of three counts of first-degree murder for ordering the 2007 slayings of Bailey and two other men. A second defendant, former bakery associate Antoine Mackey, was convicted of two counts of first-degree murder for the deaths of Bailey and Michael Wills. Devaughndre Broussard reached a plea bargain with prosecutors and testified against Bey IV, saying the leader of the black empowerment group wanted Bailey dead because the *Oakland Post* editor was working on unflattering stories about the bakery's financial problems and internal turmoil. In exchange for testifying, Broussard was sentenced to twenty-five years in prison. This is another example of a black new religious movement whose beginnings could not have foretold the trajectory of its future.

Today's hip-hop culture is informed by the legacy of black religious movements and leaders of the 1960s such as Clarence 13X, a former Nation of Islam minister, who formulated the "Five Percenter" theology. While scholars have speculated that a theological dispute or an inability to live by the NOI code of conduct led to his expulsion, the exact nature of the conflict remains unclear. In 1967, Clarence 13X established a school in Harlem that taught what he called "Five Percenter" theology. Despite his break from the NOI, Clarence 13X maintained much of the organization's instructional format. Rather than emphasizing reading and writing, teachers at the institution focused on instilling oratorical skills through question and answer sessions. The NOI has a series of introductory lessons, including such elements as the population figures for various ethnic groups around the world, the size of the earth, and the origins of the first human beings. Upon successful completion, new members are allowed to replace their "slave name" with the letter X, representing the unknown family name of their African lineage. In some cases, as members mastered higher levels of knowledge, they could petition Elijah Muhammad for an "original" designation. Five Percenter lesson plans are similar, but unfold in a different sequence and contain additional content, including Clarence 13X's *Science of Supreme Mathematics* and *Supreme Alphabet*. Underlying this system is a belief that numbers are imbued with a symbolic significance. According to Clarence 13X, to understand why life in America has historically been so oppressive for many African Americans simply required the mathematical knowledge that revealed the true meaning of names and ages as well as the hidden connections between life's events, one's relationship to the universe, and the links between the natural and supernatural realms. Once male and female members, referred to as "Gods and Earths," commit the meanings of specific numbers to memory, they are able to evaluate the validity of facts and ideas that are presented to them. For example, one might analyze the date 1964 by "ciphering" the meanings of the numbers: (1=knowledge, 9=born, 6=equality, 4=culture) to "show and prove" that in 1964 Clarence 13X demonstrated that God was a black man. Clarence was killed by gunshots on June 12, 1969.

The Five Percenters draw their organization's name from one "Lost-Found" Lesson of the Nation of Islam. From their perspective, 85 percent of the world consists of "uncivilized" people who live apart from God. Ten percent are wealthy and manipulate and oppress the poor, and the 5 percent are "the poor righteous teachers who do not believe in the teachings of the ten percent and are all-wise and know who the Living God is and teach that the Living God is the Son of Man, the Supreme Being, or the Black Man of Asia, and teach Freedom, Justice and Equality to all the human family of the planet Earth; otherwise known as civilized people, also as Muslims and Muslim Sons." Five Percenters wholeheartedly embrace the mission to bring the 95 percent to a knowledge of their true self and "civilize the uncivilized."

Five Percenter theology has spoken to social and political tension and unrest in the United States and was an important component of a burgeoning Hip-Hop culture. From 1964 to 1967, hundreds of riots and demonstrations took place across the country, from Watts to Chicago and New York. On the heels of these tensions, in New York City, a new musical genre and culture, Hip-Hop, emerged as the voice of a generation who found their experiences reflected in the lyrics and beats of new superstars such as DJ Kool Herc. By the late 1970s, rap became a national phenomenon. In 1987, Rakim Allah became the first emcee to openly declare his allegiance to the Five Percenters. However, other groups that embraced the tenets of Farrakhan's Nation of Islam, such as Public Enemy, took their message to a global audience.[13]

While new religious communities rise and dissipate every day,

---

13. Felicia Miyakawa, *Five Percenter Rap: God Hop's Music, Message, and Black Muslim Mission* (Bloomington: Indiana University Press, 2005).

the media and a post-Jonestown public accord special attention to the whereabouts and actions of new religious movements with distinctive beliefs and practices. When authorities intervene and find evidence of "unusual" approaches to religious questions, many Americans breathe easier that another dangerous "cult" has been preempted from joining the lineage of troublesome groups that ended in tragedy. With Jonestown, the Branch Davidians, and Heaven's Gate as templates, most NRMs are presumed guilty until proven innocent. With news coverage providing footage and photographs of past "cult behavior" that resulted in mass suicide in reference to your community, with websites devoted to establishing that your religion is a "cult," and where science seems to fly in the face of sacred narratives, few contemporary religious communities are given the opportunity to be understood on their own terms or move from the margins to the mainstream.

Yet, as in mainstream traditions, some NRMs also engage in troubling behaviors. Malachi Z. York, the leader of the United Nuwaubian Nation of Moors, was sentenced to 135 years in prison for improprieties with children in 2004. Rape charges were filed against Yusuf Bey, and the murder of a newspaper editor believed to be working on an investigative story on the finances of the Your Black Muslim Bakery made national headlines. In each instance, the leaders and their followers have maintained their innocence. As in mainline traditions, pedophilia, abuse, and scandal occur in new religious movements, but misdeeds in the former are often presumed to be the exception, while believed to be the rule in the latter.

Yet, the plight of many new religious movements, it seems, has less to do with their ability to respond to specific charges than it does with the dilemma of being labeled a "cult." How does a community prove that they are not a cult? The term cult—at once elusive and seemingly self-explanatory—allows the apologetic process to go on for perpetuity. There is too much at stake in the self-identity of the "mainstream" to acknowledge that the work ethic of the Nation of Islam is possibly not so different from the ambitions of the Puritans or the early Christian church. Even further, the same proof invoked to dispel rumors often fueled negative stereotypes. Rather than evidence of Father Divine's godly power, the death of the judge shortly after sentencing him to prison is a mere coincidence; rather than a devout community waiting for the advent of a supernatural spiritual event, the Nuwaubians are understood as "Space Invaders" or UFO-hunters; and rather than a belief in a sacred doctrine, black youth are presumed to be drawn to Clarence 13X's *Science of Supreme Mathematics* and *Supreme Alphabet* because of feeling disenfranchised or angry at the American system.

African American new religious movements will have to face both the obstacles that have plagued burgeoning religions in the past as well as new challenges in the future. With twenty-four-hour news cycles reporting on and constructing stories, and a skeptical audience all too willing to believe the worst, the evidence mustered to establish cult behavior is not static. The notion that "I know a cult when I see it" masks the complicated and constantly shifting grounds on which identity is questioned, constructed, and rehabilitated. Black NRMs have walked the line between maintaining their distinctiveness and embracing assimilation. If new religious traditions maintain beliefs and practices that diverge from the mainstream, they open themselves up to the range of charges of wrongdoing associated with "cult behavior." If they abandon the vision that initially brought the group together to be accepted more broadly or allow their sacred knowledge to become public, they may lose the sense of specialness that binds them together. This dilemma between maintaining authenticity while also surviving as a minority religion in America is a challenge that will likely continue well into the twenty-first century.

6

The Contemporary Scene

The Great Migration also extended westward to larger cities such as Los Angeles, California, which, in 1906, witnessed what believers would testify to as an unprecedented movement of the Holy Spirit during the Azusa Street Revival. At the time, observers suggested a number of metaphors for the phenomenon that swept through the region, but posterity would settle upon the "burned over district" to describe the wake of the spiritual movement that blazed through the city.

Pentecostalism

There were a number of factors that coincided to "spark" this revival atmosphere. The migration of southern African Americans westward, for the most part, like those who relocated northward, met unanticipated racism and difficult socioeconomic conditions upon their arrival in the West. They also constituted a sizable new population seeking a church home. Many studies speculate about the African American attraction to Pentecostalism. Some suggest that, of the Christian denominations, the Holiness–Pentecostal revival meetings most closely approximated the essence of slave religion and traditional southern worship and preaching styles. Rituals such as healing through the laying on of hands could have resonated with the practice of root work and conjure during slavery. The Pentecostal belief that a disciplined and sanctified life would lead to holiness and perfection likely offered order to lives that were beset with turmoil in a new and strange urban setting. Even further, some have concluded that the rise and popularity of Holiness-Pentecostal movements among poor African Americans was partly attributable to their need to escape from their earthly lives through the cathartic expression of emotional and exuberant worship. Yet, if these functional descriptions of religion are pressed too far, one can invalidate the real power and lasting meaning that the Azusa Street Revival brought to the lives of participants.

The origins of modern Pentecostalism occurred a few years earlier, prior to the Azusa Street Revival, on the precipice of the twentieth century. Charles Fox Parham, the founder of the Bethel Bible School in Topeka, Kansas, laid his hands upon one of his students, Agnes Ozman, to pray for her. Afterwards, according to witnesses, Ozman spoke solely in Chinese, a language with which she was previously unfamiliar, for three straight days. This marks the beginning of contemporary Pentecostalism. While a number of Christian traditions had practiced glossolalia as one of the gifts of the Holy Spirit, for example, the Holiness Movement, which separated from Methodism in the late nineteenth century, it was Parham who most adamantly made the case that speaking in tongues was the only acceptable evidence of baptism in the Holy Spirit.

One of Parham's students, William J. Seymour, brought this emphasis on glossolalia with him to the Nazarene Church in Los Angeles. His commitment to the centrality of speaking in tongues eventually caused him to be expelled from the congregation. Not long after that, Seymour, along with two former classmates from Parham's school, Lucy Farrow and J. A. Warren, began holding meetings in an abandoned Methodist church at 312 Azusa Street in Los Angeles. This would be the site of a three-year-long revival that witnessed ecstatic, charismatic experiences, speaking in tongues, and prophecy. Newspapers were captivated by the phenomenon, which drew steadily larger crowds to the meetings at the Azusa Street Mission. By late summer, gatherings regularly swelled to over twelve hundred participants. A devastating earthquake in San Francisco in April 1906 fueled the expectation that Jesus' return and the ascension of the saved to heaven was close at hand. By the end of the first year, nine Pentecostal congregations had been founded in southern California.

While Pentecostalism began as an interracial movement, the tradition has not been immune from racial tensions and schisms. Charles H. Mason founded the first legally established Pentecostal denomination, the Church of God in Christ, in Memphis, Tennessee, that ordained both white and black preachers. However, in 1914, a white exodus occurred from Mason's congregation to the Assemblies of God Church founded in Hot Springs, Arkansas. In 1916, the Assemblies of God separated into two organizations. One maintained the view that the Trinity (the Father, the Son, and the Holy Spirit) was three persons in one, while the "oneness" Pentecostals believed that all of God's blessings were bestowed upon individuals through baptism in the name of Jesus only. The latter community reorganized under the Pentecostal Assemblies of the World, but would soon also divide along racial lines as a group of white ministers left to form the United Pentecostal Church. The denomination would remain racially segregated for much of the twentieth century.

From its beginnings, women played a central role in the growth and organization of Pentecostalism. Most notably, Aimee Semple McPherson employed an innovative use of technology to spread her message. In 1918, McPherson began a revival in Los Angeles that attracted not only Pentecostals, but a wide range of evangelical Christians who came out to hear her simple and direct message, receive healing, feel the presence of the Holy Spirit, or simply be a part of the electricity she had brought to the city. McPherson emphasized that God's power could be experienced in the here and now. Her Lighthouse of International Foursquare Evangelism Bible College has trained thousands of ministers, leaving a lasting impression on Pentecostalism and American Evangelism. However, her use of radio to reach her followers in their homes throughout the day and night sets her apart as the first preacher to employ the medium as an evangelistic tool. In many ways, McPherson's life and career foreshadowed future media stars in the Pentecostal tradition. Following World War II, healing revivalism reemerged on the national scene as a number of non denominational ministries and parachurch organizations banded together to hold large protracted meetings to bring new converts into the fold. These events spawned the televangelist who brought a distinctive speaking style, fundraising methods, and a new charisma to the worship service. In the 1960s, this revival atmosphere birthed the charismatic movement. This "second wave" of Pentecostalism slowly gained increased acceptance in "mainstream" Christian churches just as conservative Evangelicals were becoming more influential in American society and politics.[1]

Spiritual Churches

In the early twentieth century, African American spiritual churches also grew in greater numbers. These communities embraced what

---

1. Gaston Espinosa, *William J. Seymour and the Origins of Global Pentecostalism: A Biography and Documentary History* (Durham, NC: Duke University Press, 2014); Matthew Avery Sutton, *Aimee Semple McPherson and the Resurrection of Christian America* (Cambridge, MA: Harvard University Press, 2009).

Hans Baer called "the manipulation of one's present condition through magico-religious rituals and esoteric knowledge." While many African American churches recognize the supernatural, spiritual churches employ methods, beliefs, and practices to harness that power in ways that many mainline black denominations, including some Pentecostal communities, would frown upon as superstition, witchcraft, or Voodoo. Scriptural recitations meant to impact one's finances, health, and relationships; blessing services that contact those who have passed away; and the use of mediums, healers, and advisors to discern spiritual causes of disorders or physical problems are all practices that would distinguish spiritual churches from other black churches. This concern about the perception of outsiders has led some formerly spiritual churches to embrace the term holiness to distance themselves from the negative connotations sometimes ascribed to spiritualism.

Examples of spiritual churches abound in African American religious history. Louis Herbert Narcisse founded the Mt. Zion Spiritual Temple in Oakland. From a small prayer meeting, the community grew to a congregation with a successful radio program, "Moments of Meditation," with over a million listeners, several records, and churches in Sacramento, Detroit, Houston, New Orleans, and Orlando. Although following a number of Baptist traditions, the communities also burned incense at home to dispel evil spirits and employed blessed oils and waters. Worship often included shouting and dancing in the aisles. Narcisse sat on a throne during services and at times drank from a golden goblet. In 1955, he was given the title "His Grace, the King of the Spiritual Church of the West Coast." Narcisse was known for his flamboyant style, wearing a crown, diamond rings, and jewelry, riding in expensive cars, and having a red carpet rolled out for him wherever he went. He lived in a large house in Oakland that was called "The Light on the Hill" and received followers in the "throne room." In a similar vein, known as a healer and "the Prophet," James F. Jones founded the Church of Universal Triumph/the Dominion of God. The community had very strict rules that included no smoking, drinking, playing games, attending other churches, or marrying without Jones's consent. Women were required to wear girdles and men to wear health belts. Like Narcisse, Jones was known for his lavish lifestyle that included a large home, cars, expensive clothing, furniture, and jewelry. He established the first community "thankful center" in 1945. Father George Willie Hurley founded the Universal Hagar's Spiritual Church in 1923. Prior to creating his own community, Hurley had a Baptist and Methodist background and eventually joined the Triumph the Church and Kingdom of God in Christ and became a minister in the National Spiritual Church. A year later he founded the School of Mediumship and Psychology and also established the Knights of the All Seeing Eye. By the time of his death in 1943 he had congregations in Michigan, Ohio, Pennsylvania, New Jersey, New York, West Virginia, Delaware, and Illinois.

Women often led spiritual churches. Mother Leafy Anderson established the Eternal Life Christian Spiritualist Church in Chicago in 1913 and the Eternal Life Spiritualist Church in the Crescent City around 1920 in New Orleans. Anderson's community attracted blacks and poor whites. She discipled leaders who led other congregations in New Orleans, Chicago, Little Rock, Memphis, Pensacola, Biloxi, and Houston as well as smaller towns. While Anderson was reticent to embrace such practices, many of her communities were the first to include elements of Voodoo and Catholicism in their services. Mother Catherine Seals founded spiritual churches in New Orleans such as the Temple of Innocent Blood, which included the use of the sign of the cross, candles, pictures, altars, and statues of saints. These were just a few of the many women who founded spiritual churches, including Mother C. J. Hyde's St. James Temple of the Christian Faith, Mother L. Crosier's Church of the Helping Hand and Spiritual Faith, and Mother E. Keller's St. James Temple of Christian Faith No. 2.

The growth of the black population in urban areas and the invention of new forms of communication and entertainment media such as radio and records spread black religious culture to ever-increasing audiences. From the 1920s, record companies produced albums of blues and jazz music as well as sermons aimed at black listeners. Baptist preachers A. W. Nix, J. M. Gates, J. C. Burnett, and Pentecostal preachers F. W. McGee and D. C. Rice gradually gained in popularity. Radio stations played black church services and sheet music of gospel songs were sold to black choirs. Some argued that this music was too secular and sounded too much like the blues, but they gradually gained acceptance. Thomas Dorsey emerged as one of the most influential gospel composers, penning popular songs such as "Precious Lord." He organized an annual convention of gospel singers that brought gospel choirs from across the country to Chicago and his songs were sung by the most popular gospel singers of the time such as Mahalia Jackson.

In the 1920s and 1930s, record companies such as Paramount, Victor, Okeh, and Columbia marketed recordings of sermons and music from southern religion to a burgeoning black middle class at the same time that storefront churches in northern urban areas began to emerge. This was a departure from the more formalized productions of the Fisk Jubilee Singers. The first preachers recorded on major labels included Reverend Calvin P. Dixon in 1925 and Reverend A. W. Nix of Birmingham, Alabama. These decades also saw the rise of religious radio preachers such as Elder Solomon Lightfoot Michaux, Mother Rosa Artimus Horn, and Reverend

Clarence LaVaughn Franklin, who took to the airwaves with their evangelizing message.[2]

The Civil Rights Movement

Religion, politics, and social reform would also come together in the nascent civil rights movement. The Montgomery bus boycott from December 5, 1955, to December 20, 1956, was organized by the Montgomery Improvement Association. Although a boycott had been discussed within the organization for months, on December 1, 1955, Rosa Parks refused to give up her seat on the bus to a white man, even after being ordered to do so by the bus driver. While the spontaneity of Parks's action is often emphasized, it was hardly a coincidence that she, a longtime NAACP activist, would play a central role in catalyzing the formation of the MIA and spark the broader civil rights movement of the 1960s. Unlike the NAACP headquartered in New York, the MIA was primarily made up of local leaders and members focused on the improvement of the conditions facing black communities in Alabama without directly challenging Jim Crow segregation. The MIA organized alternative modes of transportation for those who regularly rode the bus by purchasing vehicles and organizing car pools. In 1956, having suffered through harassment by authorities and several failed negotiations with the city and bus company, with the help of NAACP lawyers, the MIA challenged the legality of bus segregation. That same year, the United States Supreme Court affirmed an earlier decision in the case of *Browder v. Gayle*, voiding Alabama's bus segregation laws. On

---

2. Hans A. Baer, *The Black Spiritual Movement: A Religious Response to Racism* (Knoxville: University of Tennessee Press, 2001); Jonathan L. Walton, *Watch This! The Ethics and Aesthetics of Black Televangelism* (New York: New York University Press, 2009); Lerone A. Martin, *Preaching on Wax: The Phonograph and the Shaping of Modern African American Religion* (New York: New York University Press, 2014).

December 21, 1956, African Americans could sit on any available seat in the public bus system.

While technically a secular movement and organization, the MIA had religious elements interwoven into every aspect of its operations. Black ministers from a variety of denominations assumed leadership roles, made up the majority of its executive board, and wielded a strong influence in strategic planning. There were a number of reasons for this. Ministers, supported by their congregations, were less vulnerable to the retaliation of white employers for involvement in the movement. African Americans pressed their ministers, as leaders in the community, to come to the fore in advocating on their behalf. As was seen in slave religion, ministers, to a greater or lesser extent, have regularly functioned as mediators between the spiritual and material concerns of their followers. The boundaries of the sacred and secular were also blurred in the weekly meetings of the organization that were held in black churches and opened with prayers, hymns, and inspirational speeches often delivered by ministers. With the start of the Montgomery bus boycott, the MIA would thrust a young black preacher, Martin Luther King Jr., into the national spotlight as its spokesperson.

The MIA inspired and laid the groundwork for the Southern Christian Leadership Conference (SCLC), which would provide a central impetus for the civil rights movement from 1957 to 1968. Using the MIA model as a blueprint, sixty black civil rights activists met at King's Ebenezer Baptist Church in Atlanta, Georgia, from January 10th to 11th, 1957, hoping to draw upon and develop the principles that had desegregated the bus system and implement them on a broader scale. In addition to southern leadership, three activists from New York, Bayard Rustin, executive director of the War Resisters League, Ella Baker, who had directed a number of branches of the NAACP, and Stanley Levison, an attorney and businessman, were also key members of the early leadership of the SCLC. Rustin, in particular, became a key advisor for King as he sorted through his thinking about nonviolent resistance and was central in persuading King to head the new organization. However, a number of ministers participated in getting the fledgling organization off the ground, including C. K. Steele, Joseph E. Lowery, Fred L. Shuttlesworth, and Ralph D. Albernathy. Like the MIA, the SCLC had a number of religious overtones including its motto, "To Redeem the Soul of America." The early years of the SCLC were trying times for the organization. However, King was able to meet with Vice President Richard Nixon in 1957 and President Dwight Eisenhower in 1958. The student sit-in movement of 1960, the Freedom Rides of 1961, and the formation of the Student Nonviolent Coordinating Committee (SNCC) rejuvenated the SCLC. In 1963, the protests in Birmingham, Alabama, brought the civil rights movement to the attention of the national media by overflowing prisons with arrested peaceful protestors, many of whom were children. Images of young African American men and women being sprayed with fire hoses, beaten with batons, and bitten by police dogs appeared on the television screens of Americans across the country, awakening a national consciousness and debate about civil rights.

In 1963, King invited C. T. Vivian to join the executive staff of the SCLC as the director of affiliates. Vivian had participated in a lunch counter sit-in in 1947 in Peoria, Illinois and, in 1959, moved to Nashville, Tennessee to study for the ministry at American Baptist College where he became acquainted with James Lawson and the nonviolent direct-action strategies of the Nashville Student Movement. In early 1960, Vivian joined Diane Nash, James Forman, John Lewis, and other students from local universities as they staged sit-ins and other nonviolent protests throughout the city. In 1961, Vivian was among the ten Nashville students who replaced injured

Freedom Ride participants. As the director of affiliates, Vivian coordinated the activities of local civil rights groups nationwide. He also advised King and organized demonstrations during campaigns in Birmingham, St. Augustine, and Selma. In 1966, Vivian left the SCLC and moved to Chicago to direct the Urban Training Center for Christian Mission and the Coalition for United Community Action. He later founded the Black Strategies and Information Center, the National Center for Human Rights Education, and the Center for Democratic Renewal.

The success of the Birmingham demonstrations led to the "long hot summer" of protests across the United States, which eventually led to the 1964 Civil Rights Act, signed into law by Lyndon Johnson, which did away with segregation in public accommodations, banned employment discrimination, and authorized the federal government to enforce school integration. The same year, King received the Nobel Peace Prize and was named *Time* magazine's "Man of the Year." Yet, King was the first to acknowledge that the civil rights movement was not carried on his shoulders alone and would not have been possible without leaders in the SCLC like Fred L. Shuttlesworth, staff members such as Wyatt Walker, James Bevel, Andrew Young, and Dorothy Cotton, as well as the sacrifices of countless men, women, and children whose names may never be known in the historical record, but who marched, went to jail, were beaten, sprayed with fire hoses, bitten by dogs, and killed so that future generations of African Americans would have access to the promised American dream.

Martin Luther King Jr.'s outlook and approach evolved with the trajectory of the civil rights movement. Born in Atlanta in 1929, the son and grandson of Baptist preachers, King would master an oratorical style with tones and inflections that were reminiscent of the earliest slave preachers. Influenced by Walter Rauschenbusch's writings on the Social Gospel and Gandhi's theories of nonviolent resistance, King gave sermons and speeches that melded symbols of America with biblical imagery to awaken the country's conscience and hold America up to its constitutional ideals. In many ways, King was a reluctant hero who went south to live a quiet life as pastor of the Dexter Avenue Baptist Church in Montgomery, Alabama, after finishing graduate school in 1954. However, his leadership of the Montgomery bus boycott beginning in 1955, his organization of the SCLC, and marches on Selma and Washington, D.C. that led to the passage of key civil rights legislation altered the course of his career and secured his legacy as the central figure of the civil rights movement. Although the lasting image of King is his presence before the Lincoln Monument delivering his "I Have a Dream" speech, he lived for nearly five years after that poignant moment, speaking out against the Vietnam War as an immoral and senseless expenditure of resources that he felt would have better served to ameliorate poverty and uplift the downtrodden. In fact, King was planning a "Poor People's Campaign" at the time of his assassination on April 4, 1968, in Memphis, Tennessee.

While King's voice was most prominent, there were a variety of black theological perspectives on the civil rights movement. Born in 1899 in Daytona Beach, Florida, Howard Thurman attended Morehouse College, Rochester Theological Seminary, and Haverford College. In 1925, he was ordained a Baptist minister in Ohio where he studied with Quaker pacifist Rufus Jones. In 1932, Thurman joined the faculty of Howard University's School of Religion and became dean of Rankin Chapel, the first African American to be named to such a position in the United States. A 1935 trip to India with other African Americans to meet Gandhi shaped his worldview on nonviolent social activism. In 1944, Thurman relocated to San Francisco to co-pastor the Church for the Fellowship of All Peoples, an interdenominational church that sought to engage issues of race, ethnicity, class, and social justice. In 1953, he became Dean of Boston University's Marsh Chapel. Thurman mentored many young ministers including Martin Luther King Jr. as he developed his philosophy of nonviolent resistance. Thurman was friends with King's father and often visited the King home. Although King saw Thurman as part of an older generation, he carried Thurman's *Jesus and the Disinherited* with him during the Montgomery bus boycott. Published in 1949, the book argues that Jesus taught the oppressed a faith-based, unconditional love that would enable them to endure their oppression. This ideology had a wide-ranging influence on many black ministers including Jesse Jackson. However, Thurman was not on the front lines of the protest against segregation. Instead, he was, at times, criticized for being too distant and otherworldly. For Thurman, change in the world first took place within a person's inner spirit.

In 1954, Martin Luther King Jr. succeeded Vernon Johns as minister of Dexter Avenue Baptist Church. Reverend Johns had a lasting effect on King both personally and professionally. King found an example in Johns, a preacher who was able to use his religious position in the community to challenge his congregation to think broadly about issues of social justice. As Dexter's pastor from 1947 to 1952, Johns was an early proponent of civil rights activity in Montgomery, urging his congregation to challenge the traditional status quo. In response to discrimination on city buses, Johns once disembarked in protest and demanded a refund. He was well known for his controversial sermon topics, such as "It Is Safe to Kill Negroes in Montgomery." His early activism and challenges to the power structure paved the way for Dexter's congregation to receive King's socially active ministry and enabled King to take a leading role in the Montgomery bus boycott. Following his departure from Dexter,

Johns served as the director of the Maryland Baptist Center from 1955 to 1960 and was active in Farm and City Enterprises, Inc., an economic cooperative that enabled farmers to sell their goods directly to the consumer.[3]

Others questioned the effectiveness of nonviolence as a political strategy or philosophy. Minister of the United Church of Christ and pastor of the Shrine of the Black Madonna in Detroit, Rev. Albert B. Cleage Jr. argued that violence while undesirable was necessary for rapid social change to occur. For Cleage, the black church would play a central role in pressing black independence forward to fruition. He believed his own church and congregation modeled the worldview that was to come. Cleage's theology focused on Jesus as the black Messiah who preached a message of racial separation from the Roman Empire, but whose words were misinterpreted by the apostle Paul and subsequent white theologians. A number of other black leaders and organizations also questioned the nonviolent approach and actual gains brought about by the civil rights movement. Perhaps most prominently, the Black Panther Party—founded in 1966 and guided by figures such as Huey P. Newton, Bobby Seale, and Angela Davis—critiqued the effectiveness of the civil rights movement and pressed for immediate equity in housing, employment, education, and civil rights.

Black Theology

The "Black Power" movement elevated questions of black identity and institutional racism, calling for a new "racial consciousness." Concerns over the persistence of racism, despite the activism of the 1960s, swept through black churches across the country. Black liberation theology emerged out of this social and political context.

3. Martin Luther King Jr., *Stride Toward Freedom: The Montgomery Story* (Boston: Beacon Press, 2010); Aldon D. Morris, *Origins of the Civil Rights Movement* (New York: Free Press, 1986).

As the civil rights efforts of the Student Nonviolent Coordinating Committee (SNCC) gained momentum, the National Committee of Negro Churchmen issued a "Black Power" statement on July 31, 1966, in a full-page advertisement in the *New York Times*. This activism led some black clergy in predominantly white denominations to form separate caucuses to address these issues. One such organization, the National Conference for Black Churchmen, established by theologians such as Gayraud Wilmore and James Cone, produced a black liberation theology that emphasized that God was on the side of the oppressed. Even further, they asserted that God's power was most strongly present among the poor and disenfranchised, repositioning Jesus as the liberator of black people. Rather than focus on integration, these black theologians argued, dominant white ideologies needed to be challenged for their complicity in the oppression of people of color.

There were a variety of perspectives on what constituted black liberation theology. James Cone's *Black Theology and Black Power* (1969), *A Black Theology of Liberation* (1970), and *God of the Oppressed* (1975) challenged the unacknowledged white supremacy of white Christianity and its inability to speak to the needs of people of color. He described a theology based on the experiences of African Americans that could speak to their lives and liberate the oppressed. For Cone, black theology centered on the black experience.[4] James Deotis Roberts, in works such as *Liberation and Reconciliation: A Black Theology* and *Quest for a Black Theology*, challenged Cone's paradigm, arguing that black liberation must go hand and hand with reconciliation with whites. Roberts took a comparative approach, analyzing black theology within the context of other liberation theologies. Cecil Cone, James Cone's brother, and Gayraud Wilmore

---

4. James Cone, *Black Theology and Black Power* (New York: Orbis Books, 1997).

argued that black theology was too informed by European theological perspectives. Black theology, from their viewpoint, was a problematic addition to traditional European theological formulations. Both advocated for a more organic approach drawn from African American thought, practice, and intellectual traditions. Wilmore's work pointed toward African practices, beliefs, and aesthetics as powerful sources of black theology. Cecil Cone focused on the protest tradition in African American history as a foundation for black theology. The sentiment was to move from formal training from the dominant culture and toward the development of a theology that emerged from the life experiences and language of African Americans. William Jones in his *Is God a White Racist? A Preamble to Black Theology*, in 1973, challenged the notion of an inherently good and compassionate God that supported the oppressed and their quest for freedom presented by many black theologians. From Jones's reading of history, there was little evidence to support this portrayal given the continued suffering of the oppressed despite the advocacy of an omnipotent God. Jones emphasized human accountability and responsibility for moral evil rather than a focusing on the work of God in this arena. For Joseph Washington, it was assimilation and not separatism that was the appropriate response to the gospel by African Americans.[5]

Womanist Theology affirms the efforts of male theologians to critique white Christianity and to form a distinctive black theology; however, it is also mindful of the sexism that was also a part of the civil rights and Black Power movements and the ways black male hegemony replicates itself in black theology. Many black womanist theologians have asserted that the movements did not go far enough

---

5. William Jones, *Is God a White Racist? A Preamble to Black Theology* (Boston: Beacon Press, 1997); Joseph Washington, *Black Religion: The Negro and Christianity in the United States* (Boston: Beacon Press, 1964).

and have challenged black male clergy for failing to fully acknowledge the contributions and insights of African American women. Scholars such as Katie Cannon, in *Black Womanist Ethics*, and Delores Williams, in *Sisters in the Wilderness*, have analyzed the work of Zora Neale Hurston and the biblical narratives of women such as Hagar for inspiration and exemplars of the ability of women to overcome racism, sexism, poverty, and being "driven into the wilderness" by a patriarchal society.

Many womanist theologians distinguish themselves from feminists, viewing feminism as primarily a white middle-class movement. Drawing on Alice Walker's *In Search of Mother's Gardens: Womanist Prose*, Delores Williams defines womanist theology in an essay titled "Womanist Theology: Black Women's Voices":

> What then is a womanist? Her origins are in the black folk expression "You acting womanish," meaning, according to Walker, 'wanting to know more and in greater depth than is good for one . . . outrageous, audacious, courageous and willful behavior.' A womanist is also "responsible, in charge, serious." She can walk to Canada and take others with her. She loves, she is committed, she is universalist by temperament.[6]

Womanist theologians lift up the heroic qualities of black women and take seriously the roles of women in the black church and in black religious life. They shift the paradigm away from a male-centered narrative of African American religious history. In *Sisters in the Wilderness*, Delores Williams writes,

> The black church is invisible, but we know it when we see it . . . Harriet Tubman leading hundreds of slaves into freedom; Isabel, the former African-American slave, with God's help, transforming destiny

6. Layli Philips, ed., *The Womanist Reader: The First Quarter Century of Feminist Thought* (New York: Routledge, 2006), 117; Delores S. Williams, "Womanist Theology: Black Women's Voice," *Christianity and Crisis* 47 (March 2, 1987).

to become Sojourner Truth, affirming the close relation between God and woman; Mary McLeod Bethune's college starting on a garbage heap with one dollar and fifty cents growing into a multimillion dollar enterprise; Rosa Parks sitting down so Martin Luther King Jr. could stand up.[7]

The Black Power movement also impacted African American Catholics. On April 18, 1968, in Detroit, fifty-eight black Catholic priests held the inaugural meeting of the National Black Catholic Clergy only two weeks after the assassination of Martin Luther King Jr. Despite the commitment to ecumenism espoused by the Pope John XXIII during Vatican Council II (1962–1965), this group of black Catholics, led by priests Herman Porter, George Clements, and Rollins Lambert, formed the National Black Catholic Clergy Caucus to specifically address the growing anger and frustration within the black community over the racial and political climate in America. It called for black leadership training, better opportunities for black clergy, and more resources directed toward black Catholic communities. They also sought to encourage African Americans to enter the priesthood. In 1970, the group was central to the formation of the National Office for Black Catholics, which kept the church abreast of the contributions of African Americans and pushed forward the church's social justice efforts and the creation of the Institute for Black Catholic Studies at Xavier University in New Orleans, the only Black Catholic institution of higher learning. A number of other organizations emerged around the same time, including the National Black Catholic Lay Caucus, the National Black Catholic Seminarian Association, and the National Black Sisters' Conference, which created a network of support for Black Catholic Sisters and sought to improve educational and leadership opportunities and

7. Roger A. Sneed, *Representations of Homosexuality: Black Liberation Theology and Cultural Criticism* (New York: Palgrave Macmillan, 2010), 41–42; Delores S. Williams, *Sisters in the Wilderness: The Challenge of Womanist God-Talk* (New York: Orbis Books, 2013).

strengthen spiritual life. In 1983, the spiritual center Sojourner House in Detroit was founded for Catholic women and as a resource center for Roman Catholic Orders seeking to create new ministries in African American communities.[8]

The writings of Molefi Asante and other African American philosophers asserted that blacks were too often seen as objects that were acted upon in history, but not recognized as exercising any agency of their own. While western history provided ample attention to the "white" viewpoint, Asante argued that it was essential for the "black perspective" to be just as integral to the historical narratives. This philosophy is most clearly articulated in his *Afrocentricity: The Theory of Social Change*. In his work, Asante argues that because "all religions rise out of the deification of someone's nationalism," large portions of the African and African American experience have been obscured by focusing almost exclusively on European American western history. Asante asserted that an African-centered perspective was essential for raising the "consciousness" and instilling race and self-pride in all people of African descent. Asante encapsulated this shift with a concept called Njia, "The Way," which he defined as "the collective expression of the Afrocentric worldview which is grounded in the historical experience of African people." Njia is the "cumulative experience" of African and African American people "expressed concretely in the lives of a small segment." According to Asante, these new levels of knowledge evolved over time in black thinkers such as Booker T. Washington, Marcus Garvey, Elijah Muhammad, Martin Luther King Jr., Malcolm X, and W. E. B. Du Bois.[9]

---

8. Cyprian Davis, *The History of Black Catholics in the United States* (New York: Crossroad, 1995).

9. Kostas Myrsiades et al., *Race-ing Representation: Voice, History, and Representation* (Lanham, MD: Rowman and Littlefield, 1997), 26; Molefi Kete Asante, *Afrocentricity: The Theory of Social Change* (Chicago: African American Images, 2003).

The late 1960s witnessed other movements that emphasized the importance of African and African American history in the United States. Students advocated for greater representation of people of color in the faculty and curriculums of colleges across the country. One product of this movement was the creation of black studies programs in many American universities. Maulana Karenga, a professor at California State University at Long Beach, created a secular holiday in 1966, Kwanzaa, which is Swahili for "first fruits." The seven principles of Kwanzaa known as Nguzo Saba include: umoja (unity), kujichagulia (self-determination), ujima (collective work and responsibility), ujamaa (cooperative economics), nia (purpose), kuumba (creativity), and imani (faith). It is estimated that over twenty million people of African descent celebrate the harvest festival worldwide.[10]

The Nation of Islam

In the last quarter of the twentieth century, there were substantial changes in African American new religious movements. Just before his death on February 25, 1975, Elijah Muhammad bestowed the mantle of leadership upon his fifth son, Wallace Deen Muhammad. This was a somewhat surprising choice because Wallace Deen had been disciplined during his time with the NOI and seemed to be ambivalent about the mission of the movement. Shortly after being appointed as Chief Minister of the Nation of Islam, Wallace Deen sought to bring the beliefs and practices of the organization into alignment with orthodox Islam and the global Muslim community. Notions of black superiority and the demonization of whites were stricken from the theology, the color ban was lifted, and potential members of all races and ethnicities were invited to join the

---

10. Maulana Ron Karenga, *The Kwanzaa* (Los Angeles: University of Sankore Press, 1997).

movement. Wallace Deen dismantled the Fruit of Islam security force, emphasized patriotism, proudly displayed American flags at every NOI mosque and school, and encouraged military service and active participation in the American political process. Many high-ranking officials who failed to reject the theologies of the past were demoted or reassigned. In October 1976, the NOI became "The World Community of Al-Islam in the West" (WCI) and in 1980 it was renamed "The American Muslim Mission." At the same time, Wallace changed his own name to Warith Deen Muhammad, in part to distance himself from Wallace Fard and his legacy in the earlier iteration of the Nation of Islam.

For others, Warith Deen Muhammad's leadership represented "the fall" of the Nation of Islam. Born Louis Eugene Walcott in May 11, 1933, Minister Louis Farrakhan had taken over for Malcolm X as the minister of Harlem Temple No. 7 after his assassination in 1964. In 1972, Farrakhan successfully mediated a public dispute between the New York Police Department and black Harlem residents, which gained him newfound respect and authority in the NOI movement. At the time of Elijah Muhammad's illness, Farrakhan was widely speculated to be the frontrunner to be his successor. After suffering the disappointment, he fell in line under the new leadership. However, in the late 1970s, Farrakhan gathered those who felt abandoned by the new version of the NOI led by Warith Deen Muhammad and relocated his headquarters to Chicago. In 1979, Farrakhan's NOI published a new newspaper called the *Final Call*. In 1981, the reconstituted NOI held its first national convention. Among the changes that Farrakhan instituted was the deification of Elijah Muhammad, which was signified by the addition of another Saviour's Day. Today, the NOI celebrates the births of both Fard on February 26 and Elijah Muhammad on October 7 as sacred days.

Farrakhan rebuilt the NOI, strengthened its membership, and his oratorical ability and frank speaking style have made the organization one of the most prominent and controversial black religious organizations. On October 16, 1995, Farrakhan organized a "Holy Day of Atonement and Reconciliation" on the Washington Mall that was attended by hundreds of thousands of African Americans. This "Million Man March" was designed to encourage black men to be good fathers, husbands, and involved citizens in their communities. For all of the charitable work and social programs sponsored by the NOI, the publicity has not always been positive. Farrakhan has been accused of making anti-Semitic statements. Just weeks before the gathering in Washington, D.C., Farrakhan had denounced the behaviors of white Americans and been quoted as calling Jews "bloodsuckers." In 1985, he received great media attention for calling Judaism a "dirty religion" and Hitler "a very great man." In 1991, the Historical Research Department of the NOI published *The Secret Relationship Between Blacks and Jews*, which characterized Jews as playing a central role in the Atlantic slave trade, which was sharply refuted by the Jewish community and whose methodologies were challenged by a wide range of scholars. Often cast as a "hate group" in popular culture, *Time* magazine's February 28, 1994, cover declared Louis Farrakhan and the Nation of Islam a "Ministry of Rage," and the organization has often been cast as a "hate group" in popular culture. Farrakhan has continued to have a tenuous relationship with the broader Muslim community, conflicts with Elijah Muhammad's successor and son, Wallace D. Muhammad, and has faced allegations about his potential involvement in Malcolm X's assassination. As bits and pieces of NOI theology have entered the broader public sphere, controversy has accompanied Farrakhan's interpretation of Ezekiel's Old Testament vision of a fiery chariot in the sky and the role of a "mother plane" and UFOs at the apocalypse. Farrakhan has maintained his straightforward approach, suggesting to reporters that the levees in New Orleans that failed during hurricane Katrina were in fact "blown up" by the federal government.[11]

The Post-Civil Rights "Black Church"

One of the unexpected legacies of the work of the civil rights movement and the fall of Jim Crow segregation laws is the decreased centrality of the Black Church as the central meeting place for community and social activism. An increasing class split among African Americans has highlighted the diversity of black religious communities, some striving for the unrecognized dreams and promises of equity espoused in the 1960s and others finding a "gospel of prosperity" that asked "Does God want me to be rich?" For the burgeoning black middle class in the late 1970s, the question was increasingly answered in the affirmative. The creation of religious television networks enhanced the proselytizing efforts of Christian communities and their message reached ever-widening audiences. While Pat Robertson's Christian Broadcasting Network created evangelical celebrities such as Jim and Tammy Bakker, Paul and Jan Crouch's Trinity Broadcasting Network launched such prominent African American preachers as Frederick K. C. Price and T. D. Jakes.

The framework for the rise of the black megachurch stretches back to the Great Awakenings, which saw the rise of celebrity preachers such as George Whitefield, an Anglican clergyman with a background in acting, who was able to draw upon those skills from the pulpit. Whitefield became renowned for his powerful voice and ability to speak to thousands without amplification. The Second Great Awakening, while similar to the first, witnessed the professionalization of the revival enterprise. Charles Finney and other evangelists began to emphasize the human role and individual

---

11. Edward E. Curtis IV, *Islam in Black America: Identity, Liberation, and Difference in African American Islamic Thought* (Albany: State University of New York Press, 2002).

volition to choose to become a Christian. While John Calvin's and Jonathan Edwards's emphasis on the doctrine of election and salvation as a free gift from God for those who had been chosen reigned during the first Great Awakening, Finney and others put the onus on people themselves to make the decision rather than the movement of the Holy Spirit. From this vantage point, Finney instituted "new measures" that could bring about the desired results during a revival, such as advertising, the "anxious bench," and "mourner's bench" where individuals could have their souls prayed for, and the altar call, which created an urgency for people to make a decision immediately about their future salvation and accepting Jesus.

Finney's ideas were also influential on the perceived relationship between Christian communities and the secular world. If individuals ultimately controlled their salvation, they too could impact the world around them including the inauguration of the Second Coming of Jesus described in 1 Thess. 4:13–18:

> Brothers and sisters, we do not want you to be uninformed about those who sleep in death, so that you do not grieve like the rest of mankind, who have no hope. For we believe that Jesus died and rose again, and so we believe that God will bring with Jesus those who have fallen asleep in him. According to the Lord's word, we tell you that we who are still alive, who are left until the coming of the Lord, will certainly not precede those who have fallen asleep. For the Lord himself will come down from heaven, with a loud command, with the voice of the archangel and with the trumpet call of God, and the dead in Christ will rise first. After that, we who are still alive and are left will be caught up together with them in the clouds to meet the Lord forever. Therefore encourage one another with these words.

Some theologians argued that Paul's letter, written around 50 CE, struck a pastoral tone to comfort an early Christian community during a time of widespread martyrdom for those who embraced the burgeoning religion. Paul seems to be responding to a question from the Thessalonian community: "What happens to those who have died before the Second Coming of Jesus?" Paul comforts them by promising and reminding them that ultimately they will all be together with Christ in heaven. Other theologians in the 1800s began to interpret the passage as descriptive of a literal future "rapture" event that all true Christians would experience. Since the Bible could not contradict itself, many Christians asserted, careful study of the text not only empowered Christians in the present, but foretold future events that the faithful would experience, such as Luke 17:20–37:

> Once, being asked by the Pharisees when the kingdom of God would come, Jesus replied, "The coming of the kingdom of God is not something that can be observed, nor will people say, 'Here it is,' or 'There it is,' because the kingdom of God is in your midst." Then he said to his disciples, "The time is coming when you will long to see one of the days of the Son of Man, but you will not see it. People will tell you, 'There he is!,' or 'Here he is!' Do not go running off after them. For the Son of Man in his day will be like the lightning, which flashes and lights up the sky from one end to the other. But first he must suffer many things and be rejected by this generation. Just as it was in the days of Noah, so also will it be in the days of the Son of Man. People were eating, drinking, marrying and being given in marriage up to the day Noah entered the ark. Then the flood came and destroyed them all. It was the same in the days of Lot. People were eating and drinking, buying and selling, planting and building. But the day Lot left Sodom, fire and sulfur rained down from heaven and destroyed them all. It will be just like this on the day the Son of Man is revealed. On that day no one who is on the housetop, with possessions inside, should go down to get them. Likewise, no one in the field should go back for anything. Remember Lot's wife! Whoever tries to keep their life will lose it, and whoever loses their life will preserve it. I tell you, on that night two people will be in one bed; one will be taken and the other left. Two women will be grinding grain together; one will be taken and the other left.

Some theologians have interpreted this passage as depicting the immediate and literal removal of devout Christians before the coming tribulation for the unfaithful. This passage was often linked with the portrayal of the thousand-year reign of God on earth in the final days mentioned in Rev. 20:1–6:

> And I saw an angel coming down from heaven, having the key to the Abyss and holding in his hand a great chain. He seized the dragon, that ancient serpent, who is the devil, or Satan, and bound him for a thousand years. He threw him into the Abyss, and locked and sealed it over him, to keep him from deceiving the nations anymore until the thousand years were ended. After that, he must be set free for a short time. I saw thrones on which were seated those who had been given authority to judge. And I saw the souls of those who had been beheaded because of their testimony about Jesus and because of the word of God. They had not worshiped the beast or its image and had not received its mark on their foreheads or their hands. They came to life and reigned with Christ a thousand years. The rest of the dead did not come to life until the thousand years were ended. This is the first resurrection. Blessed and holy are those who share in the first resurrection. The second death has no power over them, but they will be priests of God and of Christ and will reign with him for a thousand years.

Premillennialists believed that Jesus' return would witness the removal of his followers from the world in the rapture. Those left behind would face the hardships and trials of the tribulation. At some point in the future, Jesus and the faithful would return to earth for the millennium, the one thousand-year period of righteous rule, before the final judgment. Postmillennialists believed that Jesus would return to earth after the millennium, and there would be clear separation between this age and the beginning of the millennium. Postmillennialists felt it was their duty to inaugurate the kingdom of God on earth by transforming society. However, believing that the rapture was to occur at a later unknown date, premillennialists did not necessarily feel called to such a responsibility.

After the Second Great Awakening, many Christians embraced the postmillennialist position and sought to reform society and purge it of its ills and evils. Many abolitionists, temperance movements, and advocacy for public education were driven by postmillennialist Christian notions of responsibility to the world. However, several historical factors converged to challenge these efforts for transformation. The Civil War that some postmillennialists felt would end swiftly because of their reform movements and biblically based arguments actually resulted in the unprecedented loss of human life and destruction. Industrialization brought women into the workplace, transforming the dynamics of family life. Urbanization exposed Christians from small towns to the realities of big city life. The racial, ethnic, and religious diversity that they encountered challenged notions of an evangelical majority. In addition, unemployment, disease, and political corruption all made it difficult for many Christians to maintain the idyllic notion that the world was getting better not worse.

Notions of premillennialism took center stage in the early nineteenth century, a move driven by John Nelson Darby's conception of dispensationalism or dispensational premillennialism. Dispensationalism was the notion that human history could be divided into discrete ages or dispensations and that God dealt with humanity in varying ways in the different ages. Dispensationalists asserted that God made distinctive covenants with the central figures in the Bible such as Adam, Noah, and Abraham. The current dispensation, Darby argued, called for the separation of true believers in anticipation of Jesus' premillennial return which was imminent; those left behind at the rapture would experience the wrath of God. From this perspective, the perceived deterioration of society was evidence that Jesus would return soon. Premillennialists turned their attention not to reforming society, but individual regeneration and missionary work to save souls. In many ways, evangelicals framed the temporal world as the realm of Satan from which Christians needed to separate themselves from while saving as many souls as possible through missionary work and outreach.[12]

One can see the legacy of these divisions in contemporary African American religious traditions. In many ways the seeds of the civil rights movement were sown in the emergence of the Social Gospel between the Civil War and World War I as some Protestants connected with the Progressive movement continued the efforts to transform society for the better. The Social Gospel sought to, among other things, create child-labor laws, establish the six-day workweek, and expose political corruption. Martin Luther King Jr. was influenced by these ideas, particularly the work of Walter Rauschenbusch, a key figure in the Social Gospel movement. As some African Americans began to prosper socioeconomically, many Protestants moved from traditional denominational churches to nondenominational congregations. This trend clouded statistics regarding black church attendance and skewed the reporting of membership figures. In many cases, mainline black congregations might have a large membership roster, but only a few hundred actually attended on Sundays. The opposite may be the case for black evangelical churches where their membership may be a few hundred, but thousands show up each weekend.

Increasingly the "prosperity gospel" message has resonated with middle-class black Christians. Frederick K. C. Price embraced the teachings of one of the pioneers within Pentecostalism, Kenneth E. Hagin, who popularized the "Word of Faith" doctrine that emphasized the gospel of prosperity. Price also preached and established programs that focused on social issues such as race relations, poverty, and community development among African Americans. In 1973, Price founded the independent Crenshaw

12. Randall Balmer, *The Making of Evangelicalism: From Revivalism to Politics and Beyond* (Waco, TX: Baylor University Press, 2010).

Christian Center in Inglewood, California. Price gained national notoriety through his television program launched in 1978 on the Trinity Broadcasting Network. By the late 1970s, the congregation had outgrown their fourteen-hundred-seat auditorium and relocated to a thirty-two-acre campus in downtown Los Angeles in 1984. As his ministry gained popularity, Price published numerous books and recorded audiotapes. Price's message encourages faith in God, the power of positive thinking, and practical self-help advice for African Americans.

Thomas Dexter Jakes burst onto the national stage in the 1990s. His focus on emotional healing for women and men, racial equality, prosperity, and spiritual renewal resonated across denominational lines. In 1982, Jakes began his ministry with a local radio show called "The Master's Plan," held small "Back to the Bible" conferences, and gradually gained regional acclaim for his preaching ability. By 1990, Jakes had established a hundred-member church in Montgomery, West Virginia. When the congregation relocated to Charlestown, its membership grew rapidly, breaking the one-thousand mark by 1996. However, Jakes became a phenomenon after publishing the book, *Woman, Thou Art Loosed!*, which addressed issues such as divorce, molestation, depression, and discrimination that he felt mainline black churches had long ignored in their preaching and doctrine. By 2000, more than two million copies of the book were in print and it had generated several national conferences, devotional guides, a play, gospel album, and a movie. By the late 1990s, Jakes had moved his headquarters to Dallas, and was heard regularly on the radio during his nationally syndicated program, and seen weekly on the TV show *Get Ready with T. D. Jakes*. By the turn of the century, Jakes headed one of the fastest-growing megachurches in the country, the Potter's House Church. By 2008, the church's membership had exceeded thirty thousand and met weekly in a facility that seated eight thousand.

Another in this lineage of star African American ministers is Creflo Dollar, who, like Price and Jakes, preaches a self-help doctrine, family values, and economic independence that has resonated with the experiences of many middle-class African Americans. In 1986, Dollar established his World Changers Church International in Atlanta. Bolstered by the commendations of prominent ministers such as Oral Roberts, Kenneth Copeland, and Frederick Price, Dollar's ministry has grown rapidly, establishing several businesses and social programs including a record company, a local social justice organization, and Project Change International, which provides counseling, meals, and mentoring to less fortunate African American communities.

In July 1987, Reverend Eddie L. Long was appointed pastor of New Birth Missionary Baptist Church in Decatur, Georgia. Long's references to popular culture in his sermons, and relationships with stars such as rapper T.I., have attracted young professionals as members, many of whom had not previously attended church. Eventually, Long himself became a local celebrity. Over time, the church took on a more ecstatic and experiential form of worship. By 2001, the 25,000-member New Birth was an archetypal African American megachurch, moving to a 240-acre site in Lithonia where a fifty-million-dollar facility was constructed with a television production studio, bookstore, and recreation center. The fitness center, Sampson's Gym, included four full-sized racquetball and basketball courts, saunas, and a football field. Plans included a Faith Academy for children's education, a senior/assisted living community, and an entrepreneurship school. Bishop Long's television broadcast *Taking Authority* won an Emmy and is shown nationally and internationally on Trinity Broadcast Network and Black Entertainment Television.

Long's high profile has also attracted critics. His private jet, relationship with President Bush which included participation in his faith-based initative, and flamboyant dress created tension with some African Americans. While he had led social outreach and engaged in charitable work, he was often taken to task for embracing a prosperity gospel. In 2004, as a part of his campaign for "traditional family values," Long led a five-thousand-person march against gay marriage in downtown Atlanta called "Reigniting the Legacy." However, in 2010, two former young male members of New Birth filed a civil suit in DeKalb County alleging that Long forced them to perform sexual acts while supervising them at the church's LongFellows Youth Academy. A week later, two others came forward with similar claims. These assertions undercut Long's well-known work to develop masculinity, responsibility, financial knowledge, and morality in young men. Like Ted Haggard who was the pastor of New Life Church in Colorado Springs and the former head of the National Association of Evangelicals in 2000, this was another prominent case in the media of a Christian leader who was outspokenly against gay relationships and was alleged to have engaged in homosexual acts.

Demographic shifts have played a profound role in African American religious life. The 1890 census, the first to distinguish rural and urban populations, showed that 90 percent of African Americans lived in the South and, of those, 80 percent lived in rural areas. Almost a hundred years later, in 1980, 85 percent of African Americans were in urban areas with only 53 percent residing in the southern "black belt." Yet, the "reverse migration" of African Americans from the North to the South beginning in the late 1970s has shown an appreciable increase in the black southern population in the last decades. While there are multiple reasons for this trend, increased employment opportunities, communications with relatives in the South touting its more hospitable environment, and disillusionment about life in the North marks this relocation as an about face of the Great Migration of the early twentieth century.

Many black churches are wrestling with life in the "post-denominational" twenty-first century. Most black megachurches, those with over two thousand weekly attendees, are located in sunbelt cities such as Dallas, Houston, Los Angeles, and Atlanta. Unlike white megachurches, most black megachurches are located in urban areas not suburbs. Of those megachurches that identify as denominational, Baptists make up the largest portion; however, most black megachurches are nondenominational. While there have been large black congregations dating back to the earliest independent black churches, some with over a thousand names listed on their membership rosters, weekly attendance numbers are often unavailable. Although there were rare instances of churches reporting memberships of over ten thousand in the mid-twentieth century, the black megachurch phenomenon took off in the 1980s with the formation of new congregations and the explosive growth in the membership of historical denominations. New Birth Missionary Baptist Church in Atlanta went from three hundred members in 1987 to twenty-three thousand in 1999. Windsor Village United Methodist Church in Houston, Texas, went from twenty-five in 1982 to over ten thousand in 1998. In fifteen years, St. Paul Community Baptist Church in Brooklyn grew from eighty-four to five thousand in 1993. The majority of black megachurches engage in some form of community development such as housing programs, health clinics, and job training. The anonymity offered by these extremely large church services coupled with the option to get involved in more close-knit settings such as Bible studies and classes seems to have struck the right balance for many African Americans.

The growth of black megachurches has altered the landscape of African American religion, with former department store buildings and basketball stadiums now becoming sacred spaces. Traditional pews have been replaced by theater seating, the fixed pulpit supplanted by movable stages and podiums. Rather than lengthy sermons and singing from hymnals, dramatic performances and retractable televisions convey the gospel message. These churches are particularly attentive to "seekers" who may have never attended church or are in search of something other than the traditional worship style. Other black megachurches are simply larger versions of traditional churches, and a plethora of others combine aspects of each approach. Some churches distance themselves from black theology and resist the label of a "Black Church," emphasizing their universality as a church for all people.

Scholars have employed a number of theories to try to explain the black megachurch phenomenon. Some suggest that the desire of congregants to join megachurches mirrors the trends in the broader society and the rise of mega–shopping centers that promise one-stop shopping. From this framework, religious "consumers" choose megachurches out of a desire for a church that offers a range of services that small churches are unable to provide. Others such as Mark Chaves point toward economics that make maintaining smaller churches particularly difficult, so that as they close people gravitate toward larger churches that are more economically stable. Others see megachurches as product of church-growth strategies that seek to fill a niche not being addressed by other churches. This theory suggests that megachurches seek out those who are "unchurched" or those who have had a negative experience with churches in the past. The worship style, architecture, and other aspects of the church offer these attendees an environment different from that from which they came. Others point to demographic shifts and population increases that allow churches to grow to accommodate the influx of a larger population. In suburbs, churches can often expand their size horizontally along the physical landscape because they have access to more land and space while in larger urban centers often the only option is to build vertically. With the rise of suburbanization, many people are more open to driving longer distances to attend church services.[13]

African Religions in America

As the presence of African religious expressions has grown in the United States, so too have conflicts with the surrounding communities that have resisted their presence. The Church of the Lukumi Babalu Aye came under fire by the city of Hialeah, Florida, for their performance of animal sacrifice in the early 1990s. The Santerian house practiced a ritual in which the carotid artery of a lamb or other small animal was severed with a knife. After most ceremonies involving sacrifice, the participants cook and eat the offering, but during others the animals become a surrogate for misfortune and, having absorbed the negative energy, are disposed of without being consumed. This action stimulated public concern that these dead carcasses would cause a public health hazard. Shortly after the church leased the land and announced plans to open up a house of worship, the city council held an emergency public session and enacted a number of policies. The city of Hialeah passed a series of city ordinances that prohibited "unnecessarily or cruelly killing any animal" in a "ritual . . . not for the primary purpose of food

---

13. Anthony B. Pinn, *The Black Church in the Post-Civil Rights Era* (New York: Orbis Books, 2002); Shayne Lee, *T. D. Jakes: America's New Preacher* (New York: New York University Press, 2007); Milmon F. Harrison, *Righteous Riches: The Word of Faith Movement in Contemporary African American Religion* (New York: Oxford University Press, 2005); R. Drew Smith and Tamelyn Tucker-Worgs, "Megachurches: African American Churches in Social and Political Context," in *The State of Black America 2000: Blacks in the New Millennium* (New York: National Urban League, 2000).

consumption." The legislation appeared to be directly targeting the Church of the Lukumi Babalu Aye.

The church challenged the ordinance as a violation of their First Amendment rights. They argued that animal sacrifice was an essential part of their religion. The case ultimately reached the Supreme Court, which ruled in favor of the church. Writing for the majority, Justice Anthony Kennedy noted that "[t]he suppression of Santeria was the central purpose of the law as noted by the use of terms such as 'ritual' and 'sacrifice' in the statute. Also, a resolution was passed that spoke harshly against 'practices which are inconsistent with public morals, peace or safety,' and 'reiterated' the city's commitment to prohibit 'any and all [such] acts of any and all religious groups.'" "If the main goals were to prevent animal cruelty and protect the public health," Kennedy averred, a "less restrictive ordinance" could have been passed. He concluded, "Although the practice of animal sacrifice may seem abhorrent to some, religious belief need not be acceptable, logical, consistent, or comprehensible to others in order to merit First Amendment protection."[14]

The American Society for the Prevention of Cruelty to Animals has challenged the Santerian method of slaughter and argued that it is less humane than officially licensed slaughterhouses. This issue has created unexpected alliances between Santeria, Jewish, and Christian communities who feared similar ordinances might be passed to restrict kosher slaughtering or infringe upon other religious freedoms. Today, Santeria is truly a global movement, with houses of worship around the world and with practitioners from every race and ethnicity. It was not until the 1940s, with the immigration of individual priests, priestesses, and devotees that Santeria began to be transplanted to the United States, and it was only after the 1959 Cuban Revolution that migrants came in substantial numbers. In the

14. Church of Lukumi Babalu Aye, Inc. v. City of Hialeah (508 U.S. 520).

United States, Santeria enjoyed strong growth in the second half of the twentieth century with a number of disparate immigrant groups that found a religious home in the tradition.

The last quarter of the twentieth century has also seen a transformation in the demographics of African religious communities in America. Visa requirements and immigration laws became less stringent, particularly for previously underrepresented countries, which sparked a rise in African immigration to America. Political unrest in the Congo, Somalia, Liberia, Rwanda, and the Sudan also increased the number of refugees fleeing their homelands. In the early 2000s, approximately fifty thousand Africans per year relocated to the United States. The census figures for 2003 revealed that there were over one million native Africans living in America. While the majority of these new immigrants settled in urban centers such as New York, Washington, D.C., Chicago, and Los Angeles, a significant number also chose to make their homes in smaller, more rural cities in the Midwest and Northeast.

Oseijeman Adefunmi is credited with catalyzing the growth of African American Yoruba. In 1956, he established the Order of Damballah Hwedo Ancestor Priests in Greenwich Village, New York. According to Oseijeman Adefunmi, Damballah was the snake god that linked African Americans to their African ancestors. The Order of Damballah Hwedo melded aspects of African and African American cultural practices. Oseijeman Adefunmi constructed ceremonies with a Ghanaian stool, an altar, a handmade Haitian Voodoo flag with an image of the serpent Damballah. Drawing on written sources from Africa and travel experiences, the order centered on sacred rituals that included public readings on African cultures such as the Yoruba and the Akan. Only those of African descent could attend the weekly meetings for Ancestor Priests.

These immigrants brought with them a wealth of African religious expressions. Some traditions merged African Traditional Religion and Christianity, for example, African Pentecostal and charismatic churches as well as African Initiated Churches, many of which were founded by prophetic, visionary leaders. Other African immigrant religious communities identified more closely with specific "mainstream" Christian denominations and Islamic traditions in the United States. As synagogues and churches had before them, the mosque for many African Muslims took on a variety of roles including providing religious instruction and a place of support and nurture for the community. While immigrants bring their own personal experiences of African indigenous religions with them to America, members of the priestly class in West Africa have been particularly influential in reconstituting communal religious life in America. Congregations are quite diverse, with members from all walks of life and racial and ethnic backgrounds. Through careful observation of syntax and ritual practices, studies have continued to search for resemblances between these American-based communities and their counterparts across the Atlantic in Africa.[15]

World Religions

African Americans have participated in every variety of world religions. Judaism, Christianity, and Islam have had a presence in Africa from their nascent periods. The Falasha of Ethiopia trace their lineage back to Menilek I, the son of the Queen of Sheba and King Solomon. In addition to prominent figures in entertainment such as Tina Turner and Herbie Hancock, African Americans of all stripes have embraced Buddhism and other Asian religions. As of 2008, African Americans made up twenty thousand of Soka Gakkai

15. John S. Mbiti, *African Religions and Philosophy* (Portsmouth, NH: Heinemann, 1990); Jacob K. Olupona, *Orisa Devotion as World Religion: The Globalization of Yoruba Religious Culture* (Madison: University of Wisconsin Press, 2008).

International-USA's estimated hundred thousand members. Most Buddhists in America are white and middle to upper middle class. In 1995, Korean Zen Master Samu Sunim stated that "[i]t was largely the intellectuals who were attracted to Zen Buddhism in the beginning. Even today most Zen Buddhists are college-educated, liberal-minded—they're mostly white baby boomers who couldn't make it back to their own childhood religions. We have failed to attract people from African-American communities."[16] One issue is accessibility, which requires money and leisure time. For some African Americans, Buddhism allows them to hold on to their humanness within a society that often denies it. Buddhists attest that the tradition provides ways to address the trauma of slavery that unconsciously continues to plague the souls of African Americans. Without being dealt with, they maintain, it could lead to a low self-esteem and self-hatred. Buddhism offers paths to heal those wounds. The concept of giving up attachments in the world, when focused on material goods, can cause a disconnect with those from the lower classes who often have few extraneous trappings to discard. The ability of Buddhism to acknowledge the historical impact of race but to understand race as a social construct with little real value has allowed some African Americans to assert that they have moved beyond notions of race and ethnicity.

African Americans also constitute a substantial portion of the membership of a range of religious traditions, particularly those that deemphasize racial distinctions or explicitly aim towards racial healing and reconciliation. Because of its strong focus on racial equality, the Baha'i experienced strong growth among African Americans in the 1960s, particularly in the South. Blacks have been a part of a variety of predominately white Christian traditions from

16. Marianne Dresser, *Buddhist Women on the Edge: Contemporary Perspectives from the Western Frontier* (Berkeley, CA: North Atlantic Books, 1996), 85.

the antebellum period. In the 1780s, as one of the earliest religious communities to vigorously protest the institution of slavery, the Quakers were also one of the first to admit black members such as Paul Cuffe. There are also African American Christian Scientists. The Christian Science tradition teaches that God is Absolute Mind and the only reality. The material realm indicated by our five senses is in fact an illusion. God also has personal characteristics such as love that allow humans to know God. As humans are healed they realize that illness is an illusion. In Christian Science, Resurrection is Jesus' means of bringing people to the realization that all is Absolute Mind and freeing them from death. Hell is ongoing bondage to illusory thinking and heaven is total acceptance of absolute mind, so that physical death is just a step from one radiant life to the next. Life with God in heaven is full realization, not a transition from a material to nonmaterial realm.

African Americans have had a strong influence with the Jehovah's Witnesses tradition. The 1990 National Survey of Religions found that 40 percent of Jehovah's Witnesses are African American. Emerging from the Seventh-Day Adventist tradition, the leaders of the Jehovah's Witnesses such as Charles Taze Russell (1852–1916) and Joseph Franklin Rutherford (1869–1942) focused on the Bible as the literal word of God and rejected other forms of authority in the world, including human governments and other churches, which were collectively referred to as the evil "Babylon the Great" described in the Book of Revelation. According to Russell's theology, all of the current world was under the rule of Satan as a test for humanity. Under Rutherford, the Jehovah's Witnesses continued the trend toward a distinctive understanding of the outside world. The community celebrated only the annual "Lord's Evening Meal." Drawing on the kosher laws of the Hebrew Bible and New Testament passages such as Acts 15:28–29, Rutherford prohibited members from obtaining blood transfusions. He emphasized the rejection of all symbols of secular government, including saluting the flag, joining the armed forces, voting, or jury duty.[17]

African Americans have had a complicated relationship with the Latter-Day Saint tradition. On April 6, 1830, six members of the Latter-Day Saint church met in a farmhouse to organize the nascent religion. As missionaries spread the word, in 1832, an African American named Elijah Abel responded to the message, was baptized, and was soon a missionary himself. His acceptance suggests that there was no segregation in the early church. By the end of the 1830s, Abel was ordained an elder in the priesthood of Melchizedek by the father of the prophet, Joseph Smith Sr. A year after his ordination, with the approval of the prophet, Joseph Smith Jr., Abel was elevated to the Quorum of Seventy, the second-highest governing body in the church, succeeded only by the Council of Twelve. Abel was also given a patriarchal blessing similar to those given to Abraham, Jacob, and Isaac as described in the Hebrew Bible. After Smith's martyrdom, his successor, Brigham Young, also initially expressed racial acceptance. In 1847, Young wrote, "It's nothing to do with the blood, for of one blood has God made all flesh. . . . We have one of the best Elders, an African, in Lowell, Massachusetts." However, as southerners brought their slaves with them on the migration westward the issue of slavery would remain a concern. As the territorial governor, Young had to decide what Utah's official position on slavery would be. In a legislative session, Young advocated that those already with slaves in Utah or who came with slaves be allowed to keep them. Young embraced the biblical interpretation that many southern defenders of slavery espoused,

17. Dereck Daschke, *New Religious Movements: A Documentary Reader* (New York: New York University Press, 2005); James R. Lewis, *The Oxford Handbook of New Religious Movements* (New York: Oxford University Press, 2008); Lorne L. Dawson, *Cults and New Religious Movements: A Reader* (Hoboken, NJ: Wiley-Blackwell, 2003).

which asserted that slavery was a result of the sin and disobedience of African Americans who came from the lineage of Noah's curse on his sons and the curse of Cain. As Young wrote in 1852, "The seed of Canaan will inevitably carry the curse which was placed upon them." Regarding the priesthood he declared, "If no other prophet said it before now, I say it. The seed of Cain are not entitled to the blessings of the priesthood." Two decades after Abel's ordination, the next generation of Mormon leaders asserted that blacks had no rights to the temple or to the Mormon priesthood. Although he had been a personal friend of the prophet, remained a member in good standing in the church, and had been accused of no wrongdoing or violation of any orthodoxy, in 1880, the Council of Twelve denied Abel's request to enter the temple as he had for the previous thirty years. Despite this rejection, Abel remained a committed member of the community until his death on Christmas day in 1884.

Race has been a challenging issue in the Latter-Day Saint tradition. While Noah's curse and the curse of Ham were interpretations of the Hebrew Bible, the Latter-Day Saint tradition more directly addressed the origins of darker skin. The Book of Nephi explains that while the Lamanites once had "fair" skin like the Nephites, their sins caused a darkening of their skin. Second Nephi describes: "For behold, they had hardened their hearts against [the Lord], that they had become like unto flint; wherefore as they were white, and exceedingly fair and delightsome, that they might not be enticing unto my people the Lord did cause a skin of blackness to come upon them." While the text refers to the Lamanites, the ancestors of modern-day Native Americans, racial groups including African Americans have been seen as a part of this legacy of transgression. Mormon theology has also suggested that perhaps some spirits in the pre-mortal war before humans came into existence were less valiant in the battle or had not taken sides and were "fence sitters in the preexistence." Therefore, these "fence sitters" were born of African heritage in the cursed lineage of Canaan.

These interpretations of race impact who has access to particular leadership positions in the LDS Church. Every twelve-year-old boy can be ordained into the LDS priesthood except those of African descent. This prohibition applied to women as well. An African American female pioneer, Jane Manning James, repeatedly requested to receive the sacred ordinances of the faith in the temple but was denied. Since many other Christian traditions in America had a history of racial tensions and segregation, the LDS was not distinctive in that way, but as the civil rights movement gained momentum the church's policies came under greater public scrutiny. On June 8, 1978, the revelation received by Latter-Day Saint President Spencer W. Kimball extended the priesthood to "all worthy black male members of the church . . . without regard for race or color." Yet, the biblical interpretations that undergirded the original ban remained in place. While sometimes criticized for the revelation's relatively late occurrence in light of the civil rights gains in America, this shift in perspective inaugurated an immense missionary effort to people of color around the world, making Mormonism one of the fastest-growing world religions.[18]

The response of black churches to issues of sexuality and gay marriage is also a challenging phenomenon to analyze. Given the history of black churches being at the forefront for the advocacy for equal rights for marginalized groups, one might expect the traditions to be equally outspoken for gay rights. However, historical black churches have taken some of the strongest stances against same-sex marriage, framing gay relationships as sinful. One can speculate about why this trend seems to have occurred. Some have suggested that the

18. W. Paul Reeve, *Religion of a Different Color: Race and the Mormon Struggle for Whiteness* (New York: Oxford University Press, 2015).

close reading of the Bible during slavery, such as the Exodus narrative that empowered enslaved Americans to identify with a Jesus who profoundly understood their experiences and would deliver them too from bondage as a second Moses, also informs current theological interpretations that apply the stories of the Hebrew Bible and the New Testament literally to twenty-first-century issues such as same-sex relationships.

Black families have also historically been excluded from notions of the "American family" and domesticity, which has led black churches to staunchly defend the institution. The first domestic literature in the early nineteenth century was written by and for white women. From Lydia Maria Child's *American Frugal Housewife* (1829) to Catherine Beecher's *Treatise on Domestic Economy* (1843), much of the writing about family life in America assumed a Eurocentric nuclear family as the norm. By the late 1860s, many domestic manuals assumed a level of socioeconomic success and materialism that included the ownership of a variety of appliances. Southern African Americans experienced a dramatically different family life than the American family portrayed in white evangelical domestic literature. The post–Civil War black home contained not only parents and their own children, but also an extended family of relatives, friends, and children whose own families had either died or had not been located after Emancipation. Black women responded in a variety of ways to Victorian domesticity. Enslaved African American women had little access to the material resources that came to symbolize the Victorian home. Many free northern African American women found the Victorian emphasis on family values appealing, but rejected the racial and class exclusiveness of the ideology. Even for those African Americans who did not embrace all the tenets of domesticity, many internalized the pressure to live up to Victorian domestic standards and confirm that they could assimilate into American culture.

The historical legacy of domesticity, the denigration of the black families, the upheaval of slave families, and the publishing of literature such as the government-sponsored Moynihan Report on the "Negro Family," have made the home and gender roles enduring and salient issues in African American religious communities. The nuclear family model has allowed black men to assume male privilege in the home, which has been seen as particularly important given the lack of public roles available for men to demonstrate the traditional traits associated with masculinity. The same line of thinking framed lesbians as a rejection of black masculinity. Gay relationships without the possibility of producing offspring have also been framed as a threat to the future of the African American race. Following the conclusions of the Moynihan Report, some observers made the case that a male-dominated home produced boys with masculine attributes. Therefore, by extension, female-led homes were presumed to produce more effeminate children who were thought to be more inclined to be gay. Being gay was framed as a defect in the development of black masculinity and a perversion of manhood. This position was echoed in the Afrocentric perspective as Molefi Asante writes, "The rise of homosexuality in the African-American male's psyche is real and complicated. An Afrocentric perspective recognizes its existence but homosexuality cannot be condoned or accepted as good for the national development of a strong people. It can be and must be tolerated until such a time as our families and schools are engaged in Afrocentric instructions for males. . . . The time has come for us to redeem our manhood through planned Afrocentric action."[19]

From their origins in slavery, the historically black denominations—the African Methodist Episcopal Church, African

19. Molefi Kete Asante, *Afrocentricity: The Theory of Social Change* (Chicago: African American Images, 2003).

Methodist Episcopal Zion, Christian Methodist Episcopal Church, National Progressive Baptist Church, the Church of God in Christ, National Baptist Church, USA, Inc., and the National Baptist Church of America—have taken strong theological stances on the sinfulness of homosexuality and maintained that God ordained sex to take place within the context of marriage between members of the opposite sex. It can be argued that it is anachronistic to project twenty-first-century understandings of gay relationships back upon first-century Christian communities. Few passages in the Bible address the issue of sexuality. Gen. 19:1–29 contains the story of Sodom and Gomorrah that is often cited during debates on the issue:

> The two angels arrived at Sodom in the evening, and Lot was sitting in the gateway of the city. When he saw them, he got up to meet them and bowed down with his face to the ground. "My lords," he said, "please turn aside to your servant's house. You can wash your feet and spend the night and then go on your way early in the morning." "No," they answered, "we will spend the night in the square." But he insisted so strongly that they did go with him and entered his house. He prepared a meal for them, baking bread without yeast, and they ate. Before they had gone to bed, all the men from every part of the city of Sodom—both young and old—surrounded the house. They called to Lot, "Where are the men who came to you tonight? Bring them out to us so that we can have sex with them." Lot went outside to meet them and shut the door behind him and said, "No, my friends. Don't do this wicked thing. Look, I have two daughters who have never slept with a man. Let me bring them out to you, and you can do what you like with them. But don't do anything to these men, for they have come under the protection of my roof." "Get out of our way," they replied. "This fellow came here as a foreigner, and now he wants to play the judge! We'll treat you worse than them." They kept bringing pressure on Lot and moved forward to break down the door. But the men inside reached out and pulled Lot back into the house and shut the door. Then they struck the men who were at the door of the house, young and old, with blindness so that they could not find the door. The two men said to Lot, "Do you have anyone else here—sons-in-law, sons or daughters, or anyone else in the city who belongs to you? Get them out of here, because we are

going to destroy this place. The outcry to the Lord against its people is so great that he has sent us to destroy it."

Some Christians interpret the subsequent destruction of the city of Sodom as a condemnation of gay relationships. Passages in Leviticus read, "Do not have sexual relations with a man as one does with a woman; that is detestable" (18:22) and "If a man has sexual relations with a man as one does with a woman, both of them have done what is detestable. They are to be put to death; their blood will be on their own heads" (20:13). First Cor. 6:9–10 states, "Or do you not know that wrongdoers will not inherit the kingdom of God? Do not be deceived: Neither the sexually immoral nor idolaters nor adulterers nor men who have sex with men nor thieves nor the greedy nor drunkards nor slanderers nor swindlers will inherit the kingdom of God." Other passages include Rom. 1:18–32:

> For although they knew God, they neither glorified him as God nor gave thanks to him, but their thinking became futile and their foolish hearts were darkened. Although they claimed to be wise, they became fools and exchanged the glory of the immortal God for images made to look like a mortal human being and birds and animals and reptiles. Therefore God gave them over in the sinful desires of their hearts to sexual impurity for the degrading of their bodies with one another. They exchanged the truth of God for a lie, and worshiped and served created things rather than the Creator—who is forever praised. Amen. Because of this, God gave them over to shameful lusts. Even their women exchanged natural sexual relations for unnatural ones. In the same way the men also abandoned natural relations with women and were inflamed with lust for one another. Men committed shameful acts with other men, and received in themselves the due penalty for their error.

First Tim. 1:8–11 notes:

> We know that the law is good if one uses it properly. We also know that the law is not for the righteous but for lawbreakers and rebels, the

ungodly and sinful, the unholy and irreligious, for those who kill their fathers or mothers, for murderers, for the sexually immoral, for those practicing homosexuality, for slave traders and liars and perjurers—and for whatever else is contrary to the sound doctrine that conforms to the gospel concerning the glory of the blessed God, which he entrusted to me.

Even these passages that allude to the issue were written in specific cultural contexts that are far distant from contemporary understandings of same-sex couples and relationships. Translation complicates the use of ancient documents to understand contemporary issues. The conflictedness of African American religious traditions over supporting the oppressed and faithfulness to following the proscriptions laid out in the Bible extend to other arenas as well. Many black churches wholeheartedly supported Barack Obama's presidential election campaign, but balked at his public support of same-sex marriage.[20]

Religion and Politics

The 1980s saw a significant shift in the relationship between African American religions and the American public sphere. On November 3, 1983, Jesse Jackson, a minister in the Progressive National Baptist Convention, announced his intention to run for the office of President of the United States. Jackson had been a central figure in the Southern Christian Leadership Conference, a prominent advocate for desegregation in Chicago in the 1960s, and, after King's assassination in 1968, founder of Operation PUSH, a national religious reform-oriented movement.

Jesse Jackson's National Rainbow Coalition emerged from Martin

20. Horace L. Griffin, *Their Own Receive Them Not: African American Lesbians and Gays in Black Churches* (Eugene, OR: Wipf and Stock, 2010); Kelly Brown Douglas, *Sexuality and the Black Church: A Womanist Perspective* (New York: Orbis Books, 1999).

Luther King Jr.'s Poor People's Campaign in 1967. This class-focused interracial movement sought to bring issues of poverty and racial discrimination into the American public consciousness. His presidential campaigns of 1984 and 1988 blended the cadence of a black preaching style, the call and response of a worship service, and the language of political activism. Jackson hoped to register new voters and unite human rights activists, people of color, women, and industrial and agricultural workers to force the Democrats to include their concerns in the official party platform. Yet, Jackson did not openly court white voters and embraced the support of other black leaders such as Louis Farrakhan. Jackson made a controversial remark that referred to New York City as "Hymie Town," which offended and ostracized many Jewish Americans. This relationship was further strained by his meeting with Yasser Arafat, the leader of the Palestine Liberation Organization, regarding the possibility of establishing a Palestinian homeland in Israel. Following the reelection of Ronald Reagan in 1984, Jackson refocused the National Rainbow Coalition on issues of health care and unemployment.

By 1988, Jackson was familiar to Americans from his 1984 presidential bid that had surpassed the expectations of the American public and news media by finishing third in the Democratic primaries. The surprising withdrawal of Gary Hart from the presidential race in May 1987 left Jackson as the most well known of the Democratic candidates. The media focused on the question of race and whether an African American candidate could win the election. Jackson drew upon his black preaching style to convey his message. He framed issues in terms of morality and his political rallies strongly resembled religious revivals. Strong support from religious organizations and churches formed a strong infrastructure for funding, organizational support, and leadership. However, missteps along the way dropped Jackson further and further behind in the race until ultimately Michael Dukakis claimed the nomination. In his 1988 presidential campaign, Jackson received over seven-million votes and won seven state primaries and sparked a sharp rise in African American participation in the political process.

Twenty years later, on January 27, 2008, a sermon preached by Reverend Jeremiah Wright, at his Trinity United Church of Christ in Chicago, Illinois would also elevate African American religion into the national political spotlight. Wright, presidential candidate Barack Obama's pastor and spiritual advisor, delivered a controversial talk in which he criticized everyone from black faculty who failed to fully embrace their racial identity to the actions and philosophies of Clarence Thomas, Colin Powell, and Condoleezza Rice. He condemned the "oppressive" United States government who "stole this country" from the Native Americans, defined African Americans as three/fifths of a person, and the federal court for rendering such decisions as *Dred Scott* and *Plessy v. Ferguson*. He stated, "Our country has been confused about symbols. Since we became a country, we lift up the Liberty Bell, but we're defined by the hangman's noose." In another address shortly after, he shouted, "God damn America!" These images and strong rhetoric shocked an American public and television political pundits. The backlash eventually led to Obama renouncing Wright as well as his membership in the church.[21]

In his defense, Wright asserted that the controversy over his comments stemmed primarily from those unfamiliar with the black prophetic tradition in the black church, which has historically spoken truth to power. On the one hand this is true. From the earliest slave preachers who called for abolition and social equality, Richard Allen leaving to found an independent church, Nat Turner heeding a divine call to rebel, Henry McNeal Turner stating that "God is

---

21. Barbara Dianne Savage, *Your Spirits Walk Beside Us: The Politics of Black Religion* (Cambridge, MA: Belknap Press, 2012).

a Negro," Martin Luther King Jr. proclaiming his dream, to James Cone, Cornel West, and others formulating a black theology, there are ample examples of black "prophets." Yet, as we have seen, there has never been one monolithic "black church." When the concept is invoked in the singular, as if to speak for "the" Christian voice in black communities, it denies the multivocal nature of African American religious history. Beyond Christianity, the landscape grows even more diverse. From the transmission of African Traditional Religions, Santeria, Candomble, and Voodoo to the New World, to the creative spiritual expressions of black new religious movements, African American religions have never been static, but have changed and adapted over time to meet the needs of present communities. The search for their essence will likely continue, and just as an observer believes that they have captured it, it will surely have shifted again.

Bibliography

Adeleke, Tunde. *UnAfrican Americans: Nineteenth-Century Black Nationalists and the Civilizing Mission*. Lexington: University Press of Kentucky, 1998.

Ahlstrom, Sydney. *The Religious History of the American People*. New Haven, CT: Yale University Press, 1972.

Allen, Richard. *The Life Experience and Gospel Labors of the Rt. Rev. Richard Allen*. Nashville: Abingdon Press, 1960.

Allmendinger, Blake. *Imagining the African American West*. Lincoln: University of Nebraska Press, 2005.

Aminah, Beverly McCloud. *African American Islam*. London: Routledge, 1995.

Anderson, Hugh George. *Lutheranism in the Southeastern States, 1860-1886: A Social History*. The Hague, Netherlands: Mouton, 1976.

Angell, Stephen Ward. *Bishop Henry McNeal Turner and African-American Religion in the South*. Knoxville: University of Tennessee Press, 1992.

Angell, Stephen Ward, and Anthony Pinn, eds. *Social Protest Thought in the African Methodist Episcopal Church, 1862-1939*. Knoxville: University of Tennessee Press, 2000.

Aptheker, Herbert. *The Correspondence of W. E. B. Du Bois. Vol. 1, Selections, 1877-1934*. Amherst: University of Massachusetts Press, 1973.

_____. *A Documentary History of the Negro People in the United States*. New York: Citadel Press, 1969.

_____. *The Negro in the Abolitionist Movement*. New York: International Publishers, 1941.

_____, ed. *The Souls of Black Folk*. Milwood, NY: Kraus-Thomson Organization, 1973.

Arnesen, Eric. *Black Protest and the Great Migration*. Boston, MA: Bedford/St. Martin's, 2002.

Asante, Molefi Kete. *Afrocentricity: The Theory of Social Change*. Chicago: African American Images, 2003.

Athearn, Robert G. *In Search of Canaan: Black Migration to Kansas, 1879-80*. Lawrence, KS: The Regents Press of Kansas, 1978.

Baer, Hans A. *The Black Spiritual Movement: A Religious Response to Racism*. Knoxville: University of Tennessee Press, 1984.

Bailey, Julius H. *Around the Family Altar: Domesticity in the African Methodist Episcopal Church, 1865-1900*. Gainesville: University Press of Florida, 2005.

_____. "The Final Frontier: Secrecy, Identity, and the Media in the Rise and Fall of the United Nuwaubian Nation of Moors," *Journal of the American Academy of Religion* 74, no. 2 (June 2006): 302–23.

_____. *Race Patriotism: Protest and Print Culture in the African Methodist Episcopal Church*. Knoxville: University of Tennessee Press, 2012.

Bailey, Kenneth K. "Protestantism and Afro-Americans in the Old South: Another Look," *Journal of Southern History* 41 (1975): 451–72.

Ball, Charles. *A Narrative of the Life and Adventures of Charles Ball, A Black Man*. New York: John S. Taylor, 1837.

Balmer, Randall. *The Making of Evangelicalism: From Revivalism to Politics and Beyond*. Waco, TX: Baylor University Press, 2010.

Bannister, Robert C. *Social Darwinism: Science and Myth in Anglo-American Social Thought*. Philadelphia: Temple University Press, 1979.

Becker, William H. "The Black Church: Manhood and Mission," *Journal of the American Academy of Religion* 40 (Spring 1972): 316–33.

Bederman, Gail. *Manliness & Civilization: A Cultural History of Gender and Race in the United States, 1880-1917*. Chicago: University of Chicago, 1995.

Berry, L. L. *A Century of Missions of the African Methodist Episcopal Church, 1840-1940*. New York: Gutenberg Printing, 1942.

Berwanger, Eugene. *The West and Reconstruction*. Urbana: University of Illinois Press, 1981.

Blassingame, John W. *The Slave Community*. New York: Oxford University Press, 1972.

Bluett, Thomas. *Some Memoirs of the Life of Job, the Son of Solomon, the High Priest of Boonda in Africa*. London: Printed for R. Ford, 1734.

Blumenbach, Johann Friedrich. *The Anthropological Treatises of Johann Friedrich Blumenbach*. London: Longman, Green, Longman Roberts, and Green, 1865.

Blyden, Edward Wilmot. *Christianity, Islam, and the Negro Race*. Baltimore: Black Classic Press, 1994.

Boahen, Adu, ed. *Africa Under Colonial Domination, 1880-1935*. Berkeley: University of California Press, 1985.

Boles, John B., ed. *Masters and Slaves in the House of the Lord: Race and Religion in the American South, 1740-1870*. Lexington: University Press of Kentucky, 1988.

Bracey, John H., Jr., August Meier, and Elliot Rudwick, eds. *Black Nationalism in America*. New York: Bobbs-Merrill, 1970.

Bragg, George Freeman. *The History of the Afro-American Group of the Episcopal Church*. New York: Johnson Reprint Corp., 1968.

Brauer, Jerald C. "Regionalism and Religion in America," *Church History* 54 (September 1985): 366–78.

Brown, William Wells. *The Rising Son, or, the Antecedents and Advancement of the Colored Race*. Boston: A. G. Brown, 1876.

Brown, Edgar Canter, Jr., and Larry Eugene Rivers. *For a Great and Grand Purpose: The Beginnings of the AMEZ Church in Florida 1864-1905*. Gainesville: University Press of Florida, 2004.

Bruce, Dickson D. "Ancient Africa and the Early Black American Historians, 1883-1915," *American Quarterly* 36 (Winter 1984): 684–99.

_____. "Religion, Society, and Culture in the Old South: A Comparative View," *American Quarterly* 26 (October 1974): 399–415.

Bullock, Penelope L. *The Afro-American Periodical Press, 1838-1909*. Baton Rouge: Louisiana State University Press, 1981.

Burrow, J. F. *The Crisis of Reason: European Thought, 1848-1914*. New Haven, CT: Yale University Press, 2000.

Burt, Olive. *Negroes in the Early West*. New York: Messner, 1969.

Butchart, Ronald E. *Northern Schools, Southern Blacks, and Reconstruction: Freedmen's Education, 1862-1875*. Westport, CT: Greenwood Press, 1980.

Butler, Anthea. *Women in the Church of God in Christ: Making a Sanctified World*. Chapel Hill: University of North Carolina Press, 2007.

Byrne, Donald E., Jr. *No Foot of Land: Folklore of American Methodist Itinerants*. Metuchen, NJ: Scarecrow Press, 1975.

Campbell, James T. *Songs of Zion: The African Methodist Episcopal Church in the United States and South Africa*. New York: Oxford University Press, 1995.

Carnes, Mark C., and Clyde Griffen, eds. *Meanings for Manhood: Constructions of Masculinity in Victorian America*. Chicago: University of Chicago Press, 1990.

Carretta, Vincent. *Equiano the African: Biography of a Self-Made Man*. Athens: University of Georgia Press, 2005.

Chambers, Iain, and Linda Curtis, eds. *The Post-Colonial Question*. London: Routledge, 1996.

Chidester, David. *Salvation and Suicide: An Interpretation of Jim Jones, the Peoples Temple, and Jonestown*. Bloomington: Indiana University Press, 2003.

Chirenje, Mutero. *Ethiopianism and Afro-Americans in Southern Africa, 1883-1916*. Baton Rouge: Louisiana State University Press, 1987.

Chireau, Yvonne. *Black Magic: Religion and the African American Conjuring Tradition*. Berkeley: University of California Press, 2003.

Church of Lukumi Babalu Aye, Inc. v. City of Hialeah (508 U.S. 520).

Cleage, Albert B., Jr. *Black Christian Nationalism: New Directions for the Black Church*. New York: William Morrow & Co., 1972.

Coan, Josephus R. *Daniel Alexander Payne – Christian Educator*. Philadelphia: AME Book Concern, 1935.

Coker, Daniel. *Journal of Daniel Coker, A Descendant of Africa*. Baltimore: Edward J. Coale, 1820.

Cone, James. *Black Theology and Black Power*. New York: Orbis Books, 1997.

Crummell, Alexander. *Civilization: The Primal Need of the Race*. Occasional Papers, No. 3. Washington, DC: American Negro Academy, 1897.

Cummings, Melbourne S. "The Rhetoric of Bishop Henry McNeal Turner," *Journal of Black Studies* 12, no. 4 (June 1982): 457–67.

Curtis, Edward E., IV. *The Call of Bilal: Islam in the African Diaspora*. Chapel Hill: University of North Carolina Press, 2014.

_____. *Islam in Black America: Identity, Liberation, and Difference in African American Islamic Thought*. Albany: SUNY Press, 2002.

Dallam, Marie W. *Daddy Grace: A Celebrity Preacher and His House of Prayer*. New York: New York University Press, 2009.

Daniels, Douglas Henry. *Pioneer Urbanites: A Social and Cultural History of Black San Francisco*. Berkeley: University of California Press, 1990.

Daschke, Dereck. *New Religious Movements: A Documentary Reader*. New York: New York University Press, 2005.

Davis, Cyprian. *The History of Black Catholics in the United States*. New York: Crossroad, 1993.

_____. "History of the African American Catholic Church in the United States: Evangelization and Indigenization." In *Directory of African American Religious Bodies*, edited by Wardell J. Payne, 257–63. Washington, DC: Howard University Press, 1991.

Davis, Timothy, Kevin R. Johnson, and George A. Martinez. *A Reader on Race, Civil Rights, and American Law: A Multicultural Approach*. Durham, NC: Carolina Academic Press, 2001.

Dawson, Lorne L. *Cults and New Religious Movements: A Reader*. Hoboken, NJ: Wiley-Blackwell, 2003.

Delany, Martin. *Search for a Place: Black Separatism and Africa*. Ann Arbor: University of Michigan Press, 1969.

Dickerson, Dennis C. "The Black Church in Industrializing Western Pennsylvania, 1870-1950," *Western Pennsylvania Historical Magazine* 64, no. 4 (1981): 329–44.

Douglas, Kelly Brown. *Sexuality and the Black Church: A Womanist Perspective*. New York: Orbis Books, 1999.

Douglass, Frederick. *Narrative of the Life of Frederick Douglass, An American Slave*. Boston: Anti-Slavery Office, 1845.

Dresser, Marianne. *Buddhist Women on the Edge: Contemporary Perspectives from the Western Frontier*. Berkeley, CA: North Atlantic Books, 1996.

Du Bois, W. E. B. *Black Reconstruction*. New York: Harcourt Brace, 1935.

_____. *The Philadelphia Negro: A Social Study*. Philadelphia: University of Pennsylvania, 1899.

_____. *The Souls of Black Folk*. Milwood, NY: Kraus-Thomson Organization Limited, 1973.

_____. *The World and Africa*. New York: International Publishers, 1965.

_____. *Writings*. New York: The Library of America, 1986.

Dvorak, Katherine L. *An African-American Exodus: The Segregation of Southern Churches*. Brooklyn, NY: Carlson Publishers, 1991.

Equiano, Olaudah. *The Interesting Narrative and Other Writings*. New York: Penguin Books, 1995.

Ernest, John. *Liberation Historiography: African American Writers and the Challenge of History, 1794-1861*. Chapel Hill: University of North Carolina Press, 2004.

Espinosa, Gaston. *William J. Seymour and the Origins of Global Pentecostalism: A Biography and Documentary History*. Durham, NC: Duke University Press, 2014.

Fauset, Arthur Huff. *Black Gods of the Metropolis: Negro Religious Cults of the Urban North*. Philadelphia: University of Pennsylvania Press, 2014.

Foner, Eric. *Reconstruction: America's Unfinished Revolution, 1863-1877*. New York: Harper & Row, 1988.

_____. *A Short History of Reconstruction, 1863-1877*. New York: Harper & Row, 1990.

Foner, Philip, ed. *W. E. B. Du Bois Speaks: Speeches and Addresses 1920-1963*. New York: Pathfinder Press, 1970.

_____, and Robert James Branham, eds. *Lift Every Voice: African American Oratory, 1787-1900*. Tuscaloosa: University of Alabama Press, 1998.

Frazier, E. Franklin. *The Negro Church in America*. New York: Schocken Books, 1964.

Frederickson, George M. *The Black Image in the White Mind: The Debate on Afro American Character and Destiny, 1817-1914*. Hanover, NH: Wesleyan University Press, 1987.

Fulop, Timothy E., Jr., and Albert J. Raboteau, eds. *African-American Religion: Interpretative Essays in History and Culture*. New York: Routledge, 1997.

Gaines, Kevin. *Uplifting the Race: Black Leadership, Politics, and Culture in the Twentieth Century*. Chapel Hill: University of North Carolina Press, 1996.

Genovese, Eugene D. *Roll, Jordan, Roll: The World the Slaves Made*. New York: Pantheon, 1972.

George, Carol V. R. *Segregated Sabbaths: Richard Allen and the Rise of Independent Black Churches, 1760-1840*. New York: Oxford University Press, 1973.

Grant, Colin. *Negro with a Hat: The Rise and Fall of Marcus Garvey*. New York: Oxford University Press, 2010.

Gravely, William B. "Early Methodism and Slavery: The Roots of a Tradition," *Wesleyan Quarterly Review* 2 (1965): 84–100.

_____. "African Methodism and the Rise of Black Denominationalism." In *Rethinking Methodist History: A Bicentennial Historical Consultation*. Edited by R. Richey and K. Rowe. Nashville: Kingswood Books, 1985.

Green, Augustus R. *The Life of the Rev. Dandridge F. Davis, of the African Methodist E. Church*. Pittsburgh: B. F. Peterson, Printer, 1853.

Gregg, Howard D. *History of the AME Church*. Nashville: AMEC Sunday School Union, 1980.

Gregg, Robert. *Sparks from the Anvil of Oppression: Philadelphia's African Methodists and Southern Migrants, 1890-1940*. Philadelphia: Temple University Press, 1993.

Griffin, Horace L. *Their Own Receive Them Not: African American Lesbians and Gays in Black Churches*. Eugene, OR: Wipf and Stock, 2010.

Hahn, Steven. *A Nation Under Our Feet: Black Political Struggles in the Rural*

South from Slavery to the Great Migration. Cambridge, MA: The Belknap Press of Harvard University Press, 2003.

Hall, David D. *Lived Religion in America: Toward a History of Practice.* Princeton, NJ: Princeton University Press, 1997.

Hall, Stephen G. *A Faithful Account of the Race: African American Historical Writing in Nineteenth-Century America.* Chapel Hill: University of North Carolina Press, 2009.

Handy, Robert. *A Christian America: Protestant Hopes and Historical Realities,* 2nd ed. New York: Oxford University Press, 1984.

Harrell, David E, ed. *Varieties of Southern Evangelicalism.* Macon, GA: Mercer University Press, 1981.

Harrill, J. Albert. "The Use of the New Testament in the American Slave Controversy: A Case History in the Hermeneutical Tension between Biblical Criticism and Christian Moral Debate," *Religion and American Culture: A Journal of Interpretation* 10, no. 2 (Summer 2000): 149–86.

Harrison, Milmon F. *Righteous Riches: The Word of Faith Movement in Contemporary African American Religion.* New York: Oxford University Press, 2005.

Harvey, Paul. *Redeeming the South: Religious Cultures and Racial Identities Among Southern Baptists, 1865-1925.* Chapel Hill: University of North Carolina Press, 1997.

Hatch, Nathan O. *The Democratization of American Christianity.* New Haven, CT: Yale University Press, 1988.

Heidler, David S., and Jeanne T. Heidler. *Henry Clay: The Essential American.* New York: Random House, 2011.

Herskovits, Melville J. *The Myth of the Negro Past.* Boston: Beacon Press, 1969.

Heyrman, Christine L. *Southern Cross: The Beginnings of the Bible Belt.* New York: Knopf, 1997.

Higginbotham, Evelyn Brooks. *Righteous Discontent: The Women's Movement in the Black Baptist Church, 1880-1920.* Cambridge, MA: Harvard University Press, 1993.

Hildebrand, Reginald. *The Times Were Strange and Stirring*. Durham, NC: Duke University Press, 1995.

Hill, Samuel S., Jr. *Religion and the Solid South*. Nashville: Abingdon, 1972.

Holloway, Joseph F. *Africanisms in American Culture*. Bloomington: Indiana University Press, 2005.

Hofstadter, Richard. *Social Darwinism in American Thought*. New York: Braziller, 1959.

Hutchison, William R. *The Modernist Impulse in American Protestantism*. New York: Oxford University Press, 1976.

Hutton, Frankie. *The Early Black Press in America, 1827 to 1860*. Westport, CT: Greenwood, 1993.

Isaac, Rhys. *The Transformation of Virginia, 1740-1790*. New York: W. W. Norton, 1982.

Jacobs, Sylvia M. *The African Nexus: Black American Perspectives on the European Partitioning of Africa, 1880-1920*. Westport, CT: Greenwood Press, 1981.

_____, ed. *Black Americans and the Missionary Movement in Africa*. Westport, CT: Greenwood Press, 1982.

Jacques-Garvey, Amy, ed. *Philosophy and Opinions of Marcus Garvey*. Vol 2. New York: Atheneum, 1925.

James, Joy. *Transcending the Talented Tenth: Black Leaders and American Intellectuals*. New York: Routledge, 1997.

Johnson, Michael K. *Black Masculinity and the Frontier Myth in American Literature*. Norman: University of Oklahoma Press, 2002.

Jordan, Winthrop D. *White over Black: American Attitudes Toward the Negro, 1550-1812*. Chapel Hill: University of North Carolina Press, 1968.

Joyner, Charles. "'Believer I Know': The Emergence of African-American Christianity." In *African-American Christianity: Essays in History*, edited by Paul E. Johnson, 18–46. Berkeley: University of California Press, 1994.

Kahn, Jonathan S. *Divine Discontent: The Religious Imagination of W. E. B. Du Bois*. New York: Oxford University Press, 2009.

Karenga, Maulana Ron. *The Kwanzaa*. Los Angeles: University of Sankore Press, 1997.

Killian, Charles. "Daniel A. Payne and the A.M.E. General Conference of 1888: A Display of Contrasts," *Negro History Bulletin* 32, no. 7 (1969): 11–14.

King, Martin Luther, Jr. *Stride Toward Freedom: The Montgomery Story.* Boston: Beacon Press, 2010.

King, Wilma. *Stolen Childhood: Slave Youth in Nineteenth Century America.* Bloomington: Indiana University Press, 1995.

Kirby, James E. *The Methodists.* Westport, CT: Greenwood Press, 1996.

Kurtz, Ernest. "The Tragedy of Southern Religion," *Georgia Historical Quarterly* 66 (Summer 1982): 217–47.

Lee, Jarena. *The Life and Religious Experience of Jarena Lee.* Philadelphia, 1836.

Lee, Shayne. *T. D. Jakes: America's New Preacher.* New York: New York University Press, 2007.

Leverenz, David. *Manhood and the American Renaissance.* Ithaca, NY: Cornell University Press, 1989.

Levine, Lawrence. *Black Culture, Black Consciousness.* New York: Oxford University Press, 1977.

Lewis, James R. *The Oxford Handbook of New Religious Movements.* New York: Oxford University Press, 2008.

Lincoln, C. Eric, and Lawrence H. Mamiya. *The Black Church in the African American Experience.* Durham, NC: Duke University Press, 1990.

Little, Lawrence S. *Disciples of Liberty: The African Methodist Episcopal Church in the Age of Imperialism.* Nashville: University of Tennessee Press, 2000.

Litwack, Leon F. *Been in the Storm So Long: The Aftermath of Slavery.* New York: Vintage Books, 1979.

_____. *North of Slavery: The Negro in the Free States, 1790-1860.* Chicago: University of Chicago Press, 1961.

Litwack, Leon F., and August Meier, eds. *Black Leaders of the Nineteenth Century.* Chicago: University of Illinois Press, 1988.

Logan, Rayford W., and Michael R. Winston, eds. *Dictionary of American Negro Biography.* New York: W. W. Norton, 1982.

_____. *The Negro in American Life and Thought: The Nadir, 1877-1901.* New York: Dial, 1954.

Loveland, Anne C., and Otis B. Wheeler. *From the Meetinghouse to Megachurch: A Material and Cultural History*. Columbia: University of Missouri Press, 2003.

Luker, Ralph E. *The Social Gospel in Black and White: American Racial Reform, 1885-1912*. Chapel Hill: University of North Carolina Press, 1991.

Maaga, Mary. *Hearing the Voices of Jonestown: Putting a Human Face on an American Tragedy*. Syracuse, NY: Syracuse University Press, 1998.

Maffly-Kipp, Laurie F. "Denominationalism and the Black Church." In *Reimagining Denominationalism: Interpretive Essays*, edited by Russell E. Richey, 58–73. New York: Oxford University Press, 1994.

_____. *Setting Down the Sacred Past: African-American Race Histories*. Cambridge, MA: The Belknap Press of Harvard University Press, 2010.

Magesa, Laurenti. *African Religion: The Moral Traditions of Abundant Life*. New York: Orbis Books, 1997.

Marable, Manning. *Malcolm X: A Life of Reinvention*. New York: Penguin Books, 2011.

_____. *Speaking Truth to Power: Essays on Race, Resistance, and Radicalism*. Boulder, CO: Westview Press, 1998.

Marks, George P., III, ed. and comp. *The Black Press Views American Imperialism (1898-1900)*. New York: Arno Press and the New York Times, 1971.

Martin, Lerone A. *Preaching on Wax: The Phonograph and the Shaping of Modern African American Religion*. New York: New York University Press, 2014.

Martin, Sandy D. *Black Baptists and African Missions: The Origins of a Movement, 1880-1915*. Macon, GA: Mercer University Press, 1998.

_____. *For God and Race: The Religious and Political Leadership of AMEZ Bishop James Walker Hood*. Columbia: University of South Carolina Press, 1999.

Martin, Waldo E., Jr. *The Mind of Frederick Douglass*. Chapel Hill: University of North Carolina Press, 1984.

Mathews, Donald G. "Charles Colcock Jones and the Southern Evangelical

Crusade to Form a Biracial Community," *Journal of Southern History* 41 (1975): 299–320.

_____. *Religion in the Old South.* Chicago: University of Chicago Press, 1977.

Mays, Benjamin E., and Joseph W. Nicholson. *The Negro's Church.* New York: Russell & Russell, 1969.

Mbiti, John S. *African Religions and Philosophy.* Portsmouth, NH: Heinemann, 1990.

Meier, August. *Negro Thought in America 1880-1915: Racial Ideologies in the Age of Booker T. Washington.* Ann Arbor: University of Michigan Press, 1963.

Miller, Albert G. *Elevating the Race: Theophilus G. Steward, Black Theology, and the Making of an African American Civil Society, 1865-1924.* Knoxville: University of Tennessee Press, 2003.

Miller, Floyd. *The Search for Black Nationality: Black Emigration and Colonization, 1787-1863.* Chicago: University of Illinois Press, 1975.

Miller, Kelly. "The Negro's Part." In *Radicals and Conservatives and Other Essays on the Negro in America.* New York: Schocken Books, 1968.

Mitchell, Henry H. *Black Church Beginnings: The Long-Hidden Realities of the First Years.* Grand Rapids, MI: Eerdmans, 2004.

Mitchell, Michele. *Righteous Propagation: African Americans and the Politics of Racial Destiny after Reconstruction.* Chapel Hill: University of North Carolina Press, 2004.

Miller, Perry. *Errand into the Wilderness.* Cambridge, MA: The Belknap Press, 1956.

Mixon, Winfield Henri. *History of the African Methodist Episcopal Church in Alabama: with Biographical Sketches.* Nashville: AME Church Sunday School Union, 1902.

Miyakawa, Felicia. *Five Percenter Rap: God Hop's Music, Message, and Black Muslim Mission.* Bloomington: Indiana University Press, 2005.

Montgomery, William E. *Under Their Own Vine and Fig Tree: The African American Church in the South, 1865-1900.* Baton Rouge: Louisiana State University Press, 1993.

Moon, Henry Lee. *The Emerging Thought of W. E. B. Du Bois: Essays and Editorials from The Crisis with an Introduction, Commentaries and a Personal Memoir.* New York: Simon and Schuster, 1972.

Moore, R. Laurence. *Religious Outsiders and the Making of Americans.* New York: Oxford University Press, 1986.

Morris, Aldon D. *Origins of the Civil Rights Movement.* New York: Free Press, 1986.

Morris, Calvin S. *Reverdy C. Ransom: Black Advocate of the Social Gospel.* Lanham, MD: University Press of America, 1990.

Moses, Wilson Jeremiah. *Alexander Crummell: A Study of Civilization and Discontent.* New York: Oxford University Press, 1989.

_____, ed. *Classical Black Nationalism: From the American Revolution to Marcus Garvey.* New York: New York University Press, 1996.

_____. *The Golden Age of Black Nationalism.* Hamden, CT: Archon Books, 1978.

Moss, Alfred, Jr. *The American Negro Academy: Voice of the Talented Tenth.* Baton Rouge: University of Louisiana Press, 1981.

Murphy, Larry. *Down by the Riverside: Readings in African American Religion.* New York: New York University Press, 2000.

Nash, Gary B. *Forging Freedom.* Cambridge, MA: Harvard University Press, 1988.

Newby, I. A. *Jim Crow's Defense: Anti-Negro Thought in America, 1900-1930.* Baton Rouge: Louisiana State University Press, 1965.

Newman, Richard S. *Freedom's Prophet: Bishop Richard Allen, the AME Church, and the Black Founding Fathers.* New York: New York University Press, 2008.

_____, eds. *Pamphlets of Protest: An Anthology of Early African American Protest Literature, 1790-1860.* New York: Routledge, 2001.

Numbers, Ronald L., and John Stenhouse, eds. *Disseminating Darwinism: The Role of Place, Race, Religion, and Gender.* Cambridge: Cambridge University Press, 1999.

Olupona, Jacob K. *Orisa Devotion as World Religion: The Globalization of Yoruba Religious Culture.* Madison: University of Wisconsin Press, 2008.

Painter, Nell Irvin. *Exodusters: Black Migration to Kansas after Reconstruction.* New York: W. W. Norton & Company, 1986.

Palmer, Susan. *The Nuwaubian Nation: Black Spirituality and State Control.* Burlington, VT: Ashgate, 2010.

Parfitt, Tudor. *Black Jews in Africa and the Americas.* Cambridge, MA: Harvard University Press, 2013.

Payne, Daniel A. *History of the African Methodist Episcopal Church.* Nashville: Publishing House of the AME Sunday School Union, 1891.

_____. *Recollections of Seventy Years.* Nashville: Publishing House of the AME Sunday School Union, 1888.

_____. *The Semi-Centenary and the Retrospection of the African Methodist Episcopal Church in the United States of America.* Baltimore: Sherwood & Co., 1866.

_____. *Sermons and Addresses, 1853-1891.* Edited by Charles Killian. New York: Arno Press, 1972.

_____. *A Treatise on Domestic Education.* Cincinnati: Cranston & Stowe, 1885.

Penn, I. Garland. *The Afro-American Press and Its Editors.* New York: Arno Press, 1969.

Peskin, Allan. *North into Freedom: The Autobiography of John Malvin, Free Negro, 1795-1880.* Cleveland: The Press of Western Reserve University, 1966.

Pinn, Anthony B. *The Black Church in the Post-Civil Rights Era.* New York: Orbis Books, 2002.

Porter, Dorothy ed. *Negro Protest Pamphlets: A Compendium.* New York: Arno Press, 1969.

Quarles, Benjamin. *Black Abolitionists.* New York: Oxford University Press, 1975.

Raboteau, Albert J. *A Fire in the Bones: Reflections on African-American Religious History.* Boston: Beacon Press, 1995.

_____. *Slave Religion: The "Invisible Institution" in the Antebellum South.* New York: Oxford University Press, 1978.

Rael, Patrick. *Black Identity and Black Protest in the Antebellum North*. Chapel Hill: University of North Carolina Press, 2002.

Ray, Benjamin C. *African Religions: Symbol, Ritual, and Community*. Upper Saddle River, NJ: Prentice Hall, 2000.

Redkey, Edwin S. *Black Exodus: Black Nationalist and Back-to-Africa Movements, 1890-1910*. New Haven, CT: Yale University Press, 1969.

Reeve, W. Paul. *Religion of a Different Color: Race and the Mormon Struggle for Whiteness*. New York: Oxford University Press, 2015.

Richardson, Harry V. *Dark Salvation: The Story of African Methodism as It Developed Among Blacks*. Garden City, NY: Doubleday, 1976.

Richardson, Joe M. *Christian Reconstruction: The American Missionary Association and Southern Blacks, 1861-1890*. Athens: University of Georgia Press, 1986.

Said, Omar ibn. "Autobiography of Omar ibn Said, Slave in North Carolina, 1831," *American Historical Review* 30, no. 4 (July 1925): 787–95.

Savage, Barbara Dianne. *Your Spirits Walk Beside Us: The Politics of Black Religion*. Cambridge, MA: Belknap Press, 2012.

Schneider, Gregory A. *The Way of the Cross Leads Home: The Domestication of American Methodism*. Bloomington: Indiana University Press, 1993.

Senna, Carl. *The Black Press and the Struggle for Civil Rights*. New York: Franklin Watts, 1993.

Seraile, William. *Fire in His Heart: Bishop Benjamin Tucker Tanner and the A.M.E. Church*. Knoxville: University of Tennessee Press, 1998.

_____. *Theophilus Gould Steward (1843-1924) and Black America*. Brooklyn, NY: Carlson Publishing, 1991.

Sernett, Milton C. *Black Religion and American Evangelicalism: White Protestants, Plantation Missions, and the Flowering of Negro Christianity*. Metuchen, NJ: Scarecrow Press, 1975.

_____. *Bound for the Promised Land: African American Religion and the Great Migration*. Durham, NC: Duke University Press, 1997.

Sharpe, Eric J. *Comparative Religion: A History*. La Salle, IL: Open Court, 1986.

Simmons, Charles A. *The African American Press: A History of News Coverage*

During National Crisis, with Special Reference to Four Black Newspapers, 1827-1965. Jefferson, NC: McFarland and Co., 1998.

Simmons, William J., ed. *Men of Mark: Eminent, Progressive and Rising*. New York: Arno Press and the New York Times, 1968.

Singleton, George A. *The Romance of African Methodism: A Study of the African Methodist Episcopal Church*. New York: Exposition Press, 1952.

Skinner, Elliott P. *African Americans and U.S. Policy Toward Africa, 1850-1924: In Defense of Black Nationality*. Washington, DC: Howard University Press, 1992.

Smith, Arthur L. *Language, Communication and Rhetoric in Black America*. New York: Harper & Row, 1972.

Smith, Charles Spencer. *A History of the African Methodist Episcopal Church*. Philadelphia: AME Book Concern, 1922.

Smith, David. *Biography of Rev. David Smith of the AME Church*. Xenia, OH: Xenia Gazette Office, 1881.

Smith, H. Shelton. *In His Image But...: Racism in Southern Religion, 1780-1910*. Durham, NC: Duke University Press, 1972.

Smith, R. Drew, and Tamelyn Tucker-Worgs, "Megachurches: African American Churches in Social and Political Context." In *The State of Black America 2000: Blacks in the New Millennium*, edited by National Urban League, Lee A. Daniels, Lenneal J. Henderson, William Edward Spriggs, and David W. Brown. New York: National Urban League, 2000, 171–97.

Smith, Theophus. *Conjuring Culture: Biblical Formations of Black America*. New York: Oxford University Press, 1994.

Sobel, Mechal. *The World They Made Together*. Princeton, NJ: Princeton University Press, 1987.

_____. *Trabelin' On: The Slave Journey to an Afro-Baptist Faith*. Westport, CT: Greenwood Press, 1979.

Stampp, Kenneth M. *The Era of Reconstruction, 1865-1877*. New York: Alfred A. Knopf, 1965.

Stark, Rodney, and William Sims Bainbridge. *The Future of Religion:*

Secularization, Revival, and Cult Formation. Berkeley: University of California Press, 1985.

Sterling, Dorothy. *The Making of an Afro-American: Martin Robinson Delany, 1812-1885*. New York: Da Capo Press, 1996.

Steward, Theophilus G. *Memoirs of Mrs. Rebecca Steward*. Philadelphia: Publication Department of the AME Church, 1877.

_____. *My First Four Years in the Itineracy of the African Methodist Episcopal Church*. Brooklyn, 1876.

Stuckey, Sterling. *The Ideological Origins of Black Nationalism*. Boston: Beacon Press, 1972.

Sutton, Matthew Avery. *Aimee Semple McPherson and the Resurrection of Christian America*. Cambridge, MA: Harvard University Press, 2009.

Tanner, Benjamin T. *An Apology for African Methodism*. Baltimore, 1867.

_____. *The Descent of the Negro*. Philadelphia: AME Publishing House, 1898.

_____. *The Dispensations in the History of the Church*. Philadelphia: AME Publishing House, 1898.

_____. *Hints to Ministers, Especially Those of the African Methodist Episcopal Church*. Wilberforce, OH: Industrial Student Printers, 1900.

_____. *The Negro in Holy Writ*. Philadelphia: n.p., 1902.

_____. *The Negro's Origin*. Philadelphia: AME Depository, 1869.

_____. *Theological Lectures*. Nashville: AME Sunday School Union, 1894.

Thomas, Rhondda R. "Exodus and Colonization: Charting the Journey in the Journals of Daniel Coker, a descendant of Africa," *African American Review* 41, no. 3 (Fall 2007): 507–19.

Thornton, John K. "African Dimensions of the Stono Rebellion," *The American Historical Review* 96, no. 4 (October 1991): 1101–13.

Turner, Nat. *The Confessions of Nat Turner, the Leader of the late Insurrection in Southampton, Va as fully and voluntarily made to Thomas R. Gray*. Baltimore: Thomas R. Gray, Lucas and Deaver, 1831.

Turner, Richard. *Islam in the African-American Experience*. Bloomington: Indiana University Press, 2003.

Tweed, Thomas A., ed. *Retelling U.S. Religious History*. Berkeley: University of California Press, 1997.

Walker, Clarence E. *A Rock in a Weary Land: The AME Church During the Civil War and Reconstruction*. Baton Rouge: Louisiana State University Press, 1982.

Walker, David. *Walker's Appeal*. Boston: D. Walker, 1830.

Walton, Jonathan L. *Watch This! The Ethics and Aesthetics of Black Televangelism*. New York: New York University Press, 2009.

Washington, Booker T. *The Story of the Negro*. Philadelphia: University of Pennsylvania Press, 2011.

Washington, James Melvin. *Frustrated Fellowship: The Black Baptist Quest for Social Power*. Macon, GA: Mercer University Press, 1986.

Washington, Joseph R., Jr. *Black Religion: The Negro and Christianity in the United States*. Boston: Beacon Press, 1964.

Watts, Jill. *God, Harlem U.S.A.: The Father Divine Story*. Berkeley: University of California Press, 1995.

Weisenfeld, Judith. "On Jordan's Stormy Banks: Margins, Center, and Bridges in African American Religious History." In *New Directions in American Religious History*, edited by Harry S. Stoudt and D. G. Hart. New York: Oxford University Press, 1997.

_____. *This Far by Faith: Readings in African-American Women's Religious Biography*. New York: Routledge, 1995.

Welter, Barbara. *Dimity Convictions: The American Woman in the Nineteenth Century*. Columbus: Ohio State University Press, 1985.

Wesley, Charles H. *Richard Allen: Apostle of Freedom*. Washington, DC: The Associated Publishers, 1935.

Wessinger, Catherine, ed. *Religious Institutions and Women's Leadership*. Columbia: University of South Carolina Press, 1996.

Wheeler, Edward L. *Uplifting the Race: The Black Minister in the New South, 1865-1902*. Lanham, MD: University Press of America, 1986.

White, Ronald C. *Liberty and Justice for All: Racial Reform and the Social Gospel, 1877-1925*. San Francisco: Harper & Row, 1990.

Williams, Delores S. *Sisters in the Wilderness: The Challenge of Womanist God-Talk*. New York: Orbis Books, 2013.

_____. "Womanist Theology: Black Women's Voice," *Christianity and Crisis* 47, no. 3 (March 2, 1987): 66–70.

Williams, George Washington. *History of the Negro Race in America, from 1619 to 1880*. New York: George Putnam's Sons, 1885.

Williams, Gilbert A. *The Christian Recorder, Newspaper of the African Methodist Episcopal Church: History of a Forum for Ideas, 1854-1902*. Jefferson, NC: McFarland & Co. Publishers, 1996.

Williams, Walter. *Black America and the Evangelization of Africa, 1877-1900*. Madison: University of Wisconsin Press, 1982.

Wills, David W., and Richard Newman, eds. *Black Apostles at Home and Abroad: Afro-Americans and the Christian Mission from the Revolution to Reconstruction*. Boston: G. K. Hall, 1982.

Wilmore, Gayraud S. *Black Religion and Black Radicalism*. Garden City, NY: Doubleday, 1972.

Winch, Julie. *A Gentleman of Color: The Life of James Forten*. New York: Oxford University Press, 2002.

_____. *Philadelphia's Black Elite: Activism, Accommodation, and the Struggle for Autonomy, 1787-1848*. Philadelphia: Temple University Press, 1988.

Woodson, Carter G. *The History of the Negro Church*, 3rd ed. Washington, DC: Associated Publishers, 1985.

Wright, Richard R., Jr., *The Bishops of the African Methodist Episcopal Church*. Nashville: Publishing House of the AME Sunday School Union, 1963.

X, Malcolm. *The Autobiography of Malcolm X*. New York: Ballantine Books, 1989.

Index